SKELTON
DIODORUS SICULUS

EARLY ENGLISH TEXT SOCIETY

Original Series, No. 239

1957 (for 1954), reprinted 1971

THE
BIBLIOTHECA HISTORICA
OF
DIODORUS SICULUS

TRANSLATED BY
JOHN SKELTON

EDITED BY
F. M. SALTER
AND
H. L. R. EDWARDS

VOLUME II
INTRODUCTION, NOTES,
AND GLOSSARY

Published for
THE EARLY ENGLISH TEXT SOCIETY
by the
OXFORD UNIVERSITY PRESS
LONDON NEW YORK TORONTO

Oxford University Press, Ely House, London W 1

GLASGOW NEW YORK TORONTO MELBOURNE WELLINGTON
CAPE TOWN SALISBURY IBADAN NAIROBI DAR ES SALAAM LUSAKA ADDIS ABABA
BOMBAY CALCUTTA MADRAS KARACHI LAHORE DACCA
KUALA LUMPUR SINGAPORE HONG KONG TOKYO

FIRST PUBLISHED 1957

REPRINTED 1971

REPRINTED LITHOGRAPHICALLY IN GREAT BRITAIN
AT THE UNIVERSITY PRESS, OXFORD
BY VIVIAN RIDLER, PRINTER TO THE UNIVERSITY

FOREWORD

REFERENCES to the text in the Introduction to Skelton's *Diodorus*, here following, are made to books and chapters. These are indicated in the margins of the text in Volume I. In Volume I the book numbers are in Roman capitals, in this volume in lower-case Roman figures. References in the Glossary, Notes, and Index, on the contrary, are made to page and line. The editors regret this inconsistency which at times (especially at the foot of p. xxviii where both forms of reference appear within a single line) appears to be the work of gremlins. The Introduction was written many years ago, long before it was possible to refer to page and line of the text. To convert a great many textual references to page and line, though it would contribute to consistency, would also unduly increase the cost of printing.

When a piece of work has occupied as many years as this Diodorus has done, the editors are likely to age into second thoughts. On pp. xxxii, xxxiii, xlviii, l, lii, and liii of the Introduction we have spoken of Skelton as a 'humanist'. At least one of us, and probably both, would now use that term in a more restricted sense, confining it to true Hellenists, and speak of Skelton as a Renaissance scholar and poet. Further, we look with lack-lustre eye upon the purplish passages written more than twenty-five years ago. Only the Augustans, who deprecated enthusiasm, were born old.

The editors would like to express their gratitude to Mr. R. W. Burchfield, Honorary Secretary of the Early English Text Society, who has been most helpful, painstaking, and efficient in at last bringing these volumes into comely print.

F. M. S.
H. L. R. E.

CONTENTS

INTRODUCTION

DIODORUS SICULUS	xix
POGGIO'S TRANSLATION	xx
SKELTON'S TRANSLATION	xxii
A. *Skelton's Dictionary*	xxiv
B. *Skelton's Knowledge of Greek*	xxvi
C. *Skelton's Knowledge of Latin*	xxvii
D. *Skelton's Contribution to the English Language*	xxxii
E. *Skelton and Rhetoric*	xxxiv
F. *The Essential Skelton*	xlvii
NOTES	397
APPENDIXES A, B, C, D	410
GLOSSARY	427
INDEX OF NAMES	458

INTRODUCTION

DIODORUS SICULUS

THE *Historical Library* of Diodorus the Sicilian is one of the earliest essays in a genre well known to our own day. Living in an age when the world-state seemed about to become an accomplished fact,[1] Diodorus determined to provide it with a world history—a record of events which would unite all previous narratives in one compendious whole, ranging from the origin of man to the year 59 B.C. This ambitious task involved thirty years of travel and preparation; when finished, it filled forty books, a 'Library of History'. Six books dealt with the period before the Trojan War, eleven with the period between the fall of Troy and the death of Alexander; the remainder brought the record down to Diodorus' lifetime.

Only Books I–V and XI–XX survive complete. The early books, which Poggio translated,[2] describe the lands of Egypt and Assyria, India, Scythia, Arabia, Ethiopia, and their peoples, break off to discuss the nature of the first gods and the mythology of Greece, and return to a description of the western islands, Rhodes and Crete. It is these early books, with their comparative paucity of detail, that most clearly reveal Diodorus' conception of History. In a general preface he claims the highest dignity for the subject as a means of vicarious experience and as a guide to conduct. It is History's promise of immortality, he believes, that has inspired rulers to found states, establish laws, and invent arts and sciences. Similarly, by displaying the fate which has come upon evildoers in the past, she warns men to abstain from vice. If speech is man's noblest gift, history is the noblest form of speech; it is greater than poetry and rhetoric in that it combines truth with instruction.

Such an attitude forces definite limitations upon the historian. His political history tends to become little more than a series of biographies of the great, presented with a strong moral bias. And Diodorus, an aristocrat with a rooted dislike of democracy,[3] is an

---

[1] Diodorus began writing his history 'at least as early as 56 B.C.', when Rome was mistress of the entire Mediterranean and was turning east. See C. H. Oldfather, *Diodorus of Sicily, with an English Translation* (Loeb Classical Library, 1933, 1935, 1939, 1947), i, pp. ix, xi–xii.
[2] See above, Vol. I, pp. xvi–xvii, and below, pp. xx ff.
[3] See Book I, chapter 74, paragraph 2 of this edition.

ideal exponent of this method. He presents Moeris and Sesoösis to us as types of the good ruler in Egypt, Semiramis in Assyria, while the tyrant Amasis and the effeminate Sardanapalus exemplify the sorry end of the king who abuses power. Of others the very names are withheld 'because nothing was done by them which merits mentioning'.[1] Out to instruct, he scorns to entertain; his work is quite utilitarian; and he lacks the insight into character and the narrative skill of Herodotus.

His preoccupations are still more evident in his accounts of early myths which fill up so much of the early books. A thorough rationalist, with all the rationalist's interest in comparative religion, he narrates at length the mythology of each country, equating it as far as possible with that of Greece; and his explanation is regularly a natural one. The gods of Egypt were originally the four elements, with 'spirit' ranking as a fifth. Later their names were attached to mortals who had attained lasting fame through 'the good services which they rendered to all men'.[2] His dissociation of Zeus into two distinct persons, and of Dionysus into three,[3] is a good example of his method of interpretation. It is true, of course, that Diodorus summarizes the theories of others, but the choice at least is his, and the supernatural he avoids.

POGGIO'S TRANSLATION

Such a work as the *Library of History* had a strong and immediate appeal for the humanists of the fifteenth century, and by 1449 a Latin translation of the first five books had been completed by Poggio Bracciolini.[4]

---

[1] See Oldfather, i. 423. Cf. also i. 44, 45, 60, 63 of this edition.

[2] Book I, Chapter 13.

[3] In his lengthy account of Egypt Diodorus gives some support to the diffusionist theories of the late Sir Grafton Elliot-Smith and Professor Perry, though he is careful (i. 9) not to commit himself as to the priority of the Egyptians. He expounds also the allegorical theory that Dionysus is a mere personification of the vine.

[4] There is a tradition that Poggio stole the work from an Englishman, John Free. This tradition, which has been credited to Leland (*De Script. Brit.*, Oxon., 1709, pp. 467–8) and Bale (*Index Brit. Script.*, ed. Lane Poole, 1902, p. 205), really derives from MS. Balliol 124. This manuscript contains excerpts from Pliny's *Natural History* (excerpts which have also been attributed to Free under the title *Cosmographia Mundi*) and a copy, slightly abbreviated, of Poggio's *Diodorus*, both in Free's own hand. No doubt Free's handwriting gave rise to the note in an unidentified hand of 1490–1500 on fol. 153: 'Magister Iohannes Free de Bristow natus in Italia compilavit istud opus ad dominum papam

Introduction

Poggio (1380–1459)[1] was the brilliant son of an impoverished notary of Florence. He studied Latin under John of Ravenna, whose pupils included the great Guarino, and Greek under Manuel Chrysoloras. Making his way to Rome about 1402, he served the Papal Curia as scribe and later as secretary through the most disturbed half-century of its existence, but during the worst throes of the schism Poggio was quietly accumulating antiques and rescuing manuscripts from monastic cellars. With an occasional assistant, he managed to recover the whole of Quintilian, Lucretius, Columella, a dozen comedies of Plautus, and many of Cicero's finest orations. In 1417 the election of Martin V left him temporarily without a place, and he paid a visit to England as the guest of Henry Beaufort, Bishop of Winchester.

England was a disappointment. While he drowsed through interminable dinners, on the Continent the Rhetorics of Cicero were being brought to light, with the promise of more treasures to come. He rejected an English benefice, preferring the lay 'slavery' of the papal court. Back in Rome, he relieved his secretarial duties by composing dialogues on moral themes—hypocrisy, or the unhappiness of princes. Lighter exercise was provided by the invectives which he wrote, in the fashion of the time, against Filelfo and Valla. The quarrels may or may not have been serious, but there can be no doubting the literary enthusiasm that helped to create these specimens of the art of abuse. In the same spirit of conscious craftsmanship his letters were written and in due course collected, and at the end of his life he compiled the jokes and sayings current among his colleagues of the Curia into a little volume, the *Facetiae*, as an

---

Paulum, videlicet 6 libros Diodori Siculi poetice fabulando more gentilium circa annum Christi 1465 [*sic*; but Coxe, *Catalogus*, i. 34, has 1464] et est de manu propria dicti Iohannis Free de Greco in latinum per ipsum translatus et ex merito dominus papa contulit sibi Beneficium episcopatus Bathoniensis et obiit infra mensem consequentem prefatum donum . . . .' A slightly later note in two parts (Coxe's *a* and *c*) on the same page, and to much the same effect, is in the hand of John Burton, Fellow of Balliol at the end of the fifteenth century and Vicar of St. Nicholas, Bristol, Free's home town. But as Poggio himself tells us that he had finished his translation by August 1449 (E. Walser, *Poggius Florentinus*, Leipzig and Berlin, 1914, p. 230), before Free had left England, chronology alone establishes him as the translator. Skelton, writing before 1490, had apparently never heard of Free's claim. (Cf. his references to Poggio: 'Thus endeth the prohemye of Poggius', fol. 2^v, and 'Diodori Siculi historiarum Priscarum a Poggio &c.', fol. 3^r.) (For much of this information we have to thank Professor R. A. B. Mynors.)

[2] Cf. W. Shepherd, *The Life of Poggio Bracciolini*, Liverpool and London, 1802.

example, he said, of what could be done with Latin.[1] At the age of fifty-five he abandoned a mistress and four children to marry a girl of seventeen—a disparity in age not unusual in those days—and in old age wrote a dialogue on marriage. His last years were spent in honourable retirement at Florence, where he wrote a history of the state in the vein of Livy.

In his dialogue on Avarice, which appeared in 1429, Poggio had declared that he was still not Hellenist enough to translate a classic. It was not until mid-century that he felt competent to try his hand at a Greek text, when he chose the *Cyropaedia* of Xenophon and Diodorus' *Library*. His method was half-way between translation and epitome. By omitting dialogue and set speeches he compressed the eight books of Xenophon into six, but he treated the subject-matter of Diodorus with more respect, although he showed no mercy for the rather verbose circumlocutions and moralizing passages of the Sicilian. Indeed, he carried his zeal for conciseness to a fault; and no small proportion of Skelton's errors can be traced to the ambiguity of his Latin source.

SKELTON'S TRANSLATION

Skelton's handling of Poggio sheds so much light upon his mind, his methods of work, and his character as to make it an invaluable background for any study of his poetry and career. But he is so full of difficulties and thorny problems that any approach to the general question of his humanistic status and the range of his learning craves wary walking.

The *Diodorus* was not only one of the earliest productions of Skelton himself, but one of the first English translations of the classics. That there was still much opposition to the use of the vernacular we know from many sources.[2] As late as 1561, Hoby lamented that 'our learned men for the most part hold opinion that to have the sciences in the mother tongue hurteth memory and hindereth learning'. In this depressing atmosphere, English transla-

---

[1] Skelton testifies to the fame of the *Facetiae* in the *Garlande of Laurell*, 372–3:
    Poggeus also, that famous Florentine,
    Mustred ther amonge them with many a mad tale.
[2] References have been collected by J. W. H. Atkins, *Cambridge History of English Literature*, iii. 444–5, and by L. B. Wright, 'Translations for the Elizabethan Middle Class', *The Library*, 1932–3, pp. 312 ff.

Introduction xxiii

tion could scarcely be expected to flourish; and up to 1517 the only classical works, apart from Chaucer's *Boethius*, which had been rendered direct from Latin were Burgh's *Distichs* of Cato (1477–78), two brief dialogues of Cicero (both in 1481), a phrase-book from Terence (*c.* 1483), and another from Ovid (1513).[1] It is not an impressive list; and examination of the individual items tends to confirm the verdict of Lathrop:

> As for the style of the translation, it is naïvely helpless. The writers cannot put sentences together with any regularity of syntax, or definiteness of emphasis, or clearness of connection .... [They] generally felt bound by multiplying synonyms to cover the meaning of the original words somehow, and 'resolved,' that is explained and made literal, the metaphors of the original.... Even [Caxton's] writings are immature, and most of the work of his contemporaries is simply crude. (p. 28.)

After 1513 no further translations appeared until about 1520, when Rastell translated and printed the *Menippus* of Lucian and the *Andria* of Terence, while Barclay produced a version of Sallust's *Jugurtha*. This sudden flowering drew the caustic judgement of Skelton in 1521: 'So myche translacion in to Englysshe confused.'[2]

Such an extreme poverty of material is of the utmost importance when we consider Skelton's achievement. It is true there were other, and greatly superior, prose models to be found in the *Morte Darthur* and the devotional tracts which extended back to Anglo-Saxon days.[3] But these were in a fundamentally different category from the *Diodorus*. The vocabulary of Malory's originals was Romance, that is to say familiar, if not already naturalized, to the English reader. And the tracts had behind them the great tradition of the medieval Church whenever they sought the exact equivalent for a term of ecclesiastical Latin. What finally marks off all these works from the *Diodorus* is a difference of aim. Both Malory and the devotional writers were chiefly concerned with their matter. They tried to

---

[1] H. B. Lathrop, *Translations from the Classics into English from Caxton to Chapman, 1477–1620* (University of Wisconsin Studies in Language and Literature), Madison, 1933. Only printed works are included in this survey, and Skelton's *Diodorus* is accordingly dismissed with one quotation and the comment: '[His] conscious style is of the most stuffed and swelling bombast' (p. 26).
[2] *Speke Parrot*, 444 (Rev. Alexander Dyce, *The Poetical Works of John Skelton*, 2 vols., London, 1843, ii. 22; MS. Harleian 2252, fol. 139).
[3] See R. W. Chambers, *On the Continuity of English Prose*, E.E.T.S., O.S., cxci A, 1932.

reproduce, in English, material of absorbing importance or interest; the manner of its conveyance was left to look after itself, and it did. Skelton, on the other hand, had no such exclusive interest in his subject. Translation for him was mainly a problem in communication —and in a field which was almost entirely unexplored. And to say, as Lathrop does, that his 'conscious style is of the most stuffed and swelling bombast', is to miss the point. It is to condemn a man for failing to build a tennis court when he actually intended to lay out a golf course. Surely it is only fair to Skelton to ask that he be judged within the limits of his intentions.

(A) *Skelton's Dictionary*

As a translator Skelton had to have his lexicon, and its identification may not be without interest. A gloss to *The Garlande of Laurell* reads: 'Porcus se ingurgitat ceno & luto se immergit guarinus veronencis.'[1] It was not from the Italian Guarino, however, but from the German Reuchlin that Skelton took his definition, as the following quotation shows: 'Porcus. ci. dicitur a purus. cata antifrasim. quia minime sit purus. vnde & porcus dicitur. quasi puro carens. Vel dicitur porcus. quasi spurcus & immundus. quia *ingurgitat se ceno & luto se immergit* . . . '[2] Guarino has no such statement. Skelton's error was a natural one, for the printed texts of Reuchlin were invariably bound up with Guarino's *Ars diphthongandi, punctandi, et accentuandi*, and Reuchlin's name is never given. It was known to Palsgrave in 1540, however, if his reference to the period 'a lyttel before Rheuclines days'[3] is based, as it appears to be, upon the *Breuiloquus*.

The *Diodorus* proves that Skelton knew and used his Reuchlin from very early days. For example, in Book IV. 12. 2, he recounts how 'Exion, *secretary* vnto Dame Iuno, desirid of her amorows plesure of veneriall affeccioun. Then she, *withe the son of Iuppiter*, formmyd a clowde by iuste resemblaund apparently emportynge her figure, and so offirde it as it had bene her-selfe vnto Exion. . . .' This story does not appear in Oldfather or Poggio at all; it is Skelton's interpolation. When we turn to Reuchlin, we read under *Centaurus*: '. . . Siquidem secundum fabulas poetarum xion *secretarius* Iunonis

---

[1] Dyce, i. 415–16.
[2] Reuchlin, *Vocabularius breuiloquus*, Basle, 1478.
[3] *Acolastus*, ed. P. L. Carver, E.E.T.S., O.S., ccii (1935), p. 7.

Introduction

eam interpellauit de concibitu. quę *cum filio Iouis* formauit quandam nubem in sui speciem et eam obtulit xioni....' We may be surprised at this *filio Iouis*; he is Reuchlin's own creation, for Reuchlin regularly borrowed materials from the *Catholicon*.[1] Instead of *cum filio*, Balbus has *consilio, iouis*. *Secretarius* is of course used in the regular medieval sense of a confidant or intimate.

This is not the only error of Skelton's for which Reuchlin is to blame. The first stanza of *Speke Parrot* has the line, 'Tyl Euphrates, that flode, dryueth me into Inde', with the gloss, 'Lucanus. Tigris et Euphrates uno se fonte resolvunt.' Dyce notes that the quotation is not from Lucan, but from Boethius, *de Consol. Phil.* v. 1.[2] But Skelton took the gloss directly from Reuchlin, who says, 'Euphrates ... est fluuius mesopotamię de paradiso exiens copiosissimus gemmis. qui per mediam Babyloniam influit.... *Vnde Lucanus. Tigris & euphrates vno se fonte resoluunt*....'[3] The fanciful etymology of *Katerina* in the gloss to *Speke Parrot*, 38,[4] and the use of *Menander* for *Maeander* in l. 178 of the same poem[5] can be traced to the same source.

When he translated Diodorus, Skelton relied almost exclusively upon the *Breuiloquus*. It failed him occasionally, as with *Triathericum*, Book IV. 3, which he put into his text as it stood, and *Athesian*, I. 38, for which he gave an incorrect derivation,[6] perhaps from some other reference book. But most of his definitions and comments are taken bodily from Reuchlin, as, for example, his explanations of satyr, phallus, barathrum, cynocephalus, cochlea, tragelaphus, Priapus, Muse, Hermaphroditus, Pasiphae, Libya, Hiberus, Tempe.[7] His mistranslation of *felis* as 'hind' is probably due to the same authority, while in his description of Diomedes he follows Reuchlin's confusion of the Aetolian and the Thracian. The long interpolation on the Olympic Games in Book V, which is a mere expansion of Reuchlin, actually contradicts the account given by Diodorus, but this fact is obscured by Poggio.

---

[1] Compiled by Johannes Balbus. The edition of 1495 is here quoted. It is possible, but unlikely, that Reuchlin used some other source.

[2] See Dyce, ii. 1.

[3] This also appears in Balbus, s.v. *Eufrates*.   [4] See Appendix A, 12 c.

[5] The line in Skelton is 'Alexander, a gander of Menander's pole'. The reference is to the white swans of Maeander, as in Ovid, *Heroides* 7. 2; but Reuchlin, s.v. *Olor*, gives the quotation with the same error: 'Ad vada *menandri* concinit albus olor.'

[6] See note to 54/19–20.

[7] These debts to Reuchlin are shown in the notes.

It has been doubted whether Reuchlin's 'preposterous' lexicon, which repeats so many blunders of its predecessors and adds a few of its own, could possibly have been the work of so distinguished a scholar. But Melanchthon, who should have known, tells us that the Amorbachs wanted a Latin dictionary for their new printing-house, and Capnio (as Reuchlin hellenized his name) obliged them. It was the best dictionary of its age, Melanchthon adds, and proved both popular and useful. Moreover, Reuchlin was barely twenty at the time.[1]

Modern superiority is easy, based as it is on another four or five centuries of scholarship. We should note that Skelton used the best dictionary of his day, and that whereas the 'celebrated Dr. Ruckshaw' to whom he dedicated his elegy 'Vpon the Dethe of the Erle of Northumberlande' bequeathed to his church of Lowthorpe a copy of the *Catholicon*,[2] his pupil took advantage of a more up-to-date lexicon. Nevertheless, we cannot find in Skelton's use of reference material any passionate zeal for painstaking exactitude; he was content to catch the easiest way. And this piece of knowledge about him, which is forced upon us by his work in the *Diodorus*, is a most valuable acquisition for anyone who wishes to study his subsequent poetry and career.

(B) *Skelton's Knowledge of Greek*

So far as we can judge, either from his *Diodorus* or from the remainder of his work, Skelton's acquaintance with Greek was entirely indirect—and this is not surprising. His academic career just preceded the introduction of Greek into the university curriculum both in England and at Louvain.[3] Such Greek as he could pick up by

---

[1] S. Berger, *De glossariis et compendiis exegeticis quibusdam medii aevi* . . . *diss. critica*, Paris, 1879, pp. 30–31.

[2] His will is printed in *Testamenta Eboracensia*, Surtees Society, 6 vols., 1835, &c., iv. 231.

[3] Occasional visitors may have taught Greek at Oxford—Emmanuel of Constantinople in 1455–6, Stephano Surigone before 1471, and Cornelio Vitelli *c.* 1475 (see, respectively, H. L. Gray, 'Greek Visitors to England in 1455–56', *Anniversary Essays by Students of C. H. Hoskins*, Boston and New York, 1929, pp. 81–116; R. Weiss, *T.L.S.* ix (Jan. 1937), p. 28; and Gray, loc. cit.). But there is no direct evidence. Even Grocyn, who returned in 1491 from Italy an accomplished Greek scholar, seems to have made no impression until after the turn of the century (R. W. Chambers, *Thomas More*, 1935, pp. 65–66, 81–83). He was in any case too late for Skelton. For a fully authorized Greek readership, England had to wait until 1519, when Richard Croke was appointed at Cambridge.

Introduction xxvii

himself would be elementary, and he might well consider Greek a mere handmaid to *lingua latina*. His passion for the new tongue was apparently not urgent enough to send him, later, to the feet of Politian in Florence or of Grocyn in London. Though not averse from using a word or two of the language on occasion, he did not end his poems with a fashionable TELOS in Greek characters, like his fellow court poet of the nineties, Opiciis; he never brandished an Homeric epithet in the manner of Whittinton; and he was frankly incapable of translating Lucian and Isocrates with Erasmus' pupil, the diligent young Boerio.[1] In short, if he had a nodding acquaintance with Greek, he was content with that.

(C) *Skelton's Knowledge of Latin*

Skelton himself tells us, both in his *Diodorus* and in *The Garlande of Laurell*,[2] that he translated the work from Latin and not from Greek. We should bear in mind the difficulties that confronted him. In the first place, as Chaucer has told us in his little poem addressed to Adam his own scrivener, every author who appears in manuscript is at the mercy of his scribe—and Skelton used a manuscript of Poggio which no doubt added to the difficulties and ambiguities inherent in the bare compression of his Latin style. Further, as we have seen, Skelton could not have at his command those excellent lexicons and aids to the student that now exist. Moreover, what he himself wrote comes to us in the handwriting of three somewhat

---

Erasmus' Greek lectures in 1511 were but an informal pendant to his divinity course (R. C. Jebb, *Erasmus*, Cambridge, 1890, pp. 23 ff.).

At Louvain in the early nineties Erasmus could find no teacher of Greek, but in 1498 he describes the rhetorician Francisco of Crema as *egregie litteratus*, a phrase which may or may not imply a knowledge of Greek (P. S. Allen, *Opus Epistolarum Des. Erasmi*, i. 4, ep. 204).

[1] For Opiciis' poem, dated 1497, see MS. Cotton Vespasian B. iv, fol. 23 (cf. also the colophon of Whittinton's *Vulgaria*, 1520, ed. Beatrice White, E.E.T.S., O.S., clxxxvii (1932), p. 128). Whittinton was fond of airing his Greek. The preface to his *De Consinitate gramatices* (1516) contains what is said to be the earliest Greek printed in England, and the *Antibossicon* (1521) laughs at his use of *hecatebelites*, a faulty transliteration of ἑκατηβελέτης (cf. *Iliad* i. 75). Boerio's Latin-versions of tracts by Lucian and Isocrates are in Additional MS. 19553. They were written before 1509, and the preface describes him as 'pene puer, atque in bonis litteris Tyrunculus' (fol. iv). Possibly the work is more that of Erasmus than of Boerio. See also Allen, op. cit. i. 267.

[2] See, for example, 'Thus endeth the prohemye of Poggius' at the end of Poggio's Prologue, and 'Diodori Siculi historiarum Priscarum a Poggio &c.' before the Table of Contents of Book I. In *The Garlande*, 1498–9, he speaks of 'Diodorus Siculus of my translacyon *Out of fresshe Latine* into owre Englysshe playne'.

careless and strongly individualistic scribes. And, finally, if we excuse Reuchlin for his unsatisfactory *Breuiloquus* on the ground of his youth when he compiled it, we must show Skelton the same charity. Skelton's achievement, great enough in itself, becomes greater by a consideration of the circumstances.

When we come upon the form *Euripules* (i. 7. 2) or *Erupides* (i. 39) for *Euripides*, we can safely attribute it to a scribe rather than the translator. Similarly, it is impossible to believe that Skelton wrote *Thophoceans* (i. 39. 3) for *the Phoceans*, or *Negadenes* (iii. 4) for *negardeness* (niggardliness). These are obvious errors; unfortunately, it is the less obvious scribal errors that may do harm to the translator's reputation, even though the multiplicity of readily noted scribal slips offers a continual warning.

Many errors, also, can be attributed to the manuscript of Poggio that Skelton used, though it takes a keener charity to hunt them down. When he speaks of 'The clowdy mystery of Pan' (i. 18) and 'The Clowde of the Sonne' (i. 45. 2), he has apparently read *nubem* for *urbem*; his description of Vulcan's temple-area as 'a buscage condensyd' (i. 22) may be put down to reading *lucus* for *locus*; when he refers to the moon, instead of mud (i. 36), he must have read *lunam* for *limum*; he presents a new king to history by reading *eminens* as *emineus* (i. 49); and his pathetic account of Regina's death 'by often fallyng into stremes and diches' (iii. 57) must result from a confusion between *fluminum* and *fulminum*.

Though such errors may be set at the door of Poggio's scribe, Poggio himself, though on the whole a careful translator, is by no means free from errors. He more than once confuses the Greek words for 'boundary' and 'mountain' (i. 22, 67), and he is responsible for another new king of Egypt, Ogdous (i. 50. 2). Many other errors of his are recorded in the parallel passages of this text.

But when all these mitigations have been taken into account, there remain faults which can only be attributed to Skelton. Ignorance of Greek is responsible for his treatment of terms like *cheronessus* (iii. 53. 3) and *epirus* (see note to 237/4), his misapprehension of the latter being extended to its Latin equivalent, *continens* (iii. 21, 39). And one small group of Latin words he consistently mistranslates: *aereus* 'brazen' is always rendered 'iron' (i. 96. 3; ii. 8. 2, &c.); and, more seriously, *meridies* 'south' is regularly converted into 'north' as far as iii. 41 (cf. especially 44/9–10; 55/30; 60/17), where he appears

Introduction

to have realized that there was something wrong and compromised with 'the myd-day speer'. Later he translates it 'meridian'. There are, of course, inevitable minor slips, such as 'chapters' for 'books' (i. 4. 2) and 'three' for 'four' (i. 26). Some inaccuracies spring from Latin ambiguities with which he was not familiar. Thus, on its first appearance (i. 10), he takes *lotus* to be a kind of soap—misled no doubt by Reuchlin, who gives the word only as a participle of *lavo*, 'to wash'. In the same way, when Poggio latinizes the name of a monkey as *ortus* (i.e. *hortus* 'garden') Skelton takes it to be a participle of *orior* and ingeniously translates 'Man borne' (iii. 35. 4).

The consequences of such mistakes are sometimes ludicrous. Confusion of *crassor* with *crassus* produces the exaggerated image of the soil of India manured by the blood of the slain (ii. 36. 2). In his creation of the flying island (ii. 47. 2), Skelton has anticipated Blake's *Island in the Moon*; and by a simple misunderstanding of the adverbial *una* (ii. 56), he introduces us to a soit of lady who would have enlivened the contemporary *Querelle des Femmes*. His zoology is also affected by his imperfect Latin. Whales become diving birds (iii. 41); and the ichneumon, which in i. 35 is 'a beest passynge lyke vnto a lytyl dogge', becomes a bird in i. 87. But the most instructive case is that of the hippopotamus. Diodorus says that it 'has tusks larger than those of the wild boar, three on each side, and ears ... somewhat like those of a horse'. Poggio gives this animal ears larger, rather than smaller, than those of other beasts. When Skelton has added his bit—'thre huge eris excedynge all other beestis of lengthe'— the hippopotamus is qualified for a medieval bestiary (see i. 35. 2).

Another ambiguity helps to account for a strong medieval tradition. In i. 28, 55 and iv. 15. 4 Skelton refers to the *isle* of Colchos. But the historical Colchis was not an island; how did it come to be thought one? Poggio's *qui in ponto sunt* affords an explanation. The medieval disregard for capital letters would readily permit the country of Pontus to be mistaken for *pontus* 'ocean'. Thus arose a notion which may be found in Chaucer, Gower, Lydgate, and Caxton among English writers, and which goes back at least as far as Guido delle Colonne. Similarly, Skelton refers to 'the streme that named is the watre of Thermodont in the grete see' (iii. 52). Thermodon is in Pontus; but Skelton transforms it into a river in the sea!

But in a work of this magnitude a certain number of errors is to be expected. There are, however, other problems which beset the translator. One is vocabulary. Skelton was confronted with many words and idioms which had no accepted English equivalent. He was, as we have seen, one of the earliest of modern translators, and, as we shall also see, he must have contributed largely to that great multitude of new words that came into English during the Tudor period. He would not seem to have considered very deeply the difficulties of translation before he began his work, for we find him working out solutions as he writes. In some cases he resorted to a literal translation; thus, *naues longae* 'warships' become 'shippes that be huge of lengthe', and the idiom for 'deserted' (*ordinem reliquissent*) becomes 'went out of the aray' (i. 78). Terms of measurement gave him great difficulty. He begins by rendering *stadium* as 'mile'; but after i. 46 he decides that 'furlong' would be a closer equivalent. *Iugerum* is to him an even greater puzzle. In i. 47 we get: 'so longe that seuen oxen myghte not drawe away', and a little later: 'as moche as iiij wayne of oxen may carye away.' This awkward paraphrase is shortened to 'as moche as two wayne of oxen' (i. 48) and again to 'acris' (i. 52). A few pages farther on he returns to 'more than vj wayne of oxen may drawe to-gydre' (i. 63. 2), but, still dissatisfied, he hits upon the term 'plowland' (i. 64. 2), which he retains from this point on (see ii. 10; iii. 44. 3, &c.).

His somewhat indiscriminate use of English words does not lessen the difficulty of his work. 'Pillar', for instance, is used to describe a propylaeum (i. 51. 3), a pyramid (i. 52, 89), and a stela (i. 55. 2), as well as a column (i. 66). 'Stream' does duty not only for a river but for a cataract (i. 30) and a gulf (i. 33. 2). 'Standard' may mean an obelisk (i. 57) or a colossus (i. 67); and 'stone', whose sense ranges from a precipice to a jewel, is used twice in the same sentence with totally different meanings (iii. 39. 2). A complementary habit may be seen in the translation of *heroas* as 'noble astates' (i. 23. 3), 'marcyal pryncers of renommee' (i. 44), 'noble pryncers' (i. 94), and 'pryncers, lordes' (iv. 1). *Cataractas* is rendered indifferently 'stremes' (i. 30) and 'goolis' (gullies) (i. 32. 2).

The modern reader is likely to be even more distressed by the Latin element in the syntax of Skelton's *Diodorus*. This is due both to the immense prestige of Latin and to the poverty of English at that time as compared with the classics; and a varying degree of latinity will be found in most prose of the period. But Skelton is the greatest Roman of them all.

Introduction   xxxi

His use of absolute constructions is typical. For example: 'Alle whiche maters, sommed in groos from the former yeris of olde, registred in theyr bokes of record...'(i. 44). This is apparently to be read: 'All which matters *having been* registered.' Other examples are:

    i. 95: He settynge at nought his aduertysement and counseyl, Kynge Amasus brake the triews ....

    ii. 25. 2: Thus fortune of werre vnto theymward so contrarious ....

Relative constructions, such as that of the first example above, are also frequent. An unusual instance occurs in iv. 12. 2: 'bott the flagraunt flauour ... of this lusty wyn, what thorow continuance of yers enaged, and for the myghtyly enstrengthide vehemence wherof, so hiddiously ran vppe in-to the heedis of other Centraures....' The influence of Latin *cuius* is evident here.

Word order, again, tends to follow the Latin. Phrases such as 'wilde and bestes savaige' (iii. 43. 3) are clearly echoes of Latin freedom in the position of epithets. A few sentences show an inversion which is even more un-English; e.g. 'They holde an oppynyon ... how the mone, Isis, "The Olde" as a name to her approprid eternally ...' (i. 11). It needs a little study, especially as the original lacks punctuation, before one realizes that this must mean: 'How the moon appropriated "The Old" unto herself as a name.'

But Skelton's greatest departure from normal English usage is in his omission of the subject, usually of subject pronouns. This is so regular as to constitute a definite feature of his style. Examples are:

    Poggio's Prologue (f. 3ᵛ): 'In lyke wyse these wryters behaue theymself that in theyr werkis haue regystred the fayttes & gestes of alle the world enuyron, as it were of one cyte, [   ] haue by conscripcion compacte theym to-gydre vnto a parfyght and wele encomyne.'

    i. 19. 2: 'Emonge all he named one [Nysa], a memoriall of that cyte wherin he was fostred of a tendre age; [   ] plantyd & first sette ivy.'

    i. 35: 'for he excedeth in generacion; for euery yere he hath newe, and [   ] ben but rarely taken, for as a god it is had in reuerence ....'

    i. 41: 'and that playnly is approuyd in pyttes, vawtes, & wellis of huge depenes: in the most hete [   ] ben most colde.'

To these examples from early pages may be added one late in the manuscript:

    iii. 43. 2: '... but afterwarde when [   ] began oones to fall to robberye, and as pirates vppon the see despoiled the merchauntes of the cittee of Alexandre . . . at the last yet they were taken. . . .'

This feature is so ubiquitous that we cannot consider it merely scribal. It occurs in the work of all the scribes, so that one cannot avoid the conclusion that Skelton is deliberately imitating Latin usage. In the earlier instances it may be, perhaps unconsciously, somewhat disguised, as the omission is usually confined to the latter part of a complex sentence; but it becomes definitely more noticeable as we proceed.

The qualities we find, then, in Skelton's translation of Diodorus are quite definitely those of a young and enthusiastic latinist. No other evidence than the style of this document would be needed for assigning to it the earliest possible date, and *c*. 1485 is probably nearer the truth than *c*. 1488. He has not yet learned to keep his languages separate, and Latin constructions echo through his mind and thrust themselves into his English style, warping and twisting it at times into outlandish and grotesque forms. The difficulties he encounters do not induce him to retrace his steps and correct; he is impatient of exact scholarship, but is content to make a show of learning out of the nearest available encyclopedia. With advancing years his enthusiasm may wane, it may deepen his erudition, or it may lead him to smatter widely and recklessly. The last is what actually happened: Skelton's scholarship is thin, not deep; and wide, not concentrated. Nevertheless, he is of the advance guard of humanism in England. If the child is father of the man, then the editor of Skelton's *Poems* would be well advised to give careful study to his *Diodorus*, for there we see the future Skelton as through a glass and not too darkly.

(D) *Skelton's Contribution to the English Language*

The *Oxford English Dictionary* credits Skelton with first using, or first using in special senses, more than 640 words.[1] It may be doubted whether any other English author has been so abundantly honoured by the *Dictionary*. The manifold difficulties of compiling the *Dictionary* were such, however, that probably another hundred words should have been credited to Skelton and were not. But every year adds to our knowledge of Tudor English, and it may be that in the process

[1] See F. M. Salter, 'John Skelton's Contribution to the English Language', *Transactions of the Royal Society of Canada*, Third Series, Section II, vol. xxxix (1945), pp. 119–217.

Introduction   xxxiii

of straightening out the picture many words credited to Skelton as the first user will be given to other writers. Nevertheless, there it is: 640 words apparently first used by Skelton, a fact that may be taken as roughly correct: is any further proof of Skelton's humanistic zeal necessary? For, as everyone knows, one of the constant preoccupations of the Renaissance was the enrichment of the vernacular—and if Skelton could be proved to have added fifty words, or even twenty-five, to the resources of the English language, he can be proved to have been, in that respect and to that extent, a humanist.

Now we have maintained that the mature Skelton can be seen foreshadowed in the young Skelton. Investigation reveals 816 words in his *Diodorus* which he there used fifty, seventy-five, one hundred, and even three hundred years before the first use of these words, or special senses of them, recorded in *O.E.D.*[1] The child *is* father of the man: all told, we must say that, so far as we now know or can learn, Skelton was the first person to use, either completely new or in new senses, nearly 1,500 words. Let us admit wholesale error and confusion in our knowledge of the English language in his or any period, let us say that our results are 50 per cent. wrong, and let us remember that words might be used in speech before they were used in writing, and that the first writer did not necessarily coin them, then we must believe that Skelton was the first to use in writing 750 words—or 3,000! Let us go further: let us say that our knowledge is 90 per cent. wrong, and that it is 90 per cent. wrong only in the direction favourable to Skelton; we must still say that Skelton was the first to use in English writing 150 words. In short, there is no getting round it: torture and twist the evidence as we may, there still remains to Skelton's credit a remarkable achievement. But if the 1,500 words that now stand to his credit as first user—a number large enough to form the entire vocabulary of some writers—were to be considered good enough as a rough average, then Skelton's accomplishment in finding and using and popularizing new words is absolutely amazing.

Many of these words, also, he must have coined. But in the present state of our knowledge of the English language it is idle to

---

[1] Salter, op. cit., pp. 119–84. It will, of course, be realized that in their gigantic undertaking the *Dictionary* makers could not be expected, for their harvest of words, to thresh every manuscript as well as every printed book in English. They left the sole manuscript of Skelton's Diodorus understandably untouched.

ask which, or even how many. We can, however, be certain from the many evidences as to his character and habits presented already in these pages, that the following conclusion comes fairly near the truth:

'No doubt many of his words are boisterous or fantastic nonce-words too individualistic in character ever to find sympathy with the genius of our speech; but he seems also to have drawn in and preserved for honourable careers many a folk-word of apt value, and his penchant for Anglicizing Latin terms must have given us many workaday words that still carry on the business of the world. These are words that we should probably have found for ourselves sooner or later—and we have polished the forms of not a few of them to make them a little sweeter on the tongue—nevertheless, if it were only possible to see the whole truth clearly, we may be sure that to this egocentric but conventional poet at the court of Henry VII whom life under Henry VIII and Wolsey turned rabid, we owe a large part of the phrasing of our daily walk and conversation.'[1]

(E) *Skelton and Rhetoric*

Skelton's conventionality remains largely to be seen, and it is most evident in his rhetorical ideas and practice. It will be obvious by now that in his translation of Diodorus he did not aim at literal accuracy. Nevertheless, he had an ideal—or, let us say, a developing ideal, for the last book of his translation is a very different piece of work from the first; and this ideal is best summed up in the word 'rhetorical'.

As poet laureate, Skelton was a qualified rhetorician.[2] His title of 'orator royal' is a reminder of the fact; and if we wish for outside testimony, we have only to examine Hawes's *Pastime* where, alone of the arts, Lady Rethoryke 'hadde a garlande / of the laurell grene' (658). Louvain, also, which laureated Skelton, was distinguished among universities by its Chair of Rhetoric—and Skelton's devo-

---

[1] Ibid., p. 191.

[2] William Nelson's otherwise excellent account of Laureation (*John Skelton, Laureate* (Columbia University Press, 1939) pp. 40 ff.) obscures the fact that grammar and rhetoric, although related, were distinct faculties, of which rhetoric was the superior, and that, apart from Skelton's, the only recorded grants of the laurel in English universities were made to Bulman and Whittinton—both students of rhetoric (S. Gibson, *Statuta antiqua Univ. Oxon.*, Oxford, 1931, p. lxxxviii; C. W. Boase, *Reg. Univ. Oxford*, Oxford, 1885, i. 299). It thus appears that for a brief period the laurel was the badge of a degree in rhetoric, in much the same way as the rod and birch were the insignia of a master (sometimes, though incorrectly, termed bachelor) of grammar. In all cases the rhetorician would also have studied, if he had not graduated in, grammar: hence the confusion.

Introduction

tion to the leading subject of the trivium can be traced throughout his work.

As we have noted elsewhere,[1] the technical terms of rhetoric abound in his poems. When he introduces *Speke Parrot*, he does so with a Greek rhetorical term, 'Lectoribus auctor recipit opusculy huius auxesim',[2] where *auxesis* (the Latin *amplificatio*) corresponds to the modern 'puff' or 'blurb'. Later in the same piece occurs the note: 'Sepenumero hec / pensitans psi/tacus Ego pẽ/fio [space] / Aphrosmo quia / paronomasia certe / ineprehensibilis /'[3] which apparently is to be read: 'Sepenumero hec pensitans psitacus ego patefacio aphorismo, quia paronomasia certe incomprehensibilis', referring to the 'incomprehensible word-play' of *phronesis* and *frenesis* in l. 49 of the poem. Among the Latin additions to the same work there is a distich supposed to represent an *hyperbaton*, which the scribe seems to have left unfinished. It may be amended thus:

> Psitacus heu notus ceu Persius est, puto, notus
> Nec, reor, est nec erit, licet est erit [vndique notus.][4]

Two of the four Cicero quotations in Skelton are drawn from the rhetorical *De inventione*. The Middle Ages named it the *Vetus Rhetorica*, as distinct from the *Ad Herennium*, which was the *Nova Rhetorica*. And a gloss to the *Replycacion*,[5] which is attributed to *veterum rhetoris*, is accordingly to be found in *De invent.* I. I. I. The last poem *Against Garnesche* has a reference of greater interest:

> Ye haue nat red the properte
> Of naturys workys, how they be
> Myxte with sum incommodite,
> As prouithe well, in hys Rethorikys Olde,
> Cicero with hys tong of golde.[6]

A side-note bids us consult the Prologue to Book II of the *Vetus Rhetorica* and quotes the opening words. Here Cicero relates how inhabitants of the flourishing colony of Crotona in southern Italy engaged Zeuxis to paint a masterpiece for their temple of Juno. He decided to do a Helen, and asked for a model. When they showed him their loveliest virgins, however, he chose not one but five. For nothing in nature is perfect in all its parts, but 'aliud alii commodi, aliquo adiuncto incommodo, muneratur'.

---

[1] See Appendix A, 7. [2] Here taken from Harleian MS. 2252, fol. 133^v. See Dyce, ii. 1.
[3] Fol. 134^v; Dyce, ii. 3–4.   [4] Fol. 137^v; Dyce, ii. 18.   [5] Dyce, i. 208.
[6] *Against Garnesche*, iv. 8 ff.; Dyce, i. 126. Dyce does not capitalize *Olde*.

Despite the frequent use of their names as authorities, neither Cicero nor Aristotle would have been able to recognize the medieval version of rhetoric. It had long lost its function as 'the art of giving effectiveness to truth',[1] and become little more than a standard literary technique. Its former scope still received lip service, but what medieval rhetoric actually means in practice can be seen in the most widely studied manual of the later Middle Ages—the *Poetria Noua* of Geoffrey de Vinsauf (*c.* 1210). Geoffrey conceives literature simply as the art of ornamenting a theme. He begins, it is true, with the classical subdivisions, but the vital *inventio* is dismissed with a mention, and disposition (*ordo*) gets only 116 lines (87–202). The body of the treatise is devoted to expansion. Of the two modes of emphasizing a subject, that which really concerns Geoffrey is *amplification*. This is treated in 469 lines, while 46 lines are given to *abbreviation*. The remainder of the book concerns itself with figures of style (*colores*).

An outline of the section on *amplification* (220–689) will convey the nature of the work. Eight methods of 'lingering' are prescribed. First, *interpretatio* or *expolitio*, which is nothing more than the reduplication of phrase which afflicts almost all of our early modern literature. A variant of this is periphrasis (*circuitio*)—as Geoffrey, with perfect simplicity, explains: 'Longius ut sit opus, ne ponas nomina rerum.'[2] Then comes comparison (*collatio*), followed by apostrophe (*exclamatio*), prosopopeia, digression, description, and the use of opposites, as in 675: 'Ista juventutis est et non forma senilis.' Most of these methods, with sub-species such as *collatio aperta* and *occulta*, are illustrated with lengthy examples.

Though little more than a primer of the art, and perhaps intended for schoolboys, the *Poetria Noua* was considered a standard work on rhetoric. J. M. Manly has shown[3] that Chaucer made at first a serious and later a satirical use of it; but he by no means laughed it out of existence. An anonymous poem of the early fifteenth century, describing a lady, has a long invocation which mentions:

> Englesshe geffrey with al thy colourys
> That wrote so wel to Pope Innocent.[4]

---

[1] C. S. Baldwin, *Medieval Rhetoric and Poetic*, New York, 1928, p. 3.
[2] E. Faral, *Les Arts poétiques du XIIe et du XIIIe siecle. Recherches et documents sur la technique littéraire du moyen âge*, Paris, 1924, pp. 194 ff.
[3] 'Chaucer and the Rhetoricians', *British Academy Proceedings*, xxii (1926), pp. 95–113.
[4] E. P. Hammond, 'How a Lover Praiseth a Lady', *Modern Philology*, xxi (1924), pp. 379–95 (ll. 217–18).

And 'Galfrid' remained a court of appeal right down to the sixteenth century, as we learn from the *Court of Love* (11).

That his influence was unfortunate is all too evident. His stress upon amplification explains the fatal diffuseness of much late medieval poetry. The endless catalogues of names in Gower, the worst excesses of aureation in Lydgate, were no doubt committed in his name, or in the name of the system which he represents. To say a thing in four words instead of one became the duty of every writer with pretensions to 'eloquence'. Only the man with a message, or an individual of Chaucer's genius, was strong enough to resist the invitation to dally and toy with his subject and deck it with unessential ornament.

Skelton was clearly bred in the tradition. The signs are omnipresent in his love of enigmatical ciphers, in digressions like the *cacosyntheton* of the *Garlande*, in the *Reimprosa* of his *Speculum Principis*, in his pleonasms, in his breathless inventories, and in his trick of surrounding his poems with a Latin frieze. His *Salue* is a versified exercise in *dictamen*:[1] it merely strings together the opening formulae to the specimen epistles of a Mennicken.[2] Similarly, his Latin verses on the laurel assemble all the trees of literature, with suitable epithets, in order to declare its pre-eminence. His poem to Kateryn, beginning 'Knolege, aquayntance, resort, fauour with grace',[3] is an ecphrasis in the aureate manner of Lydgate. One stanza compares her to various liquids, another to precious stones, and so on. His very proverbs are enjoined by the rhetorical text-book.

These characteristics were not derived from Cicero; their source is medieval. For it can be proved that Skelton knew his medieval *poetriae* by heart. In *The Garlande* he advises the reader to bid his mind follow the example of Janus: 'Emula sit iani retro speculetur et ante.'[4] The prophet (Vates) quoted, as indicated by the marginal note, turns out to be Geoffrey de Vinsauf, who utters this 'sentence' in his first illustration of the apostrophe (281): 'Aemula sis Jani: retro speculeris et ante.' Skelton's periphrasis for 'Ovid' in the same poem (1181) may have misled the modern critic, but it was familiar

---

[1] *Salue, &c.*, is printed by Dyce, i. 177.
[2] Cf. C. Mennicken's *Continet iste libellus epistolares quasdam formulas* (Zwollis: ? 1480) which he tells us were used by the students of Louvain residing *in pedagogio lilij*.
[3] Dyce, i. 25. Taken in order, the first letters of the first lines of the stanzas spell out K A T E R Y N.   [4] Faukes, sig. F 2ᵛ; Dyce, i. 421.

to readers of his day. The line (*Ars*, i. 8) is quoted in Geoffrey's prose *De arte versificandi*, 50, and (as 'Tiphis amoris') in his *Poetriae*, 1779, as well as by Matthew de Vendôme, *Ars versificatoria*, 61.[1]

Nevertheless, like Chaucer, though in his own personal fashion, Skelton refused to be tied down to the school rhetoric. The Northumberland elegy, indeed, is closely modelled upon Geoffrey's lament for Richard. Geoffrey, who is illustrating the use of *exclamatio*, apostrophizes first the day of death, then the murderer, then Death itself, Nature, and finally God. Skelton begins by invoking Clio, after which he rails upon the murderers. Then comes the apostrophe to the day—in spite of Chaucer's ridicule:

> O cruell Mars, thou dedly god of war!
> O dolorous tewisday, dedicate to thy name,
> When thou shoke thy sworde so noble a man to mar!...[2]

Whereupon, going one better than his master, Skelton proceeds to exclaim against the spot w ere the Earl lost his life:

> O ground vngracious, vnhappy be thy fame,
> Which wert endyed with rede bloud of the same
> Most noble erle! O foule mysuryd ground,
> Whereon he gat his finall dedely wounde!

The next stanza cries out upon Atropos and Homicide, and the poem ends with an apostrophe to the young Earl and an invocation of God, the Virgin, and 'the heuenly yerarchy'. Its conventionality and its orthodoxy are unquestionable.

By the time *Phyllyp Sparowe* was written, however, Skelton is master of his 'eloquence'. He can wear it with lightness and humour. Thus he makes Jane burst forth against the murdering cat, as he says, 'By way of exclamacyon' (274). The convention is now seen from the outside; it has become three-dimensional, vivid again. But Skelton never abandons the apostrophe. We find it when Apollo is mourning Daphne in *The Garlande*. Faukes's text runs:

> Then he assurded in to his exclamacyon
> Vnto Diana, the goddes inmortall:
> O mercyles madame ...[3]

---

[1] Faral, op. cit., pp. 293, 251, 132.
[2] Dyce, i. 10. Cf. Geoffrey's 'O Veneris lacrimosa dies! O sidus amarum!' (375 ff.), and Chaucer's parody in the *Nonnes Prestes Tale*. [3] Sig. B1 (ll. 302–4); Dyce, i. 374.

Marshe has *this* for *his*, a reading which Dyce adopts. But we can now see that Faukes was right: in Skelton's age it was expected that Apollo's dirge should be equipped with an *exclamatio*. An elegy would be incomplete without it. Here the use is serious and familiar at once. Skelton avoids banality by taking us behind the scenes, as it were, and showing us Apollo practising 'his' apostrophe and making it ready for use.

One other example will show his transmutation of the medieval formulae. The charming Commendation of Jane in *Phyllyp Sparowe* is an imitation of the first *descriptio* in the *Poetria Noua*. With his usual frankness Geoffrey explains that the figure is a device for 'expanding your piece' (*Ut dilatet opus*, 555); and he illustrates with an ideal catalogue of feminine charms. This takes the form of a list proceeding from the hair and brow steadily down, with a modest hiatus, to legs and feet. A second piece gives an equally glowing account of the clothing proper to such a beauty. This mechanical and elegant enumeration formed the basis for the description of fair women for centuries. Chaucer's Duchess only partly escaped from the mode, but Hawes follows *de cap a pé*,[1] and so does the author of *The Court of Love*, who translates his 'Galfrid' almost word for word.[2] No. LXIX of the Shirburn Ballads also preserves the tradition, and the list could be extended indefinitely.

But, like Chaucer, Skelton is too good an artist to adhere slavishly to the model. He praises Jane's features, her eyes, her 'browes bente', her veins, her white and red, her lips and mouth; but the 'warte vpon her cheke'—showing the admixture of some incommodity—might have horrified Geoffrey, and the remark about her gait, which is justly famous, certainly owed him nothing. None the less, Skelton follows the convention, at however great a distance; and the fact becomes ineluctable when we read:

> Her kyrtell so goodly lased,
> And vnder that is brased
> Such plasures that I may
> Neyther wryte nor say
> Yet though I wryte not with ynke,
> No man can let me thynke,
> For thought hath lyberte . . .[3]

---

[1] *Pastime of Pleasure*, 3846 ff. He describes the lady 'Frome toppe to too' in the manner of Geoffrey, but omits the formal concession to modesty mentioned below.
[2] 778 ff.   [3] Kele, sig. D4 (1194 ff.); Dyce, i. 87–88.

This smiling *naïveté*—so typical of Skelton, one thinks—is a paraphrase of Geoffrey's

> Taceo de partibus infra:
> Aptius hic loquitur animus quam lingua ..

This *The Court of Love* renders, more literally:

> I hold my pees of other thinges hid:—
> Here shall my soul, and not my tong, bewray.[1]

Borrowed though it be, this passage is purest Skelton. The difference in tone is absolute. It is not even parody, like Chaucer's mock invocation of Venus and 'Gaufred'. Rather we must see in it that audacity which links Skelton more surely with the Renaissance than does his learning. For, as if to emphasize the point, he repeats this little indiscretion. When Parrot is recommending the golden mean (*Speke Parrot*, 52–53), the manuscript adds a side-note: 'Apcius hic loquitur Animus quam lingua.'[2] In the very lists of political controversy, Skelton defends a principle with the solemn coyness of Geoffrey de Vinsauf!

Skelton's poems, therefore, show him a rhetorician to the end. But his mature works make a very different use of rhetoric from his early ones. By means of a dryly complex humour he converts stuffy medieval artificiality into positive virtue. His recital of his accomplishments in *The Garlande* is surely the liveliest bibliography in literature, with the possible exception of Rabelais's St. Victor catalogue. And this same poem, which is meant as a formal apologia and is stuffed bretfull of rhetorical devices, becomes the longest self-encomium a poet has ever written. Once the humour is appreciated, one can enjoy the leisurely muster of Skelton's rhetorical devices. They are disinfected of dullness.

The *Diodorus*, on the other hand, was written when Skelton was young and a candidate for the laurel; and the fact is stamped on every page of the work. In one of his rare interpolations he tells us what he conceives his task as translator to be:

> Sith it is stondyng with oure litterature of enterpretation, afforcyng thoffice by translation oure matiere to dilate, so to procede by suspensive

---

[1] *Poetria Noua*, 594–5; *Court of Love*, 806–7.
[2] Harleian MS. 2252, fol. 124ᵛ; Dyce, ii. 4. Lines 52–53 are: '*Moderata* juvant but *toto* doth excede; Dyscressyon is moder of noble vertues all.'

Introduction

contynuaunce that no thyng vnto oure proces apperteynyng be left vnremembred, we woll therfor that our stile agayne vnto Lynus be reversed. (iii. 67. 2.)

It is Geoffrey's principle, *ut dilatet opus*; and if dilation were Skelton's purpose, we must admit that he succeeded, and succeeded more abundantly as he went on.

Tautology is fundamental to dilation. Thus, 'finally' becomes 'fynally in conclusion' (ii. 25. 2), 'liken' expands to 'parifye ... by resemblaunce in symylitude' (ii. 31. 2), and the simple word is taboo. It must be, if used at all, shored up by synonyms, as 'soueraigne dame, gouernour, prynceis, and quene of all the hole lond' (ii. 20. 2), or eked out with stock epithets, like 'the furious and myghty strong lyon, savage of nature' (ii. 8. 2). There is no attempt at subtlety: in 'all to-stongen ... or ellis from the hede to the fote' (i. 77. 2), the alternative does not spring from a desire for greater accuracy or greater emphasis—it is mere repetition. The effeminate Sardanapalus, when he defeats his foes—or has them defeated for him—becomes automatically 'he that was fiers and furious of corage, of indignacion moved, and with odious rancour of malice sore fretted' (ii. 25), in contradiction to the whole account of his character.

Periphrasis is another important feature of the dilated style. True, the didactic purpose of explaining unfamiliar terms underlies it, but it contributes nevertheless to general vagueness. The Cyclades are translated as 'out isles of the sea' (i. 36. 2; 55. 2); the Argonauts become 'theym that fonde first the fayt of saylynge' (iv. C),[1] or are depersonalized into 'the first fetes that were fownde of sailyng in the see' (iii. 52). The translator was expected to vary his phrases, a ground upon which Skelton might excuse the uncertainty with which he treats certain technical terms like *iugerum*. *Olympiad* is interesting from this point of view. We get 'the solempnysed feste of Iupiter dyuulgate by name Olympiades' (i. 4. 2); 'the fest-ful solempnysacion dedicate vnto Iupiter, callyd Olympiades' (i. 44); 'Olympiade, called the feste solempnysed vnto Iubyter' (i. 68); 'the ... solennysed feest vnto Iupiter, Olimpiades by denomynation' (ii. 32); and lastly a page-long explanation of the term, taken from Reuchlin (iv. 14).

The conventional diction, in which every hill becomes 'high' and 'montuous', leads inevitably to bombast and exaggeration. The diet

---

[1] C stands for the Table of Contents preceding the book.

of Egyptian kings, which includes veal and goose, is 'but of groos vitayll' (i. 70. 2). The abettor of thieves is punished with three days' deprivation of 'mete & drynke' (i. 77), an increase in the punishment which would render it much more serious than the Egyptians intended. And the headband worn by Dionysus after he had 'waded to depe in his cruette' is transformed into 'a myter that moche was ponderous, rychely sette with stones precyous of valew' (iv. 4. 2), a somewhat drastic cure for headache. At the same time important contrasts are blurred. There is no attempt to distinguish between Egyptian and Boeotian Thebes (i. 23. 2), although the distinction is essential to the argument. In the discussion on pyramids, the antithesis is lost between the kings who built them with other men's labour and money and the architects who created them out of their own mental resources (i. 64. 4). Similarly, the distinction between the creation of the universe and the origin of man disappears in Skelton; he joins 'the first orygynal of man' with 'the first begynnynge of man' as a perfectly legitimate tautology (i. 42). In his description of the Nine Muses (iv. 7. 2) the goddesses lose individuality and become almost indistinguishable in the flood of superlatives.

As has been noted, the 'aureation' of the prose increases as we proceed. Skelton advances from a fumbling literalness in Book I to rolling periods in Book V (or IV), where Poggio's original serves only as a spring-board for leaps into eloquence, as in the following example:

> The noble actes of our former predecessours of olde suche as longe tyme were by-fore vs, as, prynces, ryall estates, & suche as were half acounted for goddis, were moche gloryously renomed, famous, & many in nombre. Whos merytorious & constant byhauour was so hyely allowed of the worldly people, ay wandrynge ful of varyaunce, that they were acounted in theyr comyn opynyon as inmortal goddis vnto whome they, with alle humylyacion of deuyne obseruaunce, rendryd sacrefyces with deuoute oblacions & offrynges of hertely affection. Whiche alle in nombre be acquyted of their moche vertuous and notable guydynge with historyous monumentis of remembraunce intermynable; whos famous names inscrybed be, wyth laureate lettres inviolably euermore to endure, emonge the celestial senatours entronanysed & crowned with the contynuel enverdured laureate leues of victoryous tryumphe in the gloryous cyte of fame. (iv. 1.)

The accumulation of variants is astounding; what is still more extraordinary is that they make so little difference to the sense. 'Former',

Introduction

'of old', 'such as long time were before us', mean exactly the same thing, but their repetition does not add emphasis or deepen the meaning. Like some histories that are to be condemned, Skelton's *Diodorus* is 'illumyned rather with ornacye of pullished termes than with the clere veritie of parfight sentence' (iii. 65. 2).

Love and the natural world are established themes for the rhetorician. Of the latter, we have a glittering instance in the account of the island where Dionysus was hidden:

... within the precynct of this ile-lande there is a contrey which among theym is accompted the contrey of terrestre pleasure and of worldely welthe, distynctly embeawted w^t medes lusty, freshly the soile ennewed with pleasaunt motles grene wherin goodly flowres grow dilectable to beholde, redolent of aire and with soueraigne swetenes reflairyng, enmoistured irriguously with the sailyng and freshly lepyng stremes of watres enwellyng and burbelyng agayne lusty Phebus radiant beme with dropes cristallyne. The soile of his owne naturall engendrure bryngeth forthe many dyuers kyndes of fruyt and vynes charged with embolmed clustres of the ruddy grape, moche replenyshed throughout with wodes of pleasure and trees passyng goodly to beholde and se. (iii. 68. 2.)

The whole of this *descriptio* should be read; it supplies a generous quota of the terms considered suitable to the beauties of nature. The detail is wholly formal, its value cumulative; the descriptive outline is lost—as it is meant to be—in arabesques of applied ornament.

But Skelton reserves his highest flight for the medieval Lord of Love. Confronted with the bare eight words of Poggio: 'Semelem Iupiter ob pulchritudinem in forma hominis cognouit', he responds:

Iupyter, so as he was moche amerous, surprised inwardly with the passynge beaute of Dame Semeles whos goodly eye, as a smaragdyne stone radyaunt, enpersyd thurgh the sterry heuen the inwarde aspecte of Iupyters hertly mynde or thought, that he, of his godly concyderacion prouoked, daygned hym-self to associate with humylyte, from his hye celestyal trone to make his progresse doun in-to this vale of myddel erthe, suche myracles to shewe by the power of his magnyfycence, transformynge hym-self in fygure of our nature humayne of purpose to be famyliarly conuersynge & frendly acqueynted with this said lady Semele whos feturis, so lustely by Dame Natures curyous operacion ennued, encyted the grete god Iupiter to resorte doun from his celestyn court of heuenly glorye with her to kepe company in her erthely couertour of this world transitorye; bytwene whome the fyry bronde of charite vnfeyned so feruently was kyndled that eche of theym to other shewed their hertes couertly wounded; and, shortly to conclude, for the sanatyf releuement of theyr preuy hurtis, eyther to other was conformable, that kyndnes for kyndnes bytwene theym was enured. (iv. 2.)

We may be grateful to Skelton that he 'concluded it shortly', for it is penance to copy or even to punctuate.

Such purple passages, however, are not the only heights of this remarkable prose. Occasionally we get effects of a less stereotyped order. The capture of a giant snake in Ethiopia seems to have excited Skelton, and he conveys that excitement to the reader:

> But when it was so they approched nere vnto hym and sawe his glasyng ien glowyng and flamyng like vnto fire, and how he lay likkyng his lippes with his towng, and the horrible sharpenes and hardenes of his scales, as often as he moved theym how they sheverd and ruskeled to-gedre like as it had bene harneis of plate, and his tuskes that stode out tusked as a tentrehoke, his lothely wide mowth discoloured vgly to beholde, they were wondrely agast. (iii. 36. 2.)

This is still rhetorical, with its alliteration and its *traductio* of 'tusks' and 'tusked', but a saving simplicity is also present in 'licking his lips with his tongue' and the 'wide mouth discolored'. The capture of this 'wild worm' is told with admirable directness:

> First they made a net with smale corde which was wondrefull myghty and strong to endure. This net was fasshend holough asmoch in quantitie as myght easily conteigne this serpent monstruous. Then espied they out the denne where he rested, and awaited the tyme by good advisement when he went ynne and when he went out; and assone as the serpent was issued out aftre his accustume of purpose to slee that bestes which toward the waters side resorted, anon they stopped the hole of his denne with erthe and with stones. They mustred then, in the brode vale there-as he shuld haue repaired by homeward to his lodgyng, such as were archours, and sumtyme had slynges, and a grete nombre of horsemen with clarions and trumpettes ordeyned of purpose for the same entent. How-be-it, noone of theym durst be so bolde to preace nygh vnto hym for drede they shuld haue fallen in the daungere as other did tofore. And when this worme savaige saw this grete people and moche ordynaunce, he casted vp his hede as high as he myght; but then, abasshed of the dartes that they piked vnto hym from afarre, and of the sight of so many horses, and what for the multitude of dogges hallowyng still by contynuaunce with terrible nois of the trumpes and clarions, he toke his passaige vnto his olde lodgyng which he fownde stopped in maner and fourme tofore recompted. Then they pursewed vppon hym in the chace with nayng of horses, with blowyng of trumpes, with showtyng of people, with hallowyng of howndes, so that the serpent was amased and ne

Introduction

wist what to doo, and drave hym into the same place whereas the nete was pight for to take hym. And thus by policye therin he was masked, and as he lay wrastlyng in it and gnawyng with his tethe of purpose to escape, with moch wondrefull hissyng and nois aftre his nature, they euermore leid vppon hym still without intermyssion. For when the nette was drawen out, and his taile venenous all to-brosed by grete force of stripes, and his tethe broken, this wilde worme by occasion therof was wondrely attamed. And thus brought they this serpent enweried vnto the citee of Alexander. . . . (iii. 37.)

The keywords of this passage are monosyllables: 'Net', 'den', 'hole', 'vale', 'worm', 'teeth', 'tail'. And though the effect is cumulative, in the manner of less exciting passages, the rhetoric is by no means empty. We may compare it with the moving comment upon the slaves in Egyptian gold-mines:

They neuer rest from this laborous travaile. Driven they be with chidyng and reheityng and iawlyng vppon, all-way with bonchyng, with betyng, so enforced vnto their work that they neuer have leisour to rest theym-self non so litle awhile. . . . And be ye wel assured there is non so harde harted a bodye beholdyng all thise how wretchedly they goo, havyng not a brat to cover-with theire taile, but he wold abhorre the sight of theym, and tendrely enpittee and have compassion vpon theym. But there nys pittee, rest, nor erthely remedye for theym, whether they be sike, or sore shakyng of the axes, or aiged man or woman, be they neuer so feble or croked. All they be curried and beten to warke still, contynually, as long as the poure myserable wrecches may drawe theire vitall breth and endure. (iii. 13.)

Skelton's *Diodorus*, it will be seen, is not all mere embroidery.

The general qualities of Skelton's prose style may nevertheless be summarized as (1) a high degree of latinity in vocabulary and syntax, (2) extreme tautology, (3) periphrasis, (4) conventional diction, (5) alliteration. The same features appear in his verse. In 1523 he was still writing lines like:

> Thus stode I in the frithy forest of Galtres,
> Ensowkid with sylt of the myry mose.[1]

'Frithy forest' can only mean forest-like forest; and, as *mose* should be *wose*,[2] 'sylt of the myry wose' is another expansion of one word into three (or five). The tag 'myry wose', incidentally, is one of those counters that passes for gold in the aureate style; it can be, and

---

[1] *Garlande*, 22–23; Dyce, i. 362.   [2] Cf. note to 18/17.

is, used over and over. From the *Diodorus* a number of such formulae can be culled, which Skelton used in his poems until the end of his days. Obvious examples are: 'blast of the pipplyng wind' and 'bremely with your bristles'.[1] And the prose introduction to the *Replycacion* shows Skelton writing, perhaps as late as 1528, the same elaborately 'polished' sentences that he affected at least forty years earlier. Though his rhetoric was often transfigured by humour or galvanized by his natural zest and vigour, its persistence in his work and the depth of its influence upon him give us a further clue to that understanding of Skelton which we seek.

That our early modern literature was 'rhetorical' is a commonplace. No gain in meaning was necessarily intended or expected from the conventional expansion and repetition. They were regarded as pure decoration. *Amplificatio* is so alien to modern standards that we find it a little difficult to believe or comprehend that a writer might in the fifteenth and sixteenth centuries aim exclusively at ornamental volubility. The latter part of the *Diodorus* is valuable as evidence of this now obsolete literary theory.

Judged from within the convention, it has much to commend it. Compare similar passages in Skelton and other writers. Here is John Kay, a contemporary poet laureate:

And also for to shewe and declare the meruaylous gretenesse of the sayde bombardes and gonnes: the grete pyles and postes strong and myghty that were stykked in the grounde behynde atte taylle of the foresayde gret bombardes gaue suche grete and myghty shakyng / that the howses of Rhodes other whyles shaked in suche a wyse lyke yf hyt hadde ben a yerth quake. But they of Rhodes alleway besy and prouydent stopped wyth trees the grete ruyne of theyre walles and made also many dyches wythinne the cytee. The turkes vexed also the Rhodyans wyth many other and dyuers instrumentes of werre, for they ordeyned rond about the foresayde Cytee of Rhodes certayn instrumentes of werre the whych ben called Slynges or Engynes / And the turkes with suche instrumentes of werre casted in to the eyere // a pype full of grete stones the whyche fel vpon the houses of Rodes and putted theym in a wrecched ruyne wyth grete murdre of theym that were within for that tyme: and forthermore they putte in a grete thoughte and sorowe alle the hole cytee of Rhodes. for noo persone was sure in hous wyth oute he were in a kaue.[2]

A parallel passage may be found in *Diodorus*, ii. 27, where Skelton's

[1] See notes to 189/29, 373/26.
[2] John Kay, *Obsidium Rhodiae urbis* [No title-page], Caxton: 1482 (?), fols. 10ʳ–10ᵛ.

superiority is unmistakable. Kay's genuine poverty of vocabulary is ill concealed under the monotonous doublets of *expolitio*: 'strong and mighty', 'great and mighty', 'busy and provident', 'other and divers', 'thought and sorrow'. The word *great* occurs no less than seven times in our brief excerpt. That is the kind of background against which we have to set the *Diodorus*.

But Skelton's concentration upon *copia*, though defensible on the ground of conventionality, brings its own revenge. When he is free to write 'it onely deuoureth not' (i. 35) for 'it not only devoureth'; 'Grekis not onely' (i. 9. 2) for 'not only the Greeks'; and 'onely is not' (i. 36) for 'is not only'; and even 'he knewe not only' (i. 39. 2) for 'he not only knew not', the result is bound to be structural anarchy. And the chief weakness of the *Diodorus* prose is a weakness of construction which renders it unfit for consecutive thought. Much the same conventional jargon can be found in later writers such as Hall; but little by little the Skeltonic *copia* disappears, and the instrument of English prose becomes more controlled, more dedicated to logical purposes.

Historically the *Diodorus* represents the end of a particular line of prose development. It is our most extreme example of 'aureation' and dilation. Renaissance prose remained rhetorical, and Renaissance rhetoric preserved the emphasis upon *amplificatio*;[1] but we never again see it so unrestrained. Even at its worst, however, it helped notably to increase our English vocabulary, and perhaps to inspire such art-forms as the masterly doublets of Shakespeare in which sound and sense are again wedded; and it is no unworthy measure of Skelton's own genius that he was able to break through the bonds of medieval convention many a time and oft, or that he could transform the 'monstruous bosse', *Amplificatio*, into the fair dame, Poesy.

(F) *The Essential Skelton*

What we have really been searching for in this long discussion of Skelton's translation, while immediately considering his dictionary, his knowledge of Greek and of the Latin language, his contribution to English, and his indebtedness to medieval rhetoric, is the ultimate object of all Skelton research—Skelton himself. There are many

---

[1] See W. G. Crane, *Wit and Rhetoric in the Renaissance*, New York, 1937, pp. 63, 76, 78, 79, 97.

puzzles in his life, and his works bristle with difficulty. How could the same man attack Wolsey with such ruthless, sustained, relentless savagery—and bow and scrape to him in a *Replycacion*? Some expert scholars have called Skelton a humanist—others, equally expert, have denied it. By some who ought to know, like Alexander Pope, his poetry has been contemptuously set aside as of little worth—others, equally valued as critics, have rated him highly. We have felt that we might come a little nearer to the essential Skelton through a study of his attainments, an investigation of his learning.

The first and most obvious of things is that he did not know Greek. But the Latin language and Latin literature Skelton knew and loved, knew intimately, in a way impossible for us of the twentieth century. His knowledge of the classics is difficult to estimate, it is true, for the mere presence or absence of a quotation or reference tells us little or nothing, particularly in a period like Skelton's, heyday as it was of the compend and the florilegium. And Skelton's peculiar technique makes investigation doubly difficult, for with his developed sense of the grotesque he brought to a fine art the trick of revitalizing clichés. Time and again we find him building up vivid, original verse out of the flattest commonplaces of the age. His vigour luxuriated in the banal, perhaps because it was so splendidly recalcitrant a medium. This habit was complicated by the medieval love of annotation that was strong in him. Most of his actual quotations appear in marginalia, and these were chosen, far more often than is usually realized, for humorous or sly comments on the text. In such cases the triteness of a tag recommends it for the purpose.[1]

A surer index to his learning will be found in those references which do not specify or quote any particular author but spring naturally from the fullness of his knowledge. An example in point is the 'Addicion' to *Phyllyp Sparowe* which Dyce thought corrupt:

> I conjure thé, Phillip Sparow,
> By Hercules that hell dyd harow,
> And with a venemous arow
> Slew of the Epidaures
> One of the Centaures,
> Or Onocentaures,
> Or Hipocentaures...   (ll. 1290–97.)

---

[1] For a list of his quotations and references see Appendix B.

Introduction

Professor Williams took 'Epidaures' to mean serpents, comparing the *serpens Epidaurius* of Horace, and understood: 'With an arrow envenomed with [the poison of] the snakes of Epidaurus.' But Skelton's meaning is not so obfuscated. Epidaurus was sacred to Aesculapius, god of medicine—the serpents were his—and the centaur slain by Achilles was Chiron, who had taught him the art. Skelton's lines are a simple inversion for 'the Epidaurian (or medical) centaur'. To his age the reference would not be unduly recondite. The next two lines are characteristically Skeltonic with their pretence of pedantic exactness in this polysyllabic aside: he will not venture to determine, on the available evidence, whether Chiron was half ass or half horse![1] The passage is quite in keeping with the tone of the 'Addicion', itself one huge parenthesis, but it also shows the familiarity with Latin of a man who can jest and play in that language.

Most of the obscurities in Skelton resolve themselves similarly. He is not, or not always, trying to be difficult; it is merely that our own education has left the traditional road to Rome. Further, with all his enthusiasm for the classics, Skelton was no purist; his Latin did not end in the Silver Age; and much that is unfamiliar in his work is due to his ready acceptance of the medieval legacy. Verses from the Breviary and the Vulgate are not his only debt to the Middle Ages; much of his Greek is medieval, and he welcomes Latin terms invented by the medieval clerk. An incomprehensible gloss in *Speke Parrot* provides a ready example:

> My deysy delectabyll,
> My prymerose commendabyll,
> My vyolet amyabyll,
> My ioye inexplicabill,
> Nowe torne agayne to me.
>
> Quid quaeritis tot capita, tot census?
>
> (ll. 246–50.)

In Reuchlin's *Vocabularius breuiloquus* we find the definition: 'Capitecensus ... corona quę in capite geritur ....' Apparently the scribe carelessly repeated the *tot*, making three words out of *capitecensus*. It is clear that after writing the stanza Skelton with some amusement asks himself, 'Why do you seek so many garlands?'

The Middle Ages could offer more, however, than a storehouse

---

[1] These terms, which might have been introduced into Appendix A, Skelton would find in Isidore of Seville (11. 3. 39, s.v. *Centaurus*) or in Reuchlin's *Vocabularius breuiloquus* (s.v. *hippocentaurus*).

l   *Introduction*

from which to draw a Skeltonesque vocabulary. From its dictionaries and schoolbooks he could draw many of his classical references and borrowings—as others than himself can be proved to have done. Thus he may have found the quotation which glosses l. 26 of *Speke Parrot* not in Martial whence it ultimately derives but in Isidore of Seville's account of the parrot (12. 7. 24), and the fine portrait of Envy in *Phyllyp Sparowe* may not have come direct from Ovid but via the long description in *The Romance of the Rose* which forms A 247 ff. of the English version. And his knowledge of vernacular literature shows not only in his familiarity with Chaucer[1] and Gower but also in his amazing catalogue of romances in *Phyllyp Sparowe*.

From the growing body of humanist literature, also, he took many items. There is, for example, the legend of Charlemagne in *Why Come Ye Nat to Courte?*, quoted from Petrarch's *Familiar Epistles*,[2] and Boccaccio is laid under tribute for the complimentary lyrics of *The Garlande of Laurell*.[3] The only Renaissance poet he quotes is Mantuan, soon to be a school author for the young Elizabethan; but Skelton borrows from the less-known *Epigrammata ad Falconem*, first published in 1489.[4] It is evident, therefore, that Skelton was a wide-ranging and voracious reader and that he kept himself up to date.

For the most part, however, he confined himself to the collectanea which were a delight of the Renaissance scholar. In 1498 Polydore Vergil published his *Proverbiorum libellus*, just preceding, as he was later careful to insist, the much more comprehensive *Adagia* of Erasmus. And one of his proverbs explains the curious device which Skelton uses twice in his *Speculum Principis* manuscript:[5] 'Tribuat michi Iuppiter Feretrius ne teram tempus apud

---

[1] Cf. the reference to Dame Prudence in his Diodorus, iii. 71, and the 'pyned goostes' of iii. 29.

[2] See Dyce, ii. 364–5, where the letter is given in full.

[3] Ibid. ii. 320–1. See also E. P. Hammond, *English Verse between Chaucer and Surrey*, Durham (N.C.), 1927, notes to *Garlande*, 827 ff.

[4] *Op. omnia*, ed. L. Cuperus, 4 vols., Antwerp, 1576, i. 97. As a gloss to *Replycacion*, 379, Skelton quotes lines 7–8: 'Dona Dei, carmen nitidum, facundia praestans, Mittitur ex astris, a superisque datur.' Mantuan's prologue has the significant title, *Contra poetas impudicè loquentes carmen*.

A similarity has been noted (W. Kerr, *T.L.S.*, 20 Dec. 1934) between *Phyllyp Sparowe* and Politian's *De Angeli puella*, but it does not really extend beyond the conventional itemizing mode of description. Politian's iambics have an obviously Catullan inspiration (cf. the *Cinaede Thalle*); they are wholly regular and unrhymed.

[5] See *Speculum*, ix (Jan. 1934), p. 37.

Eurotam.' Near the Flaminian Circus in Rome, says Polydore, Octavius had built a portico called variously Corinthian or Persian, which contained paintings of Sparta and its river Eurotas. 'The idlers lounging there were said to sit beside Eurotas: which after grew to a proverb, so that "to sit beside Eurotas" was to do nothing.'[1] Thus Skelton's prayer to Jupiter was not that he might be brought back from exile, as has been suggested,[2] but that he might be saved from the bane of every good medieval writer, idleness. Now the *Speculum Principis* volume itself and all the pieces in it are dated by the modern editor as prior to 1512,[3] a dating with which Nelson is in general agreement.[4] We have evidence, therefore, that Skelton was using Polydore Vergil's collection of proverbs within at the most a dozen years of its publication.

Skelton's debt to Erasmus' *Adagia* was, not unnaturally, larger; but there is no sign in Skelton's works of any other kind of influence of Erasmus upon him—unless he ranks as one of those in *Speke Parrot* who 'scrape out good scripture and set in a gall'.[5]

When his dates are taken into account, the items which may be ticketed 'Renaissance' in Skelton's work are relatively numerous. For translation he chose the *Diodorus* of the humanist Poggio and 'Tully's *Familiars*', by discovering which Petrarch had caused a literary furore in 1345. Of other Italians he borrowed from Mantuan and Boccaccio; of the German humanists, as we have seen, from Reuchlin; of the French, from Gaguin and Lemaire de Belges;[6] and finally from Erasmus. But analysis somewhat modifies the impression created by this shining array of names. In no case, we find, does he borrow from an 'advanced' or revolutionary volume. Even the Mantuan quotation is an Ovidian cliché. It is only the reference works of Boccaccio that he plunders. Gaguin is cited in

---

[1] 'Sedere ad Eurotam. Romae fuit porticus Corinthis inter caeteras celebris ad circum flaminium erecta a C. octauio: dicta Corinthia: propter aes corinthiacum: quod erat incolumis. dicebatur etiam porticus persei: quum Cn. octauius ex bello nauali contra persaeum triumphum rettulit. in qua porticum erat tabula picta habens lacedaemonem & eurotam fluuium laconiae auctor Plinius li. iiii. Vnde ignaui illic desidentes: dicebantur sedere ad Eurotam. hinc postea prouerbio increbuit. ut sedere ad eurotam: esset nihil agere' (*Prouerbiorum libellus*, Venice, 10 Apr. 1498, sig. d 1ᵛ-2). Pliny is the authority only for the locality of Eurotas.
[2] William Nelson, *Skelton Laureate*, New York, 1939, p. 117.
[3] See *Speculum*, ix. 30.
[4] Op. cit., pp. 246–7.
[5] For Skelton's debt to the *Adagia* see Appendix D.
[6] His *Epistres de l'amant verd* offered a number of hints for *Phyllyp Sparowe*.

Introduction

Why Come Ye Nat to Courte? only as a chronicler; Petrarch as an informal correspondent. And Erasmus' *Adagia*, though it contains many of his ideas in embryo, is primarily a *vade mecum* for the writer of Latin. Not until the very end of his life, in the *Replycacion*, do we find in Skelton an attitude which is explicitly that of a literary precisian—and, ironically enough, each cause to which he commits himself is the wrong one.[1]

At this point a distinction is clearly necessary. Unlike the typical humanist in England, Skelton was first and last a poet, not a scholar. He might tutor and translate, point with pride to his academic laurel, invoke his *almam uniuersitatem*: he was still neither a don nor a savant. The minutiae of textual criticism were not his concern; he was satisfied with a working knowledge of the texts. It is true that he keeps abreast of current discoveries, as we learn from his use of Claudius Donatus;[2] but it is useless to try to fit him into a cénacle like that of the studious London Reformers. Their enthusiasms were as foreign to him as their prejudices. Simply, his mind was not of their sort. Or, as has been said, Skelton 'was an *early* humanist who survived his age'.[3] If he had died at the turn of the century, or before 1519 when Richard Croke was appointed to teach Greek at Cambridge, there would have been no question of the fact. He was born too early for the English zealots of the humanistic movement after the turn of the century; he was born too early, moreover, for Hellenism, and his feelings toward the 'other tongue' were mixed:

> Attica dictamina
> Sunt plumbi lamina,
> Vel spuria vitulamina:
> Avertat haec Urania! (*Speke Parrot*, 272–5.)

For Skelton there were two kinds of Greek, the permanent[4] and the ephemeral;[5] and he prays to the Muse (Urania) to save us from the latter. In the same way he was quite out of sympathy with various

---

[1] See Appendix A, 9c; B, 9.
[2] See Appendix A, 11d.
[3] F. M. Salter, op. cit., p. 120. It should be acknowledged that most of the material of this Introduction has been drawn from an unpublished dissertation by H. L. R. Edwards, entitled 'The Humanism of John Skelton', in which the nature of Skelton's learning is examined at length. A copy may be seen in the Cambridge University Library.
[4] See Job (Vulgate) xix. 23–24: 'Quis mihi tribuat ut scribantur sermones mei? quis mihi det ut exarentur in libro Styło ferreo, *ut plumbi lamina*, vel celte sculpantur in silice?'
[5] See Sap. (Vulgate) iv. 2–3: '*Spuria vitulamina* non dabunt radices altas'.

Introduction

humanist efforts, Catholic and Protestant, to reform Church doctrine—a fact which may go some way toward an explanation of the *Replycacion*.

Skelton's humanism was rather of the kind common to vernacular writers of the Continent—Folengo, Pulci, Rabelais. His sense of kinship with the Roman poets gives him the same Cellinesque swagger. He has the same love for his native tongue, the same bluff and callous good humour. His very feuds might be called an Italian fashion, although his *Poems Against Garnesche* had a precedent nearer home in the flyting of Dunbar and Kennedy, a fashion which quickly spread to enliven the realm of scholarship all over Europe with *invectivae*. In all his work he reveals the budding national pride from which, at the century's close, disrupted Christendom blossomed violently into a new Europe. And in his devotion to things of this mad world, in his healthy, masculine, and secular robustness of feeling, in his independence, his satirist's clear-sightedness, in his very vulgarity, he expresses the English counterpart of the paganism—of the earthy, joyous paganism—of the high Renaissance.

It is this true Skelton, and neither the strutting court favourite of one tradition nor the rude rough railing rhymer of another, whose character sheds light upon his *Diodorus* and whose *Diodorus* sheds light upon his whole character and career.

NOTES

Page 1, line 1. *Holy Fader.* Pope Nicolas V, to whom Poggio dedicated his translation of Diodorus.

3/12. *dredeful obloquy of sclaunderous detraction.* Cf. *Speke Parrot*, 361-2: 'Detraxion, encankryd with envye, Whose tong ys attayntyd with slaundrys obliqui.'

5/25-26. *hath behold . . . world.* Cf. Homer's description of Odysseus, *Od.* i. 3.

7/1-13. *And somme . . . people.* Samuel K. Workman, *M.L.N.* lvi (1941), compares the style of this passage with the style of the same material in Caxton and Lord Berners.

7/26. The Courte of Fame is a typical Skeltonic addition.

8/2. *But alle their fayttes.* Possibly this phrase should be emended to read *For alle*, but there are so many parallel expressions in the text that one must conclude that Skelton has been influenced by nominative absolute and ablative absolute constructions in Latin.

8/34. *For it incyteth, &c.* For a somewhat elaborate illustration of this rather commonplace faith in the moral value of History, cf. Skelton's *Speculum Principis* [*Speculum*, ix (January 1934), 25-37].

11/27. *Olympiades.* Cf. Reuchlin, *Vocabularius Breuiloquus*: 'Olympias. adis. & hec olympica. ce. in eodem sensu. festum uel solemnis ludus. quod uel que fiebat ad honorem Iouis semel per quinquennium . . .'. Cf. also note to p. 382, l. 27.

13/22. *ideal.* The nearest definition in the *O.E.D.* is as follows: '*sb.*, 1623; 1. A conception of something, or a thing conceived, in its highest perfection, or as an object to be realized or aimed at; a perfect type; a standard of perfection or excellence.' But Skelton seems to be thinking of an implicit pattern or archetype in the primordial chaos, to which by an eternally continuing process the forms of heaven and earth are approximated.

18/17. *myry wose.* The frequency of this tag (cf. 42/29, 117/36, 124/3, 380/6, 395/14) and *wosy myre* of 15/6 suggests a correction of l. 23 of the *Garlande of Laurell* in the face of all texts. These have: 'Ensowkid with sylt of the myry *mose.*' Dyce takes *mose* to mean *moss* (ii. 301), but it would seem to be an error for *wose* = *ooze*. For a similar confusion of *m* and *w* in Skelton's work, cf. 226/3 where *matere* seems a better reading than *watere*. Although he takes *mose* to mean *moss* in the *Garlande*, Dyce's note is illuminating: 'The forest of Galtres (which, as already noticed, extended nearly all round Sheriff-Hutton [where the *Garlande* was written]) was, when Camden wrote, "in some places shaded with trees, *in others swampy*".' [Dyce, ii, 301.]

18/31-32. '*The sonne . . . herynge.*' Cf. Homer, *Od.* xii. 323.

19/3. *skynne of celestial variete*—i.e. the dappled fawn-skin of Dionysus.

21/3. *whyte eyen*. Oldfather notes: 'This common epithet of Athena in Homer is more generally taken to mean "gleaming-eyed".'

21/5. *the ayer is yelow*. Both Poggio's *glauci* and Skelton's *yelow* connote paleness. For *yelow* as a translation of *glaucus*, cf. *Ortus Vocab.*, 'Glaucus, ʒalo or yrne graye.' Cf. also *O.E.D.*, s.v. 'Yellow'. Cf. also *fallow* as an epithet of the sea. Reuchlin says: 'Glaucus . . . dicitur a glaucum. quod greci dicunt album. eo quod sit album . . . Glaucus ergo albus. splendidus. subniger. rubeus, flauus. viridis dicitur . . . .'

21/14. *These wordes*. Cf. *Od.* xvii. 485-7.

23/20. *a kynge*—i.e. Busiris. Cf. 65/22 ff.

24/13. *Dionisius*. As Oldfather explains (see footnote to 345/36), the name is derived from *Dios* (genitive of Zeus) and *Nysa*.

24/13. *A poete there was*. The reference, as Oldfather points out, is to *Homeric Hymns*, i. 8-9.

25/11. *not by Mynerue*. Skelton claims, *Garlande of Laurell*, 1404, to have written a poem on 'How Dame Minerua first found the olyue tre'.

27/5-6. *by enterpretacon* '. . . *disporte*'. With this 'enterpretacon', which is not in O, 1-3, cf. Reuchlin, s.v. *Satyra*: 'Sunt vero satyri leues ludificantes derisores saltores. Similiter et satyra.'

28/9-10. *shippis of thre maner of takelynge*. It is difficult to understand that Skelton could have been so in the dark as to the correct meaning of *triremis*. In 141/28 he translates it 'of iij topcastles', and in 271/24 reverts to 'iij maner of takelyng'. Reuchlin offers no clue to this puzzle, since he defines *triremis* as 'nauis que tres ordines remorum habet'.

28/19. *Reed See*. As Oldfather notes, 'Not the present Red Sea, but the Persian Gulf.'

29/11-12. *drynke of barley*. Cf. 48/13 where this Egyptian beer is called *otton*.

32/6. *festes of Bachus & Appollo*. Poggio and Diodorus mention only 'the festivals connected with Dionysus', but cf. 'Orpheus . . . apperceyued emonge theym the solempnysed mysteryes of Appollo, etc.' in 32/15 ff. Cf. also pp. 21 ff.

32/9. *emportynge signefyaunce of a dede tree*. This explanation is not in O, 1-3, but Reuchlin has 'Phalon grece. latine lignum dicitur'.

32/17. *mysteryes of Appollo*. Cf. note on *festes of Bachus & Appollo*, 32/6.

33/21-22. *places . . . of dysguysynge*. This expression, as a translation of *theatra*, suggests something of Skelton's personal background. It is likely that he assisted in the preparation of masques, revels, and 'disguisings' for the entertainment of the Court. In the *Garlande of Laurell* there are several suggestive titles, 'Diologgis of Ymagynacyoun', the 'commedy, Achademios', 'Of Vertu . . . the souerayne enterlude', and 'paiauntis that were played in Ioyows Garde', but the only dramatic work known to survive is *Magnyfycence*.

Notes 399

34/17. *Alceus.* Hercules was so named after his grandfather, Alcaeus.

37/6. *houres.* The primary sense of the Greek word, *horoi*, is 'seasons'.

38/13. *canyculer signe.* Oldfather notes: 'According to Pseudo-Eratosthenes (*Catasterismus*, 33) the star on the head of Canis Maior was called Isis as well as Sirius.'

39/17. *Colchos.* The parallels perhaps explain how Colchis came to be thought of in the Middle Ages as an island. If the initial were not written as a capital, as might happen in medieval manuscripts, the country of *Pontus* could easily be confused with *pontus*, the ocean, and Colchis be set in the latter. Examples of this error may be seen in Guido delle Colonne's *Hist. Troiana*, which refers to Colchis as *insula*, and in Chaucer, *Legende of Good Women*, 1425; Gower, *Confessio Amantis*, v. 3265; Lydgate, *Troy Book*, i. 531–2; and Caxton, *Hist. Iason*, E.E.T.S., p. 68.

39/24. *Ascij.* The point is that just as Roma was 'Urbs', and London is 'Town', so the Athenians called their city 'Asty'.

42/9. *Trogloditis.* The form, *Trogodytes*, which Oldfather, following Vogel and Kallenberg, considers preferable, appears in 53/25.

42/21. *pyplynge blaste of wynde.* This favourite expression appears not only several times in this manuscript but also in Skelton's *Replycacion*: 'the flyblowen *blast* of the moche vayne glorious *pipplyng wynde*', Dyce, i. 207.

43/7. '*The swalow of Helle*'. This 'signyficacion', which is not in O,1–3, has a parallel in Reuchlin: 'Barathrum. n. s. nomen est nimię altitudinis & profunditatis. ... Et dicitur barathrum quandoque infernus quandoque *profundissimus locus inferni*. in quo nulla est redemptio.'

43/10. *porte salew.* Cf. *Colyn Cloute*, 1262 (with Dyce's note, ii. 299), and *Garlande of Laurell*, 541, where the term 'safe harbour' is used proverbially.

45/5. *kragges or strayttes.* The term *cataractas*, which is here translated as 'kragges or strayttes', is translated a few lines later as 'straytes', and again as 'goolis', with the last of which cf. 'gullettis & fletes' for sluices or gates, 'portas', in 28/16. In 42/7 Skelton translates *cataractis* as 'stremes'.

46/4–7. *whiche signefye ... apis.* This explanation is not in O, 1–3. Reuchlin has: 'Cynocephalus . . . gens habens caput ad modum canini capitis. Et etiam quoddam genus simiarum sic dicitur.'

47/18–19. *By-cause it pretendeth ... snayles shelle.* Reuchlin, quoting from *Graecismus*, xii. 127, says: 'Cochlea ... dicitur per circulum ascensus. Vnde. Dic cochleam turris scalam testamque limacis.' Oldfather refers to Vitruvius' description of Cochlea (x. 6), as a 'screw with spiral channels, "like those of a snail shell", which turned with a wooden shaft'.

48/12. *druggis bellario.* In default of the word *dessert* (which O.E.D. first records as of 1600), Skelton used the regular Latin equivalent of *tragemata*, *bellaria*. Reuchlin does not compare them, but see Erasmus, *Colloquia*, ed. 1664, p. 136, n. 3.

48/30. *It onely deuoureth not*—i.e. it not only devoureth. The modern reader, accustomed to a fixed word order, is likely to be distressed—or

amused—by the changes Skelton rings on this formula: 'Grekis not onely . . .
but also' (16/25 ff.) for 'Not only the Greeks, &c.'; 'he knewe not only . . .
but also . . . he neuer' (57/1 ff.) for 'he not only did not, &c.'; 'This streme
onely is not beneficial . . . but also' (50/10 ff.), &c.

49/15–16. *that leyeth eggis*. The fact that 1 has *schneumon*, and 2, 3, *schueumon*
for *ichneumon*, suggests that Skelton's source also may have been corrupt at
this point. At any rate, he does not seem to connect the egg-laying monster
with the crocodile. In 117/31 he speaks as if he thought the ichneumon a
bird. Reuchlin does not define *ichneumon*.

49/22–23. *tothed . . . of lengthe*. An object lesson in the value of punctuation. Diodorus wrote: τοὺς χαυλιόδοντας ἔχει μείζους τῶν ἀγρίων ὑῶν, τρεῖς
ἐξ ἀμφοτέρων τῶν μερῶν, ὦτα δὲ καὶ κέρκον καὶ φωνὴν ἵππῳ παρεμφερῆ. It is
possible that in the text as it came to Poggio, ὑῶν was omitted. Reading it
with pauses after τρεῖς and ὦτα he translates: 'Dentes ex utroque latere tres
habet: ultra reliquas feras eminentiores aures', so that instead of projecting
tusks, the hippopotamus is said to have enormous ears. If the Poggio text
that Skelton used had a colon after *latere*, instead of after *habet*, we can
understand how his hippopotamus was endowed not with the two small ears
which one might expect, but with three enormous ones.

51/27. *out-yles*. This is Skelton's regular translation of the Cyclades (cf.
78/4). Reuchlin says (s.v. *Cycla*): 'Cyclades enim fuerunt sexagintatres
insulę circa delum in orbe sitę & ideo sic dictę sunt.'

54/19–20. *apropred . . . denomynacion*. Skelton's derivation of *Athesius*
from 'a flode that Athesis highte' is not in O, 1–3, nor in Reuchlin. The word
is actually derived from ἔτος (year) because of the periodic nature of the winds.

58/3–4. *another part . . . situacion*. Oldfather notes: 'They postulated a
south temperate zone, corresponding to the north temperate, and separated
from it by the torrid zone. The Nile, according to them, rose in the south
temperate zone. They were not in fact so far astray in the matter, the White
Nile rising just a little south of the equator, although the waters of the annual
inundation come from the Blue Nile, which has its source in the table-land
of Abyssinia.'

65/32–66/2. *ther is a poete . . . chariottis*. The reference is to *Iliad*, ix. 381–4.

66/22. *furlonge*. Skelton seems rather capricious in his treatment of all
terms used for exact measurement. Elsewhere he equates stades with miles.
Cf. 65/26.

67/20–21. *a kynges tombe whos name was Simandius*. Shelley's sonnet has
made the name of this king familiar. Oldfather notes: 'This is the great
sanctuary erected by Ramses II . . . known . . . as the Ramesseum. . . .
H. R. Hall derives the name Osymandyas from Userma-Ra . . . one of the
royal names of Ramses.'

67/23. *that seuen oxen myghte not drawe away*. Skelton's difficulties with
such a term as *iugera* serve as a reminder that translation was by no means as
easy a task in his day as in ours. Not only had the language not been enriched
by his own efforts and those of a host of others, as well as by an expanding

culture, but the medieval helps were difficult of access and frequently unsatisfactory. Reuchlin defines *iugera* as follows: 'secundum quod communiter accipitur. est spacium terrę. quod vnum aratrum potest arare in die.'

70/2–3. *veryte & trouthe*. The judge, as will be seen in 103/23 ff., has a chain about his neck, to which is attached a pendant image of Verity.

70/10–11. *Kynge Emyneus*, sprung from Skelton's mistranslation of *eminens*, perhaps with the help of a confusing text of Poggio, should act as a warning to historians—and to editors of ancient texts. For another such king as Emyneus, see Ogdous, 71/25 ff.

73/2–4. *innes or hostryes . . . a short tyme*. This ancient idea has found abundant expression through the ages, and beautifully in Masefield's line, 'Guesting awhile in the rooms of a beautiful inn' (in *Laugh and Be Merry*).

84/23. *byttoris*. Skelton uses *byttoris* where Oldfather has *quails*. Among the birds that mourn *Phyllyp Sparowe* are both 'the quayle', 416, and 'The bitter with his bumpe', 432.

87/29. *furlonge*. This pyramid was a stade, i.e. six plethra, each way at the base. The Great Pyramid previously described was seven plethra.

90/15–16. *goo ouer alle theyr dede bodyes*. Properly the translation should read, 'pass between the halves of all the dead bodies'. With reference to Genesis xv. 10, 17; Jeremiah xxxiv. 18–19; and Herodotus vii. 39, Oldfather notes that there was a primitive belief that one could 'be preserved from harm by passing between the parts of a sacrificed animal'.

91/24. *emporyens*. It is quite possible that Skelton understood *emporyens* as a race of people and that the term should be capitalized.

102/15–16. *they brynge forth encreace ayenst theyr nature*. This method of incubation, by burying the eggs in dung, is described, as Oldfather points out, by Aristotle, *Historia Animalium*, vi. 2. Sir Thomas More adopted the same method for his Utopians: 'They brynge up a greate multitude of pulleyne, and that by a mervaylouse policye. For the hennes dooe not sytte upon the egges: but by keepynge theym in a certayne equall heate they brynge lyfe into them, and hatche theym.' Everyman ed. ii. 50.

103/17–18. *prudent clergye . . . Senate*. The Areopagus and the Gerousia respectively.

103/25. *Veryte*. Cf. 70/2.

107/1–3. *And this lawe . . . dedely woo*. Alternative interpretations of this passage are possible. It may be that Skelton intends *supposed* to be taken literally from its derivation, meaning 'set under'. The passage would then mean that they considered no shame worse than that of desertion. It may be that Skelton intends *unto* to mean *comparable to*. Or a word may be omitted from the passage.

108/2–9. *For sith . . . comyn iurour*. This passage has become somewhat 'enderkyd' by translation. Diodorus offers three reasons for the preceding law of contracts: (1) that men often forsworn lose their credit, (2) that such a law morally obliges men to keep faith, (3) that if men are trusted without an oath, they should be trusted with an oath.

112/23. Skelton's translation of *felis* as *hyndes* suggests a confusion between medieval Latin *fele* and *cerua*. Reuchlin says: 'Felena . . . quędam bestia valde timida, scilicet cerua. Et pro eodem inuenitur hęc feles indeclinabile.'

118/21. *a mannes secrete membris.* Cf. Reuchlin: 'Priapus . . . iuuenis quidam de lapsato [i.e. Lampsaco] ciuitate hellesponti. vnde depulsus est propter magnitudinem virilis membri . . . Et ab illo dicitur priapus virile membrum.'

123/2. *stone of Ethiope.* Oldfather notes that the knife was probably made of obsidian or flint, 'such as are frequently found in graves with mummies'. He refers also to the description of embalming given by Herodotus, ii. 86.

124/6. *hemycicle.* Reuchlin says: 'Hemicyclus . . . dimidius circulus. . . . Vnde hemicyclus quandoque dicitur sedes dimidium circulum habens. id [est] arcum.'

127/33–128/4. *Whenne the Elienses . . . trews.* It would perhaps be more generous to Skelton to punctuate as follows: 'Whenne the Elienses, suche a maner of people so named, were ocupyed about a sedycyous debate callyd Olympyake, sente vnto hym an embacyate demaundynge in what maner of wyse this mater myght best be doon of right & equyte, yf none of the Elienses medled therwith, he ansuerde vnder this forme derkely intryked with ambiguouse sence: how the prynce of the Samyens, &c.' The punctuation of the text has been adopted because Skelton seems regularly to use *How* to introduce reported speech; but it must be pointed out that a stop after *certaret* in his text of Poggio would sufficiently account for his translation. Examples of the introductory *How* may be found in 32/15 ff.: 'They reporte how that Orpheus, &c.'; 74/26 ff.: 'They reporte that ther is xxij maner of fysshes in it, and how ther is so grete multytude taken of theym, &c.'; 143/28 ff.: 'she wele vnderstode for assuraunce how it was voide of all watche, &c.'; 175/32 ff.: 'And they repoort of the nature of that planet which among the Grecians is named Saturnus, and say how he is rigorous, &c.'; 177/1 ff.: 'They say how thise planettes, &c.'; 312/1 ff.: 'Aftre summe auctorities it is recompted how there ne was but oon Dionysius . . . and how it was he which . . . and how that through his divyne ordynaunce, &c.'

128/5–14. *entreated . . . entreate . . entreated.* Skelton uses the first two verbs in the sense of *use* or *behave towards*, the third in the sense of *pleaded with*. It would perhaps be possible also to take *frend* not as referring to Polycratus but to one of those persons whom he had abused ('haynously entreated'). But the sense of the passage seems to be that this King Amasus is a 'forcastynge man' who speaks in riddles. By virtue of a 'composicion of trews' he makes a 'frende' of Polycratus. When Polycratus abuses strangers in his land, Amasus 'paynfully entreats' him to be more kindly. Polycratus pays no attention to this remonstrance, whereupon Amasus says, 'Your misfortunes will cause you to repent, and I shall not grieve over them.' Even as he 'ansuerde vnder this forme derkely intryked with ambiguouse sense', so it fell out. Polycratus did suffer misfortunes.

130/2. *wrytynge.* The references are to *Odyssey*, xxiv. 1–2 and 11–14.

Notes 403

130/8. *They*—i.e. Homer. But, as Oldfather points out, Diodorus is in error, the only name for the Nile in Homer being *Aigyptos*. The *uocant* which must have been in Skelton's source and which appears in Poggio 1–3 is corrected to *vocat* in the edition of 1531.

130/21. *varis*. In modern Greek β is pronounced *v*. Poggio's translation is thus linguistically or phonetically interesting. Cf. *vata* for *bata*, 48/10.

131/5. *vessel*. According to Oldfather, 'a reference to the fifty daughters of Danaus who after death were condemned to the endless labour of pouring water into vessels with holes'.

139/5. *Eufrates*. As Oldfather points out, Nineveh was built on the east bank of the Tigris, not on the Euphrates.

144/19. *love and drede*. This phrase occurs again in Skelton: ''Tween love and drede, My life I lead.' See Envoy to *The Garlande of Laurell*.

149/2. *Opis which was goddes of the yerth*. Cf. Reuchlin (s.v. *Ops*): 'Opis ... Et hinc hec opis. opis. quędam dea quę putabatur opibus pręesse. ... Et dicitur ops terra. eo quod opem ferat frugibus. quę alio nomine dicitur cybele ....'

151/20. *shaft*. Reuchlin derives *obelus* (virgule) from *obelos* = sagitta. 1–3 have: quam [1: qnam] a forma obeliscum dicunt.

162/8–11. *eunuch ... estate*. Skelton does not draw this information from Reuchlin, who has: 'Eunuchus. chi ... gręcum est. id [est] spado. Et eunuchia. chię. id [est] facies. Sed eunuchię. arum sunt delitię.' Elsewhere Reuchlin has: 'Spado. donis. dicitur eunuchus. castratus. & dicitur a spadix.'

164/31. *Mennon*. Reuchlin says: 'Mennon fuit filius aurorę. rex orientalis. ...' Skelton and Reuchlin agree in the form of the name; Poggio regularly has *Memnon* which is correct.

174/19. *chateryng of birdes*. Cf. Reuchlin: 'Augur ... qui vel quę in garritu auium diuinat. ...'

182/19–20. *The beldyng ... compact*. Reuchlin says: 'Pyrama. atis ... & hic pyramis. idis. quędam alta structura quę fiebat antiquitus super sepulcrum mortuorum. & talis ędificatio surgit. vt a latitudine incipiat. & in angustum finiatur sicut ignis: Nam apud maiores. potentes. aut sub montibus vel in montibus sepeliebantur ... Item & pyramis dicitur quędam figura quę in modum ignis ab amplo in acutum consurgit.'

189/29. *pipyng*. Possibly a scribal error for *pip(p)lyng*, which is a favourite word of Skelton's. Cf. *Replycacion* (Dyce, i. 207), and 42/21, 241/19, 242/12, 250/22, 276/31, 285/13.

200/19. *wevyng in the stole*. Cf. *Garlande of Laurell*, 790: 'To weue in the stoule sume were full preste.' Dyce (ii. 318) provides a number of quotations of this phrase and supposes the *stool* to have been a weaving-frame.

208/12. *droughty soyle*. Skelton is translating too freely at this point to permit parallels to decide whether he wrote *sowle* or *soyle*. For *sowle* there is plenty of precedent, including Pseudo-Augustine's 'Anima, quia spiritus est, in sicco habitare non potest.' Cf. also 'Some dronken dastardis with their dry soules', *Garlande of Laurell*, 190.

208/13–16. *There groweth . . . naturall growyng*. As Skelton frequently alters a construction in mid-sentence, it would perhaps be better to punctuate 'There groweth in a certeyne valey of the said contrey grete habundaunce of bawme, which is vnto theym a lucrative merchaundise for-asmoch as nowhere els is noon in all the world—the plant tofore remembred hath his naturall growyng, and his vertue passyngly [is] had in cherite, &c.' It may even be that 'naturall growyng' and 'vertue' should be linked—omitting *is* as actually in the manuscript: 'the plant tofore remembred hath his naturall growyng and his vertue passyngly had in cherite, &c.'

210/16. *strute-cameles*. Reuchlin is in general agreement with Diodorus: 'Strucio. onis. gręco nomine quoddam animal in similitudine auis pennas habere videtur. tamen de terra altius non eleuatur. oua fouere negligit. sed proiecta tantummodo. fotu pulueris animantur. vt vult Isidorus . . . .' The word also occurs in the Vulgate. Cf. Leviticus xi. 16; Deuteronomy xiv. 15; Job xxx. 29; xxxix. 13, &c.

211/16. *tragelasi*. The spelling is perhaps scribal. Reuchlin defines: 'Tragelaphus. phi. . . . id [est] hircoceruus nomen est compositum a tragos quod est hircus. & laphos quod est ceruus. qui licet eiusdem speciei sit cum ceruo. villosos tamen habet armos. vt hirci. & menta barbata.'

215/5. *gibbodicili*. The word is built up perhaps from Poggio's 'nonnulli *gibbum* duplicem in dorso habent: a quo & *ditili* nominantur'; but as *dituloi* means 'double-humped', the compound was unnecessary.

218/1. *the poete maketh memoriall*. As Oldfather points out, the reference is to the *Odyssey*, vii. 120–1, where Homer describes the land of the Phaeacians.

219/6–7. *They kepe not . . . lynyally*. In Oldfather, and in Poggio 1–3, this sentence follows the discussion of letters two sentences above.

224/1–6. *Now that to-fore . . . Mount Athlas*. This introductory statement is three times as long in Diodorus. Poggio seems to have been impatient of Diodorus' long introductory, summary, and transitional statements; he cuts them all short.

229/17–18. *menyall houshold men*. Cf. 'Vpon the Dethe of the Erle of Northumberlande', 185: '. . . as menyall men of his housold' and 33: 'as meniall houshold men'.

237/4. *the ij Epirians*. Skelton regularly takes *epirus* and *continens* for the names of countries. Cf. 244/4 'a place in the see that called is Continence'. Cf. also 264/8, 270/4, 294/10.

241/28–29. *fome of the see*. Reuchlin says: 'Alga . . . secundum Hugutionem est herba frigidissima crescens in mari & est quasi fęnum disposita. & dicitur a verbo algeo. es. Etiam alga sumitur pro quolibet quod mare eijcit. vnde mare dicitur algosum eo quod algam de se proijcit. vel dicitur alga ab alligo. as. quia alligat pedes uel manus. Vnde Alga fit herba maris sed dicitur vlua paludis.'

Has Skelton misunderstood the phrase, 'quod algam de se proijcit [what the sea throws out—i.e. foam]', or does he intend 'fome of the see' descriptively as of sea-weed that floats like foam? He uses the phrase also in 236/18 and in 266/12.

243/24. *croked cammokkes*. This image, which is not in O, 1-3, occurs again in *Why Come ye Nat to Courte?* 114, 'As right as a cammocke croked', and in *Poems Against Garnesche*, i. 30, 'Crokyd as a camoke, and as a kowe calfles'.

244/4. *Continence*. See note on *the ij Epirians*, 237/4.

249/11. *he ne may bow his knee vnto the grounde*. Oldfather refers to several classical authors who share the belief that elephants could not bend their legs, and to J. E. Tennent, *The Natural History of Ceylon*, pp. 100-6, for examples of the prevalence of the idea 'both in antiquity and in the Middle Ages'.

250/21. *pyned goostes*. Cf. Chaucer, Prologue to *The Canterbury Tales*, 205.

250/25. *noyous in styngyng*. The medieval artist pictured the locust as having a scorpion's tail. This detail is added to Poggio by Skelton.

272/7. *wilde and bestes savaige*. At first sight one would suppose that *and* had been inserted by scribal error. But it is to be remembered that Skelton, like other scholars of the period, desired to enrich the language and that a construction of this type is familiar in Latin and French.

273/8-11. *Toward this see . . . holow places*. The echoic character of this passage may explain its corruption, or result from it. There is not only the minor repetition or rhyme of *where, there*; but phrases like *falling from the toppe downe, toppe . . . fallen downe* are likely to cause or result from inaccuracy of transcription.

277/20. *Ambrosia*. Skelton's interpolation may, as frequently, be based upon Reuchlin: 'Ambrosia . . . quędam herba prędulcis saporis. diuina dicta. eo quod inde pascantur equi deorum. Vnde & ambrosia dicitur quandoque nectar vel cibus deorum.'

279/4-7. *The copious abundaunce . . . abundaunce there is*. That Skelton has mistranslated the passage, the parallels prove. His text seems frequently to call for ingenious punctuation, but in this case there is a dilemma upon which the parallels shed no light. Should the text be punctuated as at present, to mean that the supply of gold is so great that the people can make tubs and barrels out of what is left over; or should it be punctuated to mean that the royal palace still survives: 'The copious abundaunce of golde and of silvere that is in the cittee of Saba where the kynges moste roiall place is that remayneth—they make vessels, as tubbes and barelles there of golde, suche plentie and abundaunce there is'? It is even possible to take *golde* with the last clause: 'there—of golde suche plentie and abundaunce there is.'

282/16-17. *daungérous stremes where monstruous of the see be resortyng, called maremaides*. The similarity between *cirenam* and *syrena*, a few lines above, has led Skelton into an identification for which, as the parallels show, Diodorus and Poggio offer no authority. It is also possible that *Marmaride* suggested *maremaides* to his mind. Reuchlin perhaps added to his ideas at this point: 'Syrtis. tis. . . . dicitur a syren quod est tractus. Et sunt syrtes loca periculosa in mari. dicta ab attractione arenę in cumulos', and 'Syrena. nę. & hec syren. renis. . . . est monstrum marinum. quod dulcedine sui cantus. nautas ad se trahit. & submergi facit . . .'. But the definition he wanted is given by Reuchlin under *Cirene*: 'Cirene regina fuit libyę. quę ex suo homine ciuitatem condidit. quam cirenen nominauit.'

297/13. *hevenly senatours*. This phrase, which Skelton uses frequently from this point onwards, is perhaps drawn from the Vesper hymn to the Apostles Peter and Paul in the Roman Breviary (29 June): 'Vitae senatum laureati possident.' He uses the verse itself as a gloss to *The Garlande of Laurell*, 1505.

299/18–19. *They say how . . . she drowned her-self*. It is curious to find only in the Poggio edition of 1531 the Latin error which must have been responsible for Skelton's mistranslation: *fluminum* for *fulminum*. See parallels.

300/32. *Marsias Frigias*. It will have been noted that Skelton's amplifications are increasing in length. From this point on Poggio frequently supplies only a hint for the 'pullished eloquence' that derives from his *History*.

305/12. *tretise of the spere*. This medieval tag derives no doubt from Johannes de Sacro Bosco's *Tractatus de Sphaera* which was used as a textbook for the B.A. degree at Oxford about 1408 [see *Munimenta Academiae Oxoniensis*, i. 241–3], or from some such textbook of astronomy.

306/14–15. *Mercurye . . . fete of marchaundise*. Cf. Reuchlin: 'Mercurius. rij deus mercatorum. sic dictus quasi mercatorum kyrios. . . . Et interpretatur sermo uel eloquentia. . . .'

306/35. *envious rancour*. Cf. *Garlande of Laurell*, 753.

309/30. *that Dionysyus had ij modres*. He was called *Dimetor*, which means 'twice-born'.

315/1–2. *such armature*. Skelton's translation is rather vague. He perhaps had in mind Reuchlin's definition of the thyrsis: 'Tirsus . . . etiam dicitur baculus uel ramus cum frondibus. quo vtuntur [*sic*] in sacrificijs bacchi.' Cf. however, 347/30–31, where Skelton translates thyrsus as 'shafte wrythen aboute with yvye', and 316/12–13 where he omits 'pro thyrso'.

320/30. *paves and wall*. Cf. 'Vpon the Dethe of the Erle of Northumberlande', 48: 'He was their bulwark, their paues, and their wall.'

321/9–10. *such as first envred to be maryners*. Reuchlin says: 'Argonauta dicitur ab argos quod est prima nauis. & nauta . . . .' Cf. 286/34.

321/3–14. *This famous Homere . . . reherced of tofore*. Skelton has considerably expanded and 'polished' this chapter. He has also confused Dionysus the god and Dionysius the historian, so that the latter's works are credited to Homer. The general context, together with the phrase which inevitably recalls Caxton's remark, 'I suppose he hath dronken of Elycons well', leads one to wonder, in the circumstances, just how serious Caxton's compliment was.

325/35. *Nymphes and Muses*. The Muses are added by Skelton. Cf. Reuchlin: 'Nympha . . . est dea aquarum. & specialiter fontium. . . . Et dicuntur nymphę eędem quę & musę. nec immerito: Nam aquę motus musam

Notes 407

efficit.' And again: 'Musa . . . dicitur a moys quod est aqua . . . quia sine humiectatione istorum non potest nasci vox.'

327/31. *skynne of the same ieopardie.* As he advances, Skelton becomes more poetical and more difficult. In this case, by metonymy, *ieopardie* must stand for the dangerous beast that has just been killed.

331/13. *the wise direction of Dame Prudence.* Cf. Chaucer's 'Tale of Melibeus'. This passage is not in Poggio.

334/11. *counterfait countenaunce.* Cf. 353/25, where this phrase occurs in connexion with Skelton's interpolated definition of tragedy. Counterfait Countenaunce is also a character in Skelton's morality play, *Magnyfycence*.

340/7–9. *Of Hercules . . . lyf.* The manuscript of Skelton's translation breaks off at iv. 19. The table of contents here given is evidence that he intended to complete the task. In *The Garlande of Laurell*, 1502, he speaks as if he had completed it: 'Sex volumis engrosid together it doth containe.' As the manuscript is not holograph, there is no reason for supposing that he failed to complete the translation.

341/1. *To vs, &c.* Skelton is becoming so 'diffuse' that it is difficult to follow the argument. Diodorus says that historians labour under four disadvantages: (1) the antiquity of events, which renders the record uncertain, (2) the insecurity of dates, (3) the multiplicity of heroes, and (4) the disagreement of the records.

342/18. *Whos, &c.* Although the sentence has been emended, it is not impossible that Skelton started with *By whos* and forgot his construction.

347/19. *Triathericum.* This word is not in Reuchlin, and Skelton's elaboration of it is not in O, 1–3.

351/24–25. As Oldfather explains, the *narthex* refers to 'the reed which formed the staff of the thyrsus'.

352/18. *many names.* Oldfather gives the derivation of all these names ad loc.

353/24. *tragedyes.* Reuchlin again serves as a possible source: 'Tragędia. dię . . . Est enim de crudelissimis rebus. sicut qui patrem vel matrem interfecit. vel comedit filium, vel econuerso. & huius modi . . . Et differunt tragędia & comędia. quia comędia priuatorum hominum continet facta. Tragędia regum. et magnatum. Item comędia humili stilo describitur. Tragędia alto. Item comędia a tristibus incipit. sed cum lętis desinit. Tragędia. econtrario.

353/24–25. *counterfete countenaunce.* Cf. note to 334/11.

354/18. *Priapus.* In the paragraphs which follow, Skelton's ideas about Priapus seem to be coloured by Reuchlin. Cf. that part of Reuchlin's definition already quoted (note to 118/21), as well as the following: '& habitus pro deo est a fęminis. Et dicitur deus hortorum propter fęcunditatem eorum . . . Item dicitur deus furum. & deus auium . . .'

356/15–16. *Hermophroditus.* Skelton again expands with the help apparently of Reuchlin: 'Hermaphroditus. ti. m. s. & hęc hermaphrodita. dicitur qui vel quę vtrunque sexum habet. & dicitur ab herma. quod est masculus. & phrodi. quod fęmina nuncupatur. Hic alio nomine dicitur androgenus. hi

dextram mammillam virilem. sinistram muliebrem habentes. vicissim coeundo
& gignunt et pariunt. Et quia talis homo nec vir. nec mulier videtur . . . Vel
hermaphroditus. dicitur ab hermes. quod est mercurius. & phrodita. quod
est venus. id [est] filius veneris & mercurij: qui commixtus ex illis vtrunque
sexum habuit.

360/6–12. *The nynthe* . . . *ben incomparable.* This sentence offers a problem
in punctuation which the editors do not claim to have solved.

367/18. *his progenytours.* As Hercules was not Theban by birth, the reading
should be, as Oldfather has it, '*their* forefathers'.

373/26. *bremly bristilde.* Cf. *bremely enbristild* a few lines above (373/13),
and also *Against the Scottes,* 161, 'Your beard so brym as bore at bay', and
Replycacion, 221, 'And bremely with your bristels'.

374/1. *as in a bande mys.* The expression seems hardly satisfactory. One is
tempted to read *abandoning,* i.e. taking into one's power, taking captive.

374/26. *Bot erst,* &c. Skelton seems a little uncertain of what actually
follows. His interpolation must actually come from Reuchlin. Under *Centaurus*
Reuchlin has: 'Siquidem secundum fabulas poetarum xion [sic]
secretarius Iunonis eam interpellauit de concibitu quę cum filio Iouis formauit
quandam nubem in sui speciem & eam obtulit xioni. quam putans ille
Iunonem esse. effudit semen in nubem. & inde nata sunt quędem monstra.
in media parte homines, & in media parte scilicet inferiori equi . . .'

380/35–381/13. *Wherof* . . . *encheson.* Reuchlin says: 'Pasiphe fingitur a
poetis fuisse quędam solis filia. quę cum tauri amore fureret Dedalo operam
dante. lignea vacca inclusa. ad nefarium inuitata est. ex qua natus est minotaurus.'

382/27. *Olympiade.* Skelton's explanation of the Olympic Games, which
is not in O, 1–3, may be taken from Reuchlin: 'Olympias. adis. & hec
olympica. cę . . . festum uel solemnis ludus. quod uel que fiebat ad honorem
Iouis semel per quinquennium. ne si vlterius pretenderetur. in negligentiam.
& obliuionem corrueret. uel si citra per quinquennium celebraretur. expensę
nimietas eos grauaret. In ipsa celebratione lex talis erat quod quicunque
victor existeret ibi in aliquo ludo haberet quodcunque munus vellet requirere.'
Note that Skelton and Reuchlin say that the prize was anything the
victor might ask, while Diodorus and Poggio, as the parallels indicate, say
that the prize was definitely a crown.

383/29. *goddesse of bataylle.* Skelton adds in each case the description of
the gods that follow. If he had not missed the significance of the phrase
'uterque insigne suae artis opus', he might not have made Pallas 'goddesse of
bataylle'.

385/5–6. *so delicate a daysye.* Cf. *The Garlande of Laurell,* 1449: 'This
delycate dasy'.

386/28. *Dyomedes.* This interpolation also may be borrowed from Reuchlin:
'Diomedes . . . Et vt narrat Papias: Diomedem pagani deum asserunt.
cuius socios in aues conuersos ita se ludificare dicunt. vt suis. id [est] gręcis

colludant. alienos verberent. & ad templum diomedis rostro aquam portant. . . .' The identification, however, is incorrect. The birds of Diomedes were connected with the king of Aetolia, the son of Tideus who so distinguished himself at Troy, and not with the king of Thrace.

387/24. *Menalyppe.* Menalippe, or Melanippê, is more than once confused with Hippolytê, probably because of the incident below when she was set free on condition that she yielded her girdle. She is called Queen by Hawes, *Pastime of Pleasure*, 11, 1761, and 4179.

388/26. *Aella.* The name in Greek signifies 'whirlwind'.

389/24–25. *Ypolite . . . in maryage.* Skelton is perhaps led into error by familiarity with 'The Knight's Tale'.

391/9. *Libia.* Concerning Libya, Reuchlin says: 'Libya. bye. filia fuit Epasi. quę regnum libye possedit. ex cuius nomine terra illa dicta est libya . . . Et dicitur libya tertia pars orbis.'

392/34. *Hyberia.* This is also Reuchlin's etymology: 'Hiberus . . . fluuius hispanię. Inde hęc hiberia. rię, dicta est hispania.'

394/33. *Tempe.* Reuchlin says: 'Tempe . . . sunt loca temperata & delectabilia & intestalia.'

APPENDIX A

Skelton's Greek

NOTE

THE following is a list of abbreviations for Skelton's works, with the text(s) used put in brackets. The form quoted is usually that of the earliest original. Readings of SP, however, are taken from Lant's print, with the exception of those portions which occur only in the manuscript, the scribe of which apparently knew no Latin. For ease of reference Dyce's numbering is followed wherever possible.

Aa	The ancient acquaintance. (Pynson.)
AgD	Against Dundas. (Marshe 1568.)
AgG	Against Garnesche. (Dyce: MS. Harl. 367.)
AgSc	Against the Scots. (Lant 1545?)
Alb	The doughty duke of Albany. (Marshe 1568.)
Ballad	Ballad of the Scottish King. (Faukes 1513.)
BC	Bouge of Court. (Wynkyn de Worde, Camb. copy.)
Bedell	Epitaph on Bedell. (Marshe 1568.)
Calli	Calliope. (Marshe 1568.)
CC	Colin Clout. (Kele 1545?)
CCLat	Latin tailpiece to CC. (MS. Harl. 2252.)
ChorG	Diss choir against the French. (Lant 1545?)
ChorSc	Diss choir against the Scots. (Ibid.)
ComC	Against a comely coistron. (Pynson.)
Compl	Complaint to the king. (MS. Addit. 26787.)
Decast	Decastichon to WCY. (Kele 1545?)
DN	Elegy on Northumberland. (MS. Reg. 18. D. ii.)
Epit	Epitaph on John Clarke. (Marshe 1568.)
ER	Elinor Rumming. (Lant 1545?)
Eul	Eulogy of his own time. (Marshe 1568.)
EulTet	Tetrastichon to Eul.
GL	Garland of Laurel. (Faukes 1523: MS. Cot. Vit. E. x.)
HVII	Epitaph for Henry VII. (Marshe 1568.)
Iliber	I liber et propera. (MS. C.C.C. (Camb.) 432.)
Kat	Knowledge, acquaintance. (Pynson.)
Laurel	Latin lines on the Laurel. (Faukes 1523.)
LCall	Latin lines on Calliope. (Marshe 1568.)
LMarg	Elegy on the lady Margaret. (Marshe 1568.)
Mag	Magnificence. (Rastell 1533?)
MMarg	Mannerly Margery. (MS. Addit. 5465.)
Palin	Palinode to the king. (MS. Addit. 26787.)
Parl	En parlament a Paris. (Faukes 1523.)

Appendix A 411

PS	Philip Sparrow. (Kele 1545?)
Qui trahis	Qui trahis ex domiti. (MS. Univ. Lib. Camb. Ee. 5. 18.)
Rep	A replication against certain young scholars. (Pynson.)
RepEpit	Epitoma to Rep.
Rose	The Rose both White and Red. (P.R.O., E 36/228.)
Salve	Salve plus decies. (Marshe 1568.)
SP	Speak, Parrot. (Lant: MS. Harl. 2252.)
Spec	Speculum principis. (MS. Addit. 26787.)
Trent	Trental for Adam Uddersall. (Marshe 1568.)
VT	Against venomous tongues. (Marshe 1568.)
WCY	Why come ye not to court? (Kele 1545?)
WCYEpit	Epitoma to WCY.
WH	Ware the Hawk. (Lant 1545?)
WomWan	Womanhood, wanton, ye want. (Pynson.)
York	On prince Henry's creation duke of York. (MS. Addit. 26787.)

Other abbreviations include:

EETS	Early English Text Society.
ESt	Englische Studien.
MLR	Modern Language Review.
MLN	Modern Language Notes.
PMLA	Publications of the Modern Language Association of America.
RES	Review of English Studies.
TLS	Times Literary Supplement.

1. GREEK PROPER NAMES

These are all to be found in Latin authors (cf. Dunbabin, *MLR*, xii (1917), 129 ff.), e.g. **Philistion** (PS 766) in Martial 2. 41; **Pherecydes** (PS 766) in Lactantius. For **Pisander**, mentioned by Macrobius, *Sat.* 5. 2, see Dyce, ii. 309, quoting Warton. For **Automedon**, see below, 11 (*a*).

2. GREEK WORDS FOUND IN CLASSICAL LATIN

(*a*) Some examples: **bacchatus, bromius, Byrsa** (= βύρσα), **Chire** (= χαῖρε), **Coaxans, Epitoma, freneses, gariopholum** (= garyophyllon), **melos, phormio** [Repn (Dyce, i. 208), ibid., SP 82, 30, Rep 118n, LMarg *sub fin*. (cf. RepEpit, WCYEpit), SP 49 (cf. Rep n (Dyce, i. 208), WCYEpit 18), SP 188, Trent 19+, SP 156].

(*b*) **Monon Calon Agaton** (SP 143); **Calon, Agaton, cum Areta.** (LMarg *sub fin*.). The first is not the sentence of an amateur Hellenist (Dunbabin, loc. cit.), but a transliteration of Cicero, *Paradoxa* 1: "Ὅτι μόνον τὸ καλὸν ἀγαθόν. The 'Areta.' of the second is probably derived from the 2nd Paradox: "Ὅτι αὐτάρκης ἡ ἀρετὴ πρὸς εὐδαιμονίαν.

Appendix A

(c) **zoekepsiche** (SP 270+). MS. has 'zoell zepsiche'; the prints: 'zoelzepsiche'. Skelton almost certainly wrote 'zoekepsiche', his *k* being mistaken for *lz*, an easy error then as now. The phrase (ζωὴ καὶ ψυχή) appears in Juvenal, *Sat.* 6, to which Skelton refers. It was also familiar from the schoolboy's *Graecismus* (ed. J. Wrobel, Uratislauiae 1887, 8. 338): 'Dic zoen animam, dic inde zoecaisychen.' (N.B. Among the eleven variants recorded by Wrobel, none has *l*, and all have *c* or *ch*; which confirms our emendation. On the other hand, none has *ps* for ψ, so that Skelton's transliteration compares favourably with the medieval product.) Skelton's translation, *vita et anima*, indicates that he was not here relying on Évrard—nor on Erasmus, *Adagia* 2. 3. 89, which deals with the phrase under *Anima & vita*, with references to Juvenal and Martial.

(d) **Myden agan** (SP 54). So MS., altered from 'Myden agayne'; the prints: 'Niden'. In the case of this tag (μηδὲν ἄγαν), so familiar that Erasmus chose it as a paradigm of the adage, it is unnecessary to look for a specific source.

3. Greek Words found in Ecclesiastical Latin

(a) Some examples: **anathematus, botrus** (botrigerus), **cacodemones, carismata, catholicus, dulia, heresiarcha, Hiperdulia, latria, ortadoxus, pseudopropheta, ydolatria** [Rep (Dyce, i. 219), SP 161, Laurel 7, Rep (Dyce, i. 218), Rep 306n, 207n, ibid., Rep n (Dyce, i. 207), Rep 207n, ibid., Rep n (Dyce, i. 207), SP 140, Rep n (Dyce, i. 209)].

(b) **Philargerya ... Castrimergia** (WCY 203, 213). These are two of Cassian's eight deadly sins: 'primum gastrimargiae, quae interpretatur gulae concupiscentia; ... tertium philargyriae, quod intelligitur avaritia, vel ut proprius exprimatur, amor pecuniae' (J. Cassianus, *De coenobiorum institutis* 5. 1 (Migne, *Patrol. Lat.* Ser. I, vol. xlix, cols. 202–3)).

(c) **fagolidorus** (LMarg *sub fin.*). So Marshe; Dyce: 'phagoloedorus' (i.e. φαγολοιδόρος). The word comes from Jerome, *Pref. to Ezekiel*, and is explained by Reuchlin, *Vocab. brev.*: 'Fagolydoros grẹce manducantes maledictum latine. Fage enim comedere. lydoros male dictum ...', i.e. a chewer of abuse. (The full note in Reuchlin occupies nearly a column.)

4. Medieval Words of Changed Form or Meaning

Capricornius (= Capricornus), **Palinodium** (= paean or, perhaps, song with refrain: cf. R. L. Greene, *Early English Carols*, Oxford, 1935, pp. xxii–xxiii), **pedagogium** (= school), **poliandrum**

Appendix A 413

(πολυάνδριον = tomb of one person: cf. Dyce, ii. 227), **sophista** (= undergraduate) SP 157, Palin *title*, SP 98, LMarg 5, WH 246 (cf. Rep 182n).

5. Medieval Personifications

(*a*) **dame philology** (SP 45): cf. Martianus' *Marriage of Philology and Mercury*, a medieval favourite.

(*b*) **sophia** (SP 165): cf. Sophie, daughter of Chaucer's Melibee and Dame Prudence.

(*c*) **Phroneses** (SP 49): cf. the arbitress in Theodulus' ninth-century eclogue between Pseustis and Alithia, found in the *Auctores octo morales* of the classroom.

6. Terms of Medieval Philosophy

Examples: **diaphonum** (= diaphanum), **energia, Gimnosophista, pneuma** [SP 195, Rep 368n, RepEpit *title*, CCLat 2–3]. For *energia* and *pneuma* see below, 12 (*d*), (*e*).

7. Greek Rhetorical Terms

Examples: **alegoria, aphrosmus** (= aphorismus), **auxesis, cacosinthicon** (= cacosyntheton), **Dilema, Enigma, hyberbato** (= hyperbaton), **metaphora, paronomasia, sarcasmos, Scema, topographia** [SP 207, 49n, *epigraph*, GL 596n, Rep (Dyce, i. 219), SP 196, 371+, 207, 49n, Rep 150n, Rep (Dyce, 219), SP 10n].

8. Greek Words found in Elementary Schoolbooks

Examples: **basileos, catholicus, Cefas, Chire, Cleros, didasculus, dulia, isagoga** (isagogicall), **latria, Perihermenias, Phroneses, sophia, zoekepsiche** [*Graecismus* 8. 45, 61, 86, 89, 53, 113; 10. 110; 8. 27, 146; Alexander's *Doctrinale puerorum* (ed. Reichling, *Mon. Germ. Paed.* xii, Berlin 1893), 542; *Graecismus* 8. 338].

9. False Quantities in Skelton's Greek

(*a*) Due to medieval tradition: **Ecclĕsia, Iacŏbus, thēologus** [Epit 7, HVII 12 (cf. 25, ChorSc 2, 13), RepEpit 3]. Cf. *Ecclĕsiarum* (*Graecismus* 9. 105), *Iacŏbique* (*Doctrinale* 1193), *thēologia* (ibid. 2630).

(*b*) Other examples: **epitōma, crōnica** [LMarg *sub fin.*, Iliber 9].

(*c*) **Sŏcrātes** (RepEpit 8). A gloss, misplaced in Pynson, reads: 'Que fiunt in / tes sociabus / sicut Acha⁊/ tes. h. Gag. &c.' Dyce printed: 'Quae fiunt inter sociabus sicut Achates. h. Gag. &c.', querying in a note 'sociatos', which sheds no light on the sense. But if we emend thus: 'Que fiunt in tes, Socrates sicut Achates. Hec Gaguinus, &c.', its relevance is patent. The note refers to the scansion of 'Socrates', whose name had been corrupted to Sortes by the medievals perhaps on account of this very difficulty of fitting it into a hexameter. The French humanist Robert Gaguin had learnt some Greek under Gregorio, who held a chair in Paris in 1458; but he does not seem to have gone much further than the elements. The Greek in his autograph copy of Suetonius has no accents, is frequently misquoted, and often unintelligible (*R. Gag. Epistole et orationes*, ed. L. Thuasne, Paris, 1903, i. 12, 19–21). As a latinist, however, he was redoubtable, and commanded the respect of the young Erasmus. Besides his great history of France—used by Skelton in WCY—Gaguin wrote an *Ars versificatoria* (Iehan Petit: Paris, 1505) which is typical of early humanism. Its three books deal, rather unmethodically, with letters and syllables, with feet, and with the different kinds of metre.

In this case Skelton is referring to the section of Book I entitled *De A in mediis syllabis correpta*, which is chiefly concerned with the exceptions, where medial *a* is long. 'Producuntur quoque hec', he says, '... Parnasus. omasum. agaso. *Achates. socrates.* nostrates. tholosates &. similis deriuationis nomina ...' (sig. A8ᵛ). Skelton's gloss, as we have reconstructed it, then translates: 'Those [nouns] which are formed in *-tes*, *Socrates* just as much as *Achates* [lengthen the medial *a*]. So Gaguin [*Ars versificatoria*, I].' The statement is incorrect, of course: the *a* in *Socrates* is short, and what is more, the *o*, which he has shortened, should be long. No doubt that is why he appeals to the Frenchman's authority.

10. SYNTHETIC GREEK WORDS

(*a*) **Satrapas** (AgG 1. 6, 13, &c.). = σατράπης. Perhaps influenced by Latin *satrapa*.

(*b*) **Policronitudo basileos** (Eul *sub fin.*, SP 36n, Iliber fol. 3ᵛ). Du Cange has *polychronia* = 'salutatio cum genuflexionȩ ex Byzantinorum more, qui in acclamationibus publicis imperatoribus aut patriarchis, Πολλά aut Πολυχρόνιον acclamabant.' *Basileos* occurs (as a nominative) in the *Graecismus*, and also in Reuchlin. Putting these together, one arrives at the translation: 'Homage to', or more freely, 'Long live the king!' The exact grammar of the phrase, however, is obscure.

11. REFERENCES INCORRECTLY TAKEN FOR GREEK

(*a*) **antomedon of loues meditacyoun** (GL 1181). A misprint, as Dyce conjectured, for 'Automedon'. Not, however, Automedon of

Appendix A   415

the Greek Anthology (F. Brie, *Archiv*, cxxxviii (1919), 226–8), but the charioteer of Ovid, *Ars amatoria*, 1. 5–8; 2. 737–8. Skelton's work was apparently a translation or adaptation of the *Art of Love*.

(*b*) **Scaloppe** . . . **Tefas** (SP 282–4). MS.'s 'Tefas' should be 'Cefas', as Dyce prints it. Not σκάλοψ, mole, and κηφήν, drone (J. M. Berdan, *MLN*, xxx (1915), 140–4), but 'the scallop' = Escalles, and 'St Peter' = Saint-Pierre or Dampierre-lez-Dunes, suburbs of Calais (W. Nelson, *PMLA*, li (1936), 68–69).

(*c*) **pandez mory** (SP 48). MS. has 'pandes mery', which Dyce rejected without explanation. Not πάντες μῶροι (R. Hughes, *Poems by John Skelton*, 1924, n. ad loc.), but French *pandez morie* = *prenez folie*. (I have to thank the late Prof. L. M. Brandin, of University College, London, for this solution.)

(*d*) **In Affryc tongue / Byrsa is a thonge of lether** (SP 82). Dunbabin comments that a Greek scholar would have known βύρσα is Greek for a hide. But Skelton is not talking Greek. The Vergilian commentator Claudius Donatus writes as follows on *Aeneid*, 1. 367: '(Byrsa) et lingua graeca, unde Dido fuit, *et punica* . . . significat corium. byrsa quippe graeca appellatione corium est et bursaft punica elocutione corium significatur' (ed. Teubner, Leipzig, 1905–6, 1. 367). This Donatus was a fifteenth-century discovery; his notes on Vergil were first found by Giovanni Pontano, and were not printed until 1535 (Smith, *Class. Dict.*, *sub nom.*). So that—except for a rare chance—Skelton could not have known his work complete. But from 1487 (Teubner ed., i, p. xix) Landino began to introduce extracts into his Vergil; and it soon became the fashion to print the poet with five commentaries, those of Servius, Landino, Mancinelli, Donatus, and Domitius. And Landino's edition of 1487 contains the gloss: 'Do-[NATUS]:·byrsa: qu*o*d et lingua greca unde fuit Dido: et punica. i*d* [est]. ipsius regionis: in qua res est gesta / coriu*m* significat' (*In P. Vergilii Interpretationes Prohemium* . . ., Florence, 18 March 1487, unpaginated, ad loc.). The rest of Donatus' note is crowded out, so that until 1535 only a handful of antiquaries like Landino could know that the Punic for 'hide' was not *byrsa* but *bursaft*.

As far as contemporary scholarship went, therefore, Skelton was right. Moreover, he must have known very well that the word was also Greek; it is the exceptional, the out-of-the-way fact that excites his comment, and for that very reason. In just the same way he brings in the Hebrew name 'Iereboseth' because it was an exotic new-comer to the Vulgate (*PMLA*, liii (1938), 617, n. 7).

But that is only the surface meaning of verse 82. Like so much of SP it really refers to Wolsey, the burse or purse being still one of the Lord

Chancellor's insignia. 'Affryc' is also meant to remind us of Dido's fraud, which won for her people the site of Carthage (*Aeneid*, 1. 367):

> mercatique solum, facti de nomine Byrsam,
> taurino quantum possent circumdare tergo.

And Skelton's play on the double meaning of *corium* (the regular translation of *byrsa*) as 'hide' or 'thong' is a reference to the old proverb, *De cute non propria maxima corrigia*, translated in the *Proverbs of Hending*, 'Of un-boht hude men kerueth brod thong', and explained by Cotgrave, 'To spend freely on another man's purse' (W. W. Skeat, *Early English Proverbs*, Oxford, 1910, no. 86). The reflection on Wolsey's enormous fortune is subtle—and devastating.

12. MISCELLANEOUS

(*a*) **creticus** (Rep 256n, WCYEpit 16). A difficult word. Reuchlin has: 'creticus . . . iudex vel medicus. & dicitur a crisis quod est iudicium. quia secundum crisim iudicat de infirmo. an debeat euadere nec ne. vel dicitur a cerno. nis. Inde creticus. a. um. id [est] iudicialis vel determinatiuus. vt creticus dies. in quo sumitur iudicium infirmitatis.' It is clearly a medieval form of the classical *criticus* (like *crisis*, from the Greek κρίνω), which occurs in both the medical and judicial senses. But Skelton's use of it is curiously ambiguous. In the *Replication* gloss he invokes a curse on the *heretici cretici frenetici* he is attacking. Here it seems to have the derived medical sense of 'feverish'—the equivalent, more or less, of *frenetici*.

But in the *Epitoma* to *Why Come* Wolsey is denounced as

> Dominus male Creticus
> Aptius Dictus Tetricus
> Phanaticus freneticus
> Graphicus sicut Metricus
>   Autumat,
> Hoc gènus dictaminis
> Non egit examinis
> In centiloquio néc centimetro
> Honorati
> Grammatici
> Mauri

(So Kele: Dyce emends 'egit' to 'eget'). The train of thought is hard to follow. At first sight *male creticus* means simply 'of ill judgement', Wolsey being of course Lord Chancellor. But the final sentence is confusing. As Dr. Nelson has pointed out to us, it refers not to Terentianus Maurus but to the more famous Servius, whose full name was Marius Servius Honoratus Grammaticus Maurus. Now, is Servius the

Appendix A   417

'graphic metrist' of the previous sentence? If so, the last words are a note on what has just been said. (They may even have crept into the text from the margin. There are examples of this in VT and the manuscript of SP.) Can it be that *creticus* is connected with the 'cretic' measure (*dictamen*), which was traditionally derived from those frenzied ministers of Cybele, the Cretan Corybantes? As it happens, the cretic is mentioned by Servius (without comment) only in his treatise on the Horatian metres; while Terentianus actually praises the foot. But if one remembers the reputation of Crete for lying (Ovid, *Ars*, 1. 298; St. Paul's *Ep. to Titus*, 1. 12; and the proverbial '*cretiza cum Cretensi*, lie to a liar', Erasmus, *Colloquia*, Leyden, 1664, p. 359) and Juvenal's choice (*Sat.* 2. 66, 77) of the name Creticus for his harsh and voluptuous judge, as well as the connexion with delirium, it seems possible that Skelton was drawing on a vague memory of such unpleasant connotations for the word *creticus*, which, as it was also a prosodic term, he assumed would be in Servius. Some such involved history, at least, appears the best explanation for these verses.

(*b*) **Perihermenias latine interpretatio.** &c. (Rep n (Dyce, i. 209)). Pynson has 'Perihermōias', but 'Perihermeniall' in text. A transliteration of Aristotle's περὶ ἑρμηνείας. The *Graecismus* has *periarmenias* (8. 27); but Skelton uses the correcter form of Reuchlin: '*Peri hermenias* sunt duę partes. Peri enim gręca prępositio est. & valet tantum quantum de. hermenias est gręcus genetiuus a nomine gręco hermenia. quod *latine* sonat *interpretatio*.' As may be seen, Skelton defines the whole by its part, either through carelessness or merely to save space in the margin.

(*c*) **Katerina vniuersalis vicii ruina grecum est** (SP 38n). Dunbabin's 'portmanteau-word compounded out of Cath-olicus, καθαρός and *ruina*' is over-ingenious. This was the accepted definition of the time; cf. Reuchlin: 'Katerina nę. proprium nomen cuiusdam sanctę virginis. & dicitur a cata. quod est vniuersum & ruina quasi vniuersalis ruina. Omne enim ędificium diaboli in ea vniuersaliter corruit. . . .'

(*d*) **pneuma** (CCLat 2–3). MS. (fol. 153ᵛ) reads:

> Colin*us* Clout*us* q*uanquam* mori carmina mvltis
> sordescu*nt* stult*is* sed puevinate sunt rare cult*is*
> pue vinat*is* altisem diuino flamina falt*is*

As I have pointed out (*TLS*, 19 Dec. 1936), *puevina-* is a corruption of *pneuma-*. The passage should most probably read:

> Colinus Cloutus, quanquam mea carmina multis
> sordescunt stultis, sed pneumatisant bene cultis,
> pneumatis altisoni diuino flamine flatis.

E

(The differences between the present version and that proposed in *TLS* are the fruit of a stimulating discussion with Mr. D. W. Pye, of Llandovery College.) 'My poems have their faults,' says Colin, 'but their echo in the mind, like the prolonging of an antiphon, brings out their real value; for they breathe the holy air of the Spirit from on high.' If our reading is correct, Skelton began with the medieval sense of *pneuma* as the drawn-out close of a plainsong melody; and this led him, by a kind of pun, to the Holy Ghost (*pneuma sanctum*). (*Altisonus* may mean either 'high-sounding' or 'sublime'.) The sentiment recurs at the end of the *Replication*, where he talks of poets as 'Ante alios omnes divino flamine flatos' (Dyce, i. 223).

(*e*) **Energia** (Rep 367n). Pynson: 'Energia grece latine efficax operatio. Int*er*noq*ue* quodam spiritus impulsu inopinabiliter originata. &c.' This definition is not in Skelton's usual works of reference, nor in Boccaccio. Skelton appears to be quoting from a 'Boke of Good Aduertysement' (Rep 360–1; cf. GL 1186)—possibly some Renaissance defence of poetry which he had translated. The word *energia* seems to have come into Latin through Rufinus' translation of Origen's *De principiis* (3. 3. 3). This describes certain *virtutes spiritales* which operate the wisdom of this world: 'ut sit propria quaedam *energia* ac virtus, quae inspiret poeticam, alia quae geometriam', and so on. This, he continues, is why the Greeks thought it impossible to have poetry without insanity, and why they describe their *vates* as filled with a spirit of madness, their seers (*divinos*) as uttering oracles in artful verse, and their magicians as with the aid of demons causing even children to speak marvellous poetry (Migne, *Patrol. Graec.* xi, col. 316A–B; cf. *Thesaur. Lat.*, s.v. 'energia').

APPENDIX B

Skelton and the Latin Classics

THE following list makes no claim to completeness, but it does present the great majority of Skelton's borrowings from classical authors. Merely nominal references are omitted, but repeated quotations and false attributions both find a place in it. The last are marked with an asterisk, and are excluded from the totals.

Totals

VERGIL. *Ecl.* 1 and 3 (GL 1076 ff.); 2. 54 (Laurel 12), 57 (GL 1497 and n); 3. 64 (GL 1495n), 64–65 (SP 257n), 76 (Palin 10); 4. 2 (Laurel 11); 5. 16 (GL 601); 7. 26 (GL 751), 61 ff. (Laurel 1 ff.); 10. 1 (PS 860). *Georg.* 1. 18–19 (GL 1404n). *Aen.* 1. 215 (GL 1240n), 367 (SP 82), 740 ff. (GL 688 ff.); 4. 154–5 (GL 1408n), 373 (GL 1179n), 511 (PS 1363–6); 6. 101 (GL 1472n); 10. 284 (GL 1397n), 501 (GL 1402n) 21

OVID. *Ars* 1. 5–8 and 2. 737–8 (GL 1181); 1. 57–59 (Salve 6–7); 3. 549–50 confused with *Fast.* 6. 5 (Rep 375n). *Amor.* 1. 9. 1 (GL 1387n); 2. 6 (PS 387 ff.); 2. 6. 21 (SP 18). *Her.* 1. 12 (GL 1181n); 7. 2 (SP 178), 20. 6, 97 and 21. 111–13 (GL 885). *Met.* 1. 129–31 (GL 1196n), 452–567 (GL 290–322); 2. 753 ff. (GL 49n [*MS. only*]), 775 (PS 905); 3. 232 (PS 296); 15. 547 ff. (PS 1151) . . . 15

JUVENAL. 1. 18 (LMarg 25–26), 30 (WCY 1208, Spec fol. 17ᵛ), 167 (GL 748); 6. 46 (Rep 297n), 191 ff. (SP 271); 8. 129 (GL 597–8), 140 (WCY 1224) 8

HORACE. *Carm.* 1. 1. 2 (Palin 10, Eul 32); 3. 4. 65 (SP 42–43: n. *refers to* 73 ff.). *Ars* 5 (GL 1433n), 71–72 (GL 1182n), 333 (GL 1246n). *Ep.* 1. 16. 79 (GL 1176n). [GL 1500n = Persius]* . . . 7

PERSIUS. *Prol.* 8 (SP 30); 1. 65 (SP 339); 5. 52 (GL 1500: attrib. Hor.), 76 (GL 742), 184 (GL 751) 5

MARTIAL. 1. 4. 8 (SP 268), 1. 109 (PS 210 ff.); 14. 73 (SP 27) . 3

SENECA. *Phaed.* 773 (SP 17n); *Troad.* 257 (SP 52) . . . 2

CLAUDIAN. *In Eutrop.* 1. 181 (Decast 10) 1

MAXIMIAN. *El.* 5 (GL 360–1) 1

LUCAN. *Phar.* 3. 256–8 (SP 4n) = BOETHIUS, *De cons. Phil.* 5, met. 1* 1

CICERO. *De invent.* 1. 1. 1 (Rep. p. 208n), 2. 1–3 (AgG 4. 11–12, GL 892). *Parad.* 1 (SP 143). *De off.* 1. 22. 77 (GL 1185n) . 4

LIVY. 1. 34 (LMarg 7); 2. 9–14 (WH 208–10) 2

SALLUST. *Cat. con.* 2. 7 (GL 1177n) 1

VAL. MAXIMUS. 3. 3 (WH 198–9). RepEpit 9n* 1

JUSTIN. 11. 10 (WCY 540 ff.) 1

PLINY SECUNDUS. *Hist. nat.* 10. 2 (PS 536 ff.)* 0

NOTES

1. *Vergil.* That Vergil heads the list by no means implies that he was Skelton's favourite author. It is largely a tribute to his eminence; even more, perhaps, it is the result of his ubiquity in the grammar books. The Vergilian tag sprang naturally to the pen of a schoolmaster looking for an apt quotation. The epic note of the *Aeneid* also lent itself to humour, as in the *Garland* 1240n, 1408n, 1472n. True to his age, however, Skelton's chief enthusiasm was for the *Eclogues*. They account for more than half his borrowings, and for the ones most woven into the stuff of his verse.

> Dulce meum decus est. illi hanc ego phillida mitto./

he writes of the king in his *Palinodium* (MS. fol. 28ᵛ). The first phrase is Horatian (*Carm.* I. I. 2); but the second can only be a memory of *Ecl.* 3. 76:

> Phyllida mitte mihi: meus est natalis, Iolla.

No doubt the poem was written for the king's birthday. Again, a marginal note in the *Chronique de Rains* which Skelton gave to Henry reads:

> Vltor celestis da. cur ruit iste scelestus?
> Quod petis instanter. Thome loca sacra loquantur

(MS. C.C.C. 432, fol. 7). This refers to the death of Henry II, who according to the chronicler was found 'estrangle. les raignes ton froin entor son col'. Skelton declares it was a divine judgement for the murder of Becket. In writing his gloss, however, he has chosen the rare *da* for *dic* which he found in *Ecl.* 1. 18:

> sed tamen iste deus qui sit da, Tityre, nobis.

If the *Garland* may be trusted, he even modelled upon the *Eclogues* a work now lost, which told 'how iollas louyd goodly phillis' (Faukes, sig. F2: l. 1497).

2. *Ovid.* In his marked fondness for Ovid Skelton was also a child of his period (cf. D. Bush, *Mythology and the Renaissance Tradition in English Poetry*, Minneapolis, 1932, *passim*). He may have translated the *Art of Love* (see App. A, 11(*a*), above); possibly the *Heroides* as well:

> Of louers testamentis and of there wanton wyllis (GL 1496).

(But the typical pun on 'will' (cf. PS 681) reminds us that 'testament' also means 'witness', as in Usk's *Testament of Love*. Villon offers another possibility; but the plural 'testamentis' points more definitely to Ovid.) Certainly the Ovidian tricks, as interpreted by the Middle Ages, are

Appendix B 421

everywhere in Skelton's Latin verse—the recurrences, the closed antithetic couplet, the accumulation of similes (which in the *Salve* becomes active borrowing). Even where Vergil is the primary source, as in GL 290–322, the finest lines in the passage:

> He sange also how the tre as he did take
> Betwene his armes he felt her body quake (300–1)

come straight out of Ovid (*Met.* 1. 553–4).

3. *Maximian.* As a contemporary of Boethius, though entirely pagan in spirit, this poet should perhaps be omitted from our list. But his fifth elegy complements the erotic flippancy of Ovid in a way which the later Pamphilus (whom Skelton also knew: SP 239 and n) does not. Despite a popularity which gave us the word *pamphlet*, the *De amore Galateae* is mere Ovid-and-water. In the later Middle Ages Maximian was no less a household name (cf. Alexander's contrast of his *Doctrinale* with the *nugis Maximiani*, ll. 3, 25), and he is decidedly more significant a literary figure.

4. *Martial.* It seems probable that the miracle of Jane's sampler (PS 210 ff.) derives from the painting of Publius' lap-dog (1. 109):

> hanc ne lux rapiat suprema totam,
> picta Publius exprimit tabella,
> in qua tam similem videbis Issam
> ut sit tam similis sibi nec ipsa . . . .

5. *Seneca. Moderata iuuant* (SP 52) is probably a reminiscence of *Moderata durant* (*Troad.* 257), which in the 1506 ed. of Seneca is capitalized as a 'sentence'.

6. *Justin.* If not from a medieval source, Skelton's account of Abdalonimus is more probably from Justin than from Quintus Curtius (4. 1. 19), who makes a point of his royal descent.

7. *False attributions.* (*a*) In his account of the phoenix's rebirth Pliny makes no mention of 'incyneracyon'. This indeed appears to be a post-classical elaboration of the myth.

(*b*) The Philostratus reference may be dealt with here, as Skelton obviously has a Latin version in mind. Malicious tongues, he says (VT (Marshe, sig. Aa2): Dyce, i. 134), are

> More stinging the*n* scorpions y[t] stang Pharaotis

and he directs us, in a note which Marshe put into the text, to 'philostratum de vita tyanei Apollonij'. But the Phraortes of Philostratus did not die of scorpions' stings, nor (so far as I have found) did anyone else of a comparable name. Even the astounding list of deaths in J. Textor's encyclopaedic *Officina partim historijs | partim poeticis referta disciplinis*

(Paris, 1520: fol. 25), with its thirty-seven categories, gives no Phraortes among the thirteen *Occisi a serpentibus*.

(*c*) The erroneous reference to Lucan is apparently due to Reuchlin (see Introduction, p. xxiv).

8. *False quantities*. Apart from those which have been dealt with in App. A, 9, there remain only a few cases in which a short syllable occupies the first half-foot in a pentameter—a perfectly legitimate medieval practice, as Dunbabin has noted—and one serious double error in PS 1091 (Kele, sig. D1):

> Quid petis filio / mater dulcissi[m]a ba ba

This much-criticized hexameter should come under suspicion immediately, as it takes the place filled, everywhere else in the poem, by a quotation, and is indeed almost meaningless as an original. It is actually the garbled refrain of a very charming religious ditty of the period, which represents a dialogue between the Infant Jesus and his Mother:

> 'Quit petis, o fily?'—'mater dulcissima, ba ba!'
> 'quid petis, o fili?'—'michi plausus, oscula da da!'

(MS. Addit. 31922, fol. 112^v: my punctuation. There is no need to emend, with Dyce, *ba ba* to *babae*! The term is familiar Tudor for 'kiss'.) This discovery at once explains the metrical error as due to Skelton's printer, and supplies a meaning to the verse in harmony with the context.

9. *Incorrect spelling*. There is one interesting example. In Pynson line 101 of the *Replication* reads: 'Necq*ue* negatiuis', and the gloss: 'Necq*ue* non neque legas'. Dyce, who regularized Skelton's Latin by nineteenth-century standards, failed to make sense of this, reading *neque* throughout, and transcribing the gloss: 'Neque non, neque legas.' But clearly Skelton believed that *neque* was derived from *nec* plus *-que* enclitic, and should be spelt accordingly. His usual sources do not discuss the word.

10. Spec offers a number of references which might be added to our list, e.g. Regulus (fol. 4: ? Val. Max. 4. 4. 6); Cincinnatus (fol. 4: ? Liv. 3. 25); Fabricius and Pyrrhus (fol. 5^v: ? Val. Max. 2. 9, &c.); St. Augustine, *De civ. Dei* 5. 12—not 13, as Skelton has it (fol. 6); an untraced reference to Scipio (fol. 7); Horace on the princely virtues (? a reminiscence of lines such as *Carm.* 3. 24. 25–30, 4. 4. 33–36, 4. 15. 9 ff.; *Ep.* 2. 1. 245–50); and a group of noble leaders: Marcellinus (the virtuous fifth-century general), Caesar, Pompey, Alexander, the good emperors Titus and Theodosius, Themistocles, Carridius Cyrus, Lucius Valerius, Trajan, and Brutus. For the references to Cato's Distichs see App. C.

APPENDIX C

Skelton's Debt to Cato's Distichs

ON the influence of this amazingly popular textbook, which extended from the fifth to the nineteenth century, see W. G. Crane, *Wit and Rhetoric in the Renaissance*, New York, 1937, pp. 24-25. In the later Middle Ages it was prefaced by a series of shorter aphorisms—according to Warton (qu. Dyce, ii. 344), by one Daniel Church, 'a domestic in the court of Henry the Second', which became known as the *Cato Parvus*, and is mentioned in SP 183. An interesting example of its use in didactic literature may be seen in the aphorisms which Skelton added for the guidance of Prince Henry at the end of the *Speculum*. Parallels are given below. (Unnumbered quotations are from the *Cato Parvus*.)

Spec (fols. 19ᵛ-23)	*Cato*
Ante omnia gulam abhominare.	Indulgere gulae noli . . . (4. 10).
Crapulam proscribe.	Vino tempera.
Luxuriam detestare.	Luxuriam fugito . . . (2. 10).
Prostibulum scortorum fuge.	Meretricem fuge.
Coniugem tibi delige . . .	Coniugem ama.
Non sis immemor beneficii.	Benefici accepti esto memor.
Facile non credas omni spiritui . . .	Nihil temere credideris.
Affabilis esto.	Blandus esto.
Non sis parcus.	. . . Fuge nomen auari . . . (4. 16).
S⟨c⟩is cum ratione munificus largus benignus et dapsilis.	Dapsilis interdum notis et largus amicis,
	Cum fueris, dando semper tibi proximus esto (1. 40).
Iram cohibeas.	Iracundiam rege.
Neminem irrideas.	Neminem riseris.
Fidem serua.	Iusiurandum serua.
Diu delibera, loquere pauca.	Inter conuiuas fac sis sermone modestus,
Libenter audias, tarde discucias.	Ne dicare loquax, cum vis urbanus haberi (3. 19). (Cf. 4. 20: Prospicito tecum tacitus quid quisque loquatur. . . .)
Famulos respice . . .	Familiam cura. (Cf. 4. 44.)
. . . clemens mitis et humilis . . .	Clemens et constans . . . esto (1. 7).
	Verecundiam serua.

Appendix C

Spec (fols. 19ᵛ–23)	Cato
Esto fortis in aduersis, cautus in prosperis.	Tranquillis rebus semper diuersa timeto, Rursus in aduersis melius sperare memento (4. 26).
Deum obsecra.	Deo supplica.
Libros lege.	Libros lege.
. . . manda memorie, noli obliuisci . . .	Quae legeris, memento.

APPENDIX D

Skelton's Debt to the Adagia of Erasmus

1. Iuuenes sanguinolenti propter libidinem dominandi et gloriam fame / frequenter fieri solent sediciosi. hec dias. (Rep, p. 209n). So Pynson, followed by Dyce. But the only recorded utterance of Dias of Ephesus (Philostratus, *Vit. Soph.* 1. 3) in no way resembles this dictum. It is a misprint for 'Bias', and the note is taken from Erasmus on *Ne quid nimis* (1. 6. 96): 'Aristotiles tertio Rhetoricorum libro ad Biantem auctorem refert, tractans de juvenum immoderatis affectibus, quos ait, ubique nimia vehementia peccare: nam & amare nimium, pariter & odisse nimium....' But Erasmus in turn has made two errors. He refers to the wrong book of the *Rhetoric*, and he confuses two of its chapters. *Rhet.* 2. 13, which deals with the nature of old men, has the observation: 'And on this account they neither love nor hate with great earnestness, but, *conformably to the remark of Bias*, they both love as though about to hate, and hate as though about to love' (Bohn trans.). The previous chapter discusses the 'passions and habits of the young', and says: '... by reason of their ambition they cannot endure a slight, but become indignant... and they are ambitious indeed of honour, but more so of victory; for youth is desirous of superiority....' Later on comes the remark: 'And all their errors are on the side of excess and too great earnestness, *in contravention of Chilo's rule*....' With so similar a context the epigrams of Chilo and Bias became telescoped in Erasmus' memory, and he conferred Chilo's *ne quid nimis* on the latter. There is no such confusion in Trapezunzio's Latin (*In Rhetoricarum Aristotelis libros prefatio* ..., Paris, 15—, *ad loc.*). Erasmus seems, however, to have established the mistake: cf. Puttenham's reference to 'the saying of *Bias*: *ne quid nimis*' (*Arte of English Poesie*, ed. Willcock and Walker, Cambridge, 1936, 3. 7). It may be noted that the adage is itself quoted a little earlier in Skelton's poem (Rep, p. 208).

2. Syr capten of catywade / catacumbas of cayre (AgG 1. 16). 'Cayre' is not Cairo (Dyce), but Caria (cf. Skelton's *Diodorus*, fol. 50^v). *Adagia* 4. 3. 3 describes *Caricum sepulchrum* as a term used 'de re magnifica, sumptuosaque. Sumptum a Mausoli sepulchro, quod est apud Caras.' Skelton's meaning is now obvious. 'Sir captain of Cattawade' evokes a Suffolk Napoleon of Notting Hill; and to underline the mockery the hamlet with its little shrine (described as 'the great God

of Catwade', probably also with comic intent, in *The Four PP*, 1. 46) is likened to that wonder of the ancient world, the Mausoleum. The phrase is not classical; and Isidore, followed by Reuchlin and the *Catholicon*, refers to Mausolus as a king of Egypt (15. 11. 3). So there can be little doubt whence Skelton obtained the phrase. None of Garnesche's recorded interests bring him very near to Cattawade, but as a Suffolk man he may have lived or had property there.

3. **omni Spartano liberior** (LCall *sub fin*.). Marshe has 'Spartane', corrected by Dyce. Cf. *Adagia* 2. 8. 61: *Generosior Sparta*, i.e. 'freer than Sparta', which was proverbial for the proud independence of its citizens. 'Dicebatur', comments Erasmus, 'excellenti animo, minimeque timidus aut humilis.'

4. **Solus sapis** (Spec, fol. 10). Cf. *Adagia*, 2. 3. 53: *Solus sapit*. Derived from Homer, *Od*. 10. 495, where it is said of the seer Teiresias that he alone of the dead has understanding, while the others flit about as shadows.

5. **Hec res acu tangitur** (SP 57). Cf. *Adagia* 2. 4. 93: *Rem acu tetigisti*.

6. **Asinus Qui pinxit mulum** (Bedell 16–17). Marshe has 'vixit multum'. Emended by Dyce, who noted (ii. 214) that the phrase is from *Adagia* (ed. 1606), p. 1663: *Mulum de asino pingere*, which is explained by Erasmus as representing foolishness by other foolishness or supporting lies by means of lies. 'Magna similitudo inter asinum et mulum est.'

GLOSSARY

This Glossary is a glossary of 'hard words'. No attempt is made to record every appearance of such words as are listed, but the range of their meaning is exemplified.

Variant spellings created by substitution for each other of such letters as *i* and *y* (*barbarian* and *barbaryan*; *yrous* and *irous*), *u* and *v* (*inuencion* and *invention*, *auayll* and *avail*), *c* and *s* (*base* and *bace*), and initial *c* and *k* (*carayne* and *karen*) are not recorded. The prefixes *em-* and *en-* seem freely interchangeable in Skelton (as in *embesy* and *enbesye*). Cross-references are therefore not given from variants to the main entry of such words. The prefixes *em-* and *im-* are similarly interchangeable, as are *en-* and *in-*, *im-* and *in-*, and are similarly treated. The form chosen for the main entry is usually that which appears most frequently in the Diodorus, but this form is sometimes rejected in favour of one more easily checked in the O.E.D. The reduced definite article *th-*, which is often combined with a following noun (as in *thacquytayl*), is disregarded (thus *acquytayl*). Similarly disregarded is the reduced *t-* (for *to*) combined with an infinitive. Regular forms of plurals, past tenses, and participles are not recorded.

abandonynge *pr. p.* subjugating 366/2; *pt.* 337/18; *pp.* 333/7, 366/24, 372/25.
abashement *n.* fear, dread 6/36, 101/9, 105/32, *etc.*; shame 347/27; sudden confusion 144/1, 160/3, *etc.*; *pl.* fears 316/9.
abasshyd *pp.* ashamed 139/34, 370/17; confounded 116/19, 158/1, 160/21, *etc.*; frightened 158/11, 161/17, 206/15, *etc.*; *v. refl. pt.* feared 366/1.
abiect, abiected *pp.* cast out 239/32; rejected 191/14.
abraide *pp.* startled 291/23, 299/7.
abusion *n.* spirit of abuse 290/6; perversion of truth 386/36.
accombred, accunbride *pp.* oppressed, overwhelmed 184/31, 244/18, 314/24, *etc.*
acertayned, acerteigned, adcerteyned *pp.* made certain, assured 95/20, 156/15, 327/36, *etc.*
acquytayl *n.* repayment 377/33.
acquyte *v.* take revenge upon 328/4; avenge 355/20; repay 329/31, 331/27, 376/5; *pr. p.* repaying 334/7; ~ed (*of*) *pp.* repaid (for) 342/24; *v. refl. pr. p.* giving account of (himself) 337/15.
adaunt *v.* moderate 25/21, 242/13, 262/19; put down 348/9; *pr. p.* quelling 191/7; moderating 374/1; *pt.* quelled 34/25.
a dayes *adv.* nowadays 15/2.
adcerteyned. See **acertayned.**
addresse *v.* prepare, set in order 190/6; 286/29; direct 1/5, 134/2; *pr. 3 s.* directs 7/19; *pt.* fitted out 76/16, 159/17; *pp.* prepared, set in order 123/22, 145/8; directed 125/28; fitted out 156/21; *v. refl.* prepare 226/24, 228/31, *etc.*; apply (ourselves, *etc.*) 61/5, 77/12; *pr. p.* setting (himself, *etc.*) 46/26, 152/11; clothing (herself) 143/12; *pt.* clothed (himself) 166/6; betook (himself) 178/14; prepared (himself) 137/18; applied (themselves) 99/32; undertook 156/35, 182/14, 190/32, *etc.*; *pp.* furnished (themselves) 187/2.
addycion *n.* title 385/20.
adioynaunt, adiunant, *etc., adj.* adjoining 60/15, 243/17, 244/24, *etc.*

Glossary

adioyned *pt.* added 303/17; joined 310/10.
admyracion *n.* wonder 85/35, 320/2, 364/31.
admyratyve *n.* wonder 372/18.
admyxtion *n.* mixture 249/30.
adnulled *pt.* annulled 229/9.
aduenture, auenture *n.* chance 90/22, 105/5; incident 113/33; outcome 144/20; *of* ~, *on* ~ by chance 139/25, 152/6, 161/13.
aduenture *v.* risk 168/18.
aduertence *n.* heedfulness 313/27, 373/29.
aduertise *v.* give counsel 176/9; *pr. p.* taking heed 9/3; *pt.* counselled 169/10; *pp.* 126/2.
aduertisement *n.* observation 6/12, 90/8, 143/22, *etc.*; counsel 97/20, 98/20, 128/9, *etc.*
adunyd *pt.* united 77/19; *pp.* 179/7 (cf. Lat. *adunare*).
adust, adusted *pp.* scorched, parched 58/17, 244/1, 281/31.
adustion *n.* scorching, parching 224/15.
aduysed *pp. we may be* ~ we may consider (cf. 'Le roi s'avisera' as a formula for courteous refusal), 56/14, 394/17.
aduysion. See **avisyon.**
advisament, aduysement, auysement *n.* deliberation 96/28, 156/37, 170/6, *etc.*
advoide. See **avoide.**
affection *n.* inclination 175/25, 308/16.
affectionat *adj.* partial 104/15, 394/20; inclined 305/17.
afferreth *pr. 3 s.* confirms 165/18.
affiaunce *n.* credence 221/17; testimony 53/24.
affiaunsyng *pr. p.* pledging 292/29, 332/9, 339/11; **affyaunced** *pt.* 29/30, 329/11, 368/17; *pp.* 316/30, 363/19; allied 335/33.
afforce, enforce *v.* undertake 12/18, 137/26, 157/1, *etc.*; *pr. 3 s.* 56/22; *pr. p.* 3/35, 342/9; *pt.* 26/31, 144/10, 181/2, *etc.*; *pp.* 3/11, 9/6, 191/32, *etc.*; *v. refl.* undertake 164/3, 193/34, 196/17, *etc.*; *pr. p.* 102/25;
pt. 7/31, 37/19, 260/33, *etc.*; betook (himself) 160/25, 187/11.
affrayed *pp.* frightened 168/35, 317/15, 331/7.
afore-gayne, aforgaynste *adj.* opposite 269/6, 274/2.
aforthe *v.* afford 209/8.
agrest *adj.* rude 25/19, 243/16, 244/13, *etc.*
alaye, alayer *n.* admixture 349/1, 8, 351/30.
alaye *v.* dilute 351/27.
algarysme, augrym *n.* arithmetic 24/30, 178/13, 321/15, *etc.*
alientes *n. pl.* aliens 295/23.
alighed. See **allyed.**
allective *n.* allurement, inducement 93/29, 144/10, 196/17, *etc.*; *pl.* 182/1; benefits 342/5, 360/3.
allective *adj.* enticing 166/10.
allectuary *adj.* enticing 62/21.
allectuarye *n.* spice 209/17; *pl.* 99/16, 208/27; aromatic perfumes 123/20, 276/34, *etc.*; **electuaries** allurements 296/4.
allonely *adv.* only 59/4.
allowed *pt.* accepted 32/22, 33/19; *pp.* commended 2/30, 73/21, *etc.*; approved 58/2; accepted 52/31, 59/2, *etc.*
all to-brekyth, all to-brosed, alle to-flappe, all to-rent, altoreveth, all to-stongen, alle totere. See **to-brekyth, to-brosed,** *etc.*
alludyng *pr. p.* suggesting 277/17.
allyed, alighed, alyed *pp.* allied 84/4, 296/36, 301/10, *etc.*
allynges *adv.* altogether 282/24, 311/12.
amased *pp.* demented 155/9, 303/25, 369/36; dumbfounded 169/24, 262/6; terrified 144/5, 345/22.
ambiguite *n.* doubtfulness 3/22, 16/29, 53/22, *etc.*
ambiguous *adj.* doubtful 69/30, 128/3, 196/1, *etc.*
amersyd *pp.* fined 102/32, 109/16.
amplyated *pp.* amplified 393/29.
and *conj.* if 57/3.
anell *n.* ring or hoop 226/28.
anenst *prep.* among 3/13, 73/21, *etc.*; toward 7/33, 105/1.

Glossary 429

annexynge *pr. p.* adding 343/6;
annexed *pp.* united 394/3.
annoy *v.* injure 150/20, 221/9;
 hamper 200/32; *pt.* injured 171/15;
 pp. damaged 194/25; afflicted 203/
 31, 229/21, *etc.* See **ennoye**.
annuary *adj.* annual 11/3, 330/2,
 341/12, *etc.*
anoiaunce *n.* harm, injury 194/27,
 220/6, *etc.*; injuriousness 208/1.
 See **ennoyaunce**.
anoy *n.* injury 246/29.
aourned *pp.* furnished 29/8.
appalleth *pr. 3 s.* tarnishes 208/1.
apparative *adj.* capable of making
 evident 212/26.
apparayllynge *pr. p.* making use of
 16/5; apparayllyd *pp.* fitted out
 65/1, 114/33.
apparceyue *v.* observe 56/7; learn
 95/19; *pr. p.* learning 57/33, 102/3;
 pt. learned 52/8; *pp.* learned 22/25,
 101/33; seen, perceived 57/28, 96/
 28.
appertly *adv.* openly 57/32.
appetyte *n.* desire 77/1, 82/2, 96/23,
 etc.
appoyntement, oppoyntement *n.*
 agreement 316/27, 317/5.
apprehensive *n.* understanding
 285/31, 322/6.
approbate *n.* proof, 373/22.
approbate *pp.* approved 128/32.
approchment *n.* means of approach
 or access 373/20.
appropre *v.* assign, appropriate 20/
 10, 53/34, 177/22; *pt.* 20/8, 24/24,
 enpropred 27/15, *etc.*; *pp.* 19/5,
 19/30, 21/4, *etc.*; appropried *ppl.
 a.* 214/5.
approuyth *pr. 3 s.* proves 346/2; *pp.*
 52/30, 59/20, 112/2, *etc.*; ap-
 prouyd *ppl. a.* 15/9.
aranyes, arenyes *n.* spiders 252/2,
 6.
arblaste *n.* cross-bow 370/12; *pl.*
 171/22.
arenes *n.pl.* sands 57/20.
arette. See **arrect**.
armature *n.* armour 289/19, 315/2,
 367/20, *etc.*
armure *n.* arms 338/14, 350/27, *etc.*

arrect, arette *v.* turn, direct, lift up
 82/18, 97/19, 112/11, *etc.*; *pr. p.*
 141/2, 175/10, 338/25; *pt.* 126/5,
 180/15, 189/7, *etc.*; *pp.* 117/8, 173/
 4; *pt.* ascribed 339/16.
arrest *n.* seizure (usually in phrases:
 *batayllle of arreste, ioustis of areste,
 etc.*) 331/35, 332/32, 339/3, *etc.*
arrette. See **arrect**.
arryuage, aryuage *n.* landing 381/
 22, 387/27.
ascence, ascens *n.* ascent 154/4,
 207/7.
assigne *v.* specify 391/8; *pp.* signed
 7/3.
assourded. See **assurd**.
assoyllynge *pr. p.* resolving 53/22.
assumpt *pp.* taken up (into Heaven)
 299/23.
assurd, assurdir *v.* burst forth,
 spring up 187/36, 373/3; *pr. 3 s.*
 184/25, 272/21; *pp.* 55/33.
astate, estate *n.* rank 97/5, 137/27,
 139/25, *etc.*; noble 130/4, 150/23;
 pl. nobles, heroes 33/25, 63/19, 91/
 29, *etc.*
astonyed, astowned, astoynd,
 etc., *pp.* astounded 86/25, 158/1,
 160/5, *etc.*
astronomyens *n.* astronomers 71/6.
atasted *pp.* tasted 232/26.
attamed *pp.* tamed 262/15.
atteigned *pp.* obtained 194/28.
attemperat *adj.* temperate 25/3.
attemperaunce *n.* temperateness
 18/13, 98/3, 194/4, *etc.*
attempre *v.* moderate 331/10; *pp.*
 qualified by admixture 349/10.
attones, attonys *adv.* at once, 42/
 31, 364/28, 367/35, *etc.*
attratyue *adj.* attractive (*vertue* ~
 drawing power) 55/13.
atwene *prep.* between 380/8.
aualeth *pr. 3 s.* subsides 51/20, 22.
auauncement, avaunsement *n.*
 furtherance 327/1, 339/15, 350/24,
 etc.; advancement 8/36; advantage
 90/6, 328/32, 343/19; praise 311/
 28, 357/28; *pl.* 334/15.
auaunse *v.* give advantage to 156/
 30; *pr. 3 s.* 185/15; *pt.* increased
 138/9, 296/11; elevated 29/3, 191/

15; exalted 131/27; raised 117/3, 168/28; *pp.* exalted 36/18, 190/18; extolled 31/7, 126/8; *v. refl.* thrust (himself) forward 192/17; *pt.* advanced 142/20, 191/28, 199/19.
auaunt *n.* boast 125/18, 322/10.
auauntage *n.* benefit 9/11, 101/37, 117/14.
auauntageth *pr. 3 s.* assists 20/6; *pt.* benefited 158/16.
auauntyng *pr. p.* boasting 170/13; **auaunted** *pp.* rendered foolhardy 159/30.
auenture. See **aduenture.**
augrym. See **algarysme.**
aultiere, awtiere *n.* altar 293/32, 299/25, 304/17.
auoultresse *n.* adulteress 89/19.
auydious *adj.* avid 156/35, 182/4, 279/27, *etc.*
auydiously *adv.* avidly 354/27, 360/3.
auysement. See **advisament.**
available, auayllable *adj.* useful 6/23, 10/17, 23, *etc.*
availl *n.* advantage 192/13.
avenquyssyng *pr. p.* vanquishing 138/10.
avisyon, aduysyon, avysion, aduysion, *etc., n.* apparition 90/9; dream 90/19; forewarning given in dream 36/4, 76/8, 83/17, *etc.*
avoide, advoide *v.* escape 43/16, 244/34, 326/12; depart 256/33; flee away 210/28; keep away from 267/30, 287/23, 367/9, *etc.*; remove 266/29; empty 380/1; *pr. p.* escaping 81/5; emptying 364/35; *pt.* escaped 116/22, 317/33, 327/20, *etc.*; subsided 52/8; *pp.* driven away 300/14; cleansed 264/29.
avoutrye *n.* adultery 301/23.
avow *n.* vow 37/26, 120/16, 159/8, *etc.*; *pl.* 112/16.
awaite *n.* watchfulness 230/2, 373/30.
awayte (after) *v.* studiously observe 39/11.
awtiere. See **aultiere.**
awtraijd. See **outray.**
axes *n.* fever, ague 236/1, 255/20, 314/8, *etc.*

bakhalf *n.* hinterland 199/1.
bale *n.* torture 386/5.
bande *n.* bond 374/1.
bandon *n.* control 191/7, 192/1.
baratours *n. pl.* quarrelsome persons 348/17.
baratous, barratous *adj.* quarrelsome 245/29, 279/30.
barbarian *adj.* non-Greek 184/25, 189/34, *etc.*
barbarians, barbaryns *n. pl.* non-Greeks 60/24, 175/5, 207/23, *etc.*
barbarik *adj.* non-Greek 9/19, 166/17, 167/24.
barbary *n.* the non-Greek world 8/14, 40/14, 202/30, *etc.*
barbary *adj.* non-Greek 11/6, 13, 16/28, *etc.*
barratyng *vbl. n.* brawling 241/9.
bayne *n.* bathe 97/32.
baynes, baynys *n. pl.* baths 99/16, 218/25.
beawteynge *pr. ⁀.* beautifying 98/31.
becomme *v.* go 251/23.
behalf, behalue, bihalue *n.* half, side 186/1; respect or particular (*in som* ~ in some respect) 10/17, 25/24, 43/28, *etc.*; *of his fadres* ~ in respect of his father, because of his father 24/12; *for theyr* ~ in their behalf or interest 104/1.
behavour, byhauour, byhauoyr *n.* demeanour 64/9, 97/9, 307/33, *etc.*; class in society, way of life 39/32, 40/6, 41/9; skill 321/29.
behoef, byhoeff *n.* benefit 7/4, 17/22, 24/1.
behoefful, byhoeffull *adj.* advantageous 29/6, 40/15.
behold *pp.* beheld 5/25, *etc.*
benefayt, bienefayt *n.* benefit 21/35, 386/3, 5, *etc.*; *pl.* 22/20, 30/25, *etc.*
beseen, besene, bysene *pp.* provided, furnished 65/1, 66/2, 19, *etc.*
besynes *n.* busyness 27/18, 265/6; business 52/4, 111/26; occupation 102/24, 163/25, 192/35, *etc.*; labour 313/26.
bewrap *v.* wrap 233/9.
bewrayed *pt.* betrayed 107/7; *pp.* revealed 301/18.

Glossary

bienfayt, bienefayt. See benefayt.
bladdered *pp*. blistered 256/26.
blastered *pp*. shrivelled 256/26.
blasty *adj*. gusty 56/5.
(at a) blushe at once 281/5, 347/27.
bonchyng *vbl. n.* thumping 235/16; bunchynges *pl.* 240/29.
borall *adj*. civilized 315/20.
bosse *n*. a fat woman 182/23.
bothes *n. pl.* temporary huts 194/21, 214/7, 249/24.
botries *n. pl.* butteries 238/21.
bourde *n*. freeboard, gunwale 266/17, 267/12, 16; *pl.* boards 236/9 (burdes), 12.
boyng *vbl. n.* lowing (as of oxen) 239/10.
boystous *adj*. massive 34/12; powerful 89/22.
brat *n*. rag 235/29.
bray *v*. grind to powder 218/21, 235/23, 236/10.
brede *n*. breadth 44/20, 66/22, 83/18, etc.
breme *adj*. fierce 261/6.
breme *adv*. fiercely 254/1.
bremely, bremly *adv*. fiercely 332/26, 373/13, 26.
brenne *v*. burn 209/4, 368/6; brennynge *ppl. a.* 376/15; brenned, brente *pt.* 66/28, 83/13, 327/8, *etc.*; brent *pp.* 106/10, 155/22, 247/17, *etc.*; brenned *ppl. a.* 327/9.
brest, breste *pt.* burst 83/28, 303/14.
bribed *pp*. robbed 265/15.
bribery, briboury *n*. robbery 283/18, 308/18.
bribours *n. pl.* robbers 215/33.
brose *v*. crush 238/31, 245/19. See to-brosed.
brosoure *n*. bruising, wound 246/29, 378/22.
brothelles *n*. loose women 315/28.
bruser *n*. (?) grinding toil 79/17.
brute *n*. fame, reputation 6/32, 41/10, 203/15, *etc.*
bruted *pp*. bruited 4/6, 37/18, 65/17, *etc.*; famed 94/33, 178/26; ~ of known by 29/2.
brutows *adj*. fame-worthy 373/37.
bummyng *vbl. n.* humming, buzzing 246/11.

bunchynges. See bonchyng.
burdes. See bourde.
buscage *n*. thicket 31/8.
bushmentes *n*. surprise parties 247/19, 249/3; groups 253/25.
buske *v*. bustle 247/8; *pt.* 261/5.
busyer *adj*. more intricate 68/5.
by & by in order or succession 48/18, 64/22, 97/7.
byfore-seson *adv*. formerly 80/11.
by-pertely *adv*. near by 49/7.
bysette *pp*. studded 103/24.
bysplyttyd *pp*. split 84/21.
bystadde *pp*. bestead (*sore* ~ hard pressed) 376/5, 380/8.
byttor *n*. bittern 118/5; *pl.* 84/23.

calvy *n*. mud-fish 237/31.
cammokkes *n*. knees of timber 243/24.
can *v*. know 214/19.
canicvler *adj. dayes* ~ dog-days 27/27; ~ *signe* dog-star 38/13, 246/6.
captivous *adj*. of the nature or quality of vassalage 191/33.
carayne, karen *n*. carrion, dead body 114/9, 283/6; *pl.* 88/8, 301/26 (carens).
cast (vp) *v*. abandon, leave 102/25; castyng *pr. p.* pondering 143/23, 346/31; castid, kyste, casted *pt.* planned 75/30, 103/6, 202/5, *etc.*; threw 163/12; caste *pp*. planned 91/4; defeated 303/10; dropped by the dam, or born 115/1.
caste *n*. calculation 24/30; plan 85/4.
casuall *adj*. accidental 175/24.
casualte *n*. chance 371/10.
causatyf *n*. cause 7/8, 18/14, 19/31, *etc.*; causatyues *pl.* 52/23, 28, 60/12, *etc.*
causes *n. pl.* legal cases 97/30, 103/15, 25, *etc.*
celestyne *adj*. celestial 299/25, 308/30, 325/20, *etc.*
cered *pp*. anointed 99/23.
ceryous, ceryously. See serious, seriously.
cestrens *n. pl.* cisterns 150/20.
chaas, chace. See chese.
chafed, chafynge. See chauffeth.

chaffar *n.* merchandise 333/24.
champayn, champen, *etc., n.* open country 17/24, 42/14, 44/34, *etc.*; *pl.* fields, meadows 129/23; plains 183/29.
champayn, champen, chaumpen, chaumpeen, *etc., adj.* level, flat, 51/24, 153/27, 197/37, *etc.*
chapitres *n. pl.* chapters 13/8, 61/11, 134/6, *etc.*
chare *n.* chariot 81/22; *pl.* 66/6, 77/3, 141/15.
charge *n.* responsibility 25/28, 163/25, 171/31, *etc.*; expense 3/32, 89/10, 98/32, *etc.*
chargeable *adj.* onerous 93/22; heavy 215/8; expensive 122/25.
chargyd *pp.* burdened 101/3.
chase. See **chese.**
chauffeth *pr. 3 s.* warms 14/6; *pr. p.* 15/6; *pp.* 212/36.
chaumpeen, chaumpen. See **champayn.**
chaungyng *vbl. n.* exchange, trade 279/1. See **choppynge and chaungynge.**
cherete, cherte, chierte *n.* affection 98/24, 302/8, 320/4, *etc.*; favour 208/17, 209/6.
chese *v.* choose 153/13, 227/33, 232/6, *etc.*; **chaas, chace, chase** *pt.* 26/19, 39/8, 72/10, 293/10, *etc.*
cheste *n.* coffin 99/24, 125/12, 14.
chesten *n.* chestnut tree 210/3.
chestid *pp.* coffined 124/15.
cheuyssaunce *n.* trade 107/32, 207/14, 275/35, *etc.*
chierte. See **cherete.**
chirme *n.* the jargoning of birds 325/24.
choppynge and chaungynge buying and selling 107/32, 207/14, 214/21.
chow *v.* chew 238/30; *pp.* 140/18.
chynche *n.* niggardliness 86/6.
clarete *n.* clearness (of weather) 60/30.
close *v.* enclose 112/18, 113/5; *pt.* 157/31.
cloyster *n.* enclosure 71/31.
coaction *n.* compulsion 229/4.

coactives *n. pl.* compelling causes 216/30.
coarted *pt.* constricted 393/34; *pp.* compelled 206/7.
coclea *n.* the screw of Archimedes 47/19.
cognition *n.* knowledge 4/13, 5/27, 296/15, *etc.*
cognysance *n.* badge, heraldic device 26/17, 32/3, 332/16, *etc.*
colaterall *adj.* neighbouring 5/30, 179/7, 182/7, *etc.*
colaterally *adv.* side by side 197/23, 225/23.
colaterallyth *pr. 3 s.* lies contiguous with 321/26.
cole *n.* coal; *the wynde . . . bloweth no grete cole* the wind . . . barely breathes (ref. is to blowing upon embers to brighten a fire) 250/4.
colestockis *n. pl.* cabbages 109/36.
collocke *n.* ale-pot 349/6.
collusion *n.* deceit, fraud 8/31, 29/34, 271/1, *etc.*
comeberous *adj.* cumbrous, vexatious 277/35.
comfortatyf, confortative *adj.* medicinal 208/30, 348/33.
commen (vnto) *pp.* reached 251/37.
commened, commenyd. See **communed.**
commestyble *adj.* edible 50/8.
com(m)odious, commodyous *adj.* useful, profitable 9/11, 71/34, 101/32, *etc.*; fruitful 71/28, 150/4, 156/17, *etc.*
commodiously *adv.* profitably 244/7; abundantly 251/35.
commoditie, comoditie *n.* usefulness 4/4, 50/12, 143/17, *etc.*; fruitfulness 17/15, 22/25, 42/1; article of economic value 208/28; *pl.* benefits 182/12; articles of economic value 208/23.
communed (of), commenyd, *etc. pp.* discussed 43/8, 60/27, 170/5.
communion *n.* assembly 142/2.
commyng-in, commyng into, commyng vnto *n.* entrance 67/21, 68/4, 150/5, *etc.*
commyng-out *n.* exit 237/5.
commyse, comyse *v.* commit, per-

Glossary

form, or perpetrate 337/28, 351/33, 367/8, *etc.*; *pt.* 107/23, 374/25; *pp.* 106/19, 318/26 (conmysed), 361/15, *etc.*; ~ *bataylle* join battle 159/19, 390/32.
commyxtion *n.* commingling 8/30, 13/28; sexual union 14/24.
compacte *pp.* combined, compacted 6/10, 13/29, 150/17, *etc.*
compassyng *pr. p.* weighing in mind 143/29; compassed *pp.* contained 177/27; ~ *ppl. a.* contrived 155/1, 164/8, 168/9.
competency *n.* due 70/18.
competently *adv.* sufficiently 4/3, 54/13, 122/25.
composicion *n.* agreement or treaty 90/28, 128/4, 181/1, *etc.*
comprehende *v.* include 11/8; *pr. 3 s.* 12/6, 277/24.
comynalte *n.* commonalty, the common people 40/3, 391/34.
comynte *n.* the common people 82/1.
concalefaction *n.* heating 212/37.
concavous *adj.* concave, hollow 178/1, 273/12.
conceipt, conceyte, consayte *n.* favourable opinion 8/37, 33/21, 165/9, *etc.*; mind 324/17; belief 19/10, 34/4; opinion 54/6, 382/5, *etc.*
concentive *n.* consent 190/32, 224/11, 298/2, *etc.*
concentyf *adj.* agreeing 357/23.
conceyte. See conceipt.
concite *adj.* concealed 324/9.
concluded *pp.* refuted 55/5; agreed 310/27; *pt.* 303/9, 388/14, *etc.*
condensate *ppl. a.* thickened 55/8.
condenseth *pr. 3 s.* thickens 213/5; *pp.* 31/8, 183/28, 211/3, *etc.*
condiscende *v.* agree 388/7; *pp.* 374/6.
conducte *n.* guide 351/19.
conduyte *v.* conduct 2/13; *pp.* 42/26.
confections *n. pl.* spices 215/32.
confeteraunce *n.* confederacy or conspiracy 229/36, 317/2, 367/15, *etc.*
confluence *n.* junction of streams 188/12, 395/6; multitude 182/7, 383/1; concourse 15/26, 151/18.

confortative. See comfortatyf.
confuse *n.* confusion 10/21, 296/23.
confuse *adj.* confused 15/21.
congeste *n.* compendium 10/18, 321/13; sum total 231/13.
congested *ppl. a.* heaped up 393/30.
(of or for a) congruence fitting, proper 58/33, 126/6, 174/3, *etc.*; fittingly 5/15, 12/13, 18/12, *etc.*
congruency *n.* propriety 81/25.
coniunctyf *adj.* favourable 356/32.
conmysed. See commyse.
connynge *n.* learning 95/17, 19, 100/23, *etc.*; skill 63/15, 124/33, 133/16, *etc.*
connynge, konnyng *adj.* learned 13/14, 85/18; skilful 85/19, 145/5.
connyngly *adv.* skilfully 68/14.
consayte. See conceipt.
conscribyd *pp.* enrolled 11/3.
conscripcion *n.* compilation 6/10.
contagiously *adv.* noxiously 303/27.
contagyous *adj.* noxious 390/28.
contrarious *adj.* adverse 293/24, 294/23.
contrauersid *pt.* turned against 79/27.
contryuer out *n.* discoverer, inventor 63/15.
contumacie *n.* rebelliousness 277/34.
contynuance *n.* repetition or prolongation (of time) 73/9, 82/14, 110/13, *etc.*
contynued *pp.* expressed at length 164/21, 342/6; expressed 173/12.
conuencion *n.* agreement, contract 122/33; as a collective noun, (law of) contracts 107/32.
conuersacion *n.* behaviour 2/5, 7/24, 8/20, *etc.*
conuersaunt *adj.* dwelling 10/34, 133/1, 204/34, *etc.*
conueyaunce *n.* management 111/8; expression 363/14.
conueyed *pp.* recounted 11/11.
coost, coste *n.* edge, border 42/3, 6; region 24/17, 27/30, 41/23; *etc.*; *pl.* regions 10/30, 38/20, 43/23, *etc.*
cooste *v.* extend 77/14; *pr. 3 s.* 66/10, 80/15, 147/9, *etc.*; *pr. p.* 294/31, 346/5.

F

434   Glossary

copye *n.* abundance 79/2, 91/26, 184/18, *etc.*
corage *n.* spirit, desire 97/19, 99/32, 101/8, *etc.*; disposition 96/21, 116/20, *etc.*; *pl.* 2/5.
coragious *adj.* spirited 157/5.
costage, costaige *n.* cost 50/27, 65/12, 209/7, *etc.*
costiousnes *n.* expensiveness 88/22.
costuouse, costyous *adj.* expensive 73/11, 89/5, 153/27, *etc.*
costyously *adv.* expensively 114/32.
cotidiane *adj.* daily 185/27, 202/35, 366/17.
couched, couchyd *pp.* placed 150/18, 237/16; inset 275/33, 358/11.
couenable *adj.* appropriate, useful 1/5, 8/34, 23/22, *etc.*
couenably *adv.* conveniently 10/11, 308/34.
couert *n.* hiding place 349/30, 371/29, 378/33.
couerte *adj.* hidden 52/12, 78/18, 136/31, *etc.*
couertly *adv.* secretly 39/2, 83/29, 116/13, *etc.*
couertour *n.* covering 345/2.
couetyse *n.* covetousness 86/3, 97/11, 98/9, *etc.*
countermaunde *v.* attack 261/18.
couragith *pr. 3 s.* incites, encourages 6/30; *pt.* 167/32; *pp.* 52/27, 125/28, 136/13, *etc.*
coursyd *pp.* ridden 75/16.
craftely *adv.* cleverly 8/31.
crafty *adj.* skilled 40/4, 47/3, 66/31, *etc.*
crampisshed *ppl. a.* (?) curving 332/27 (cf. **crampand** Sc. obs., curling, curly).
cratgyd *pt.* scratched 352/2.
crea(u)ncer *n.* tutor 322/28, 326/14, 335/26, *etc.*
creveis *n.* crayfish 237/30.
crocottes *n. pl.* wolf-dogs 259/21.
crudelitie *n.* cruelty 144/35, 149/20, 246/4.
cruet(te) *n.* bowl, drinking vessel 92/1, 167/13, 350/34; *pl.* 92/4; ornamental bosses 279/16.
cure *n.* care 1/9.

curiositie *n.* cleverness 85/1; delicacy 188/31.
curried *pp.* beaten 236/2.
curyous *adj.* expert, skilled 66/31, 68/5, 8, *etc.*
curyously *adv.* skilfully 23/25, 91/10, 147/7, *etc.*
customable *adj.* customary 3/23, 75/14, 167/28, *etc.*
cyder *n.* cedar 123/17.

darreyne, dereyne *v.* engage (battle) 141/6, 177/10, 329/14, *etc.*; *pt.* 33/34, 180/23, 292/23, *etc.*; *pp.* 30/1, 94/28, 181/15, *etc.*
dasyeth *pr. 3 s.* dazzles 264/13.
daunger *n.* difficulty 69/30, 169/10, 170/35; jeopardy 76/32, 118/4; hostility 116/22, 161/19; captivity 171/38; injury 172/34; *in his* ~ at his mercy, under his control 159/10, 198/24.
debate *n.* strife, contention, or combat 127/34, 131/13, 161/8, *etc.*
decernynge *pr. p.* laying down or decreeing 108/35.
decoction *n.* cooking to preserve 185/11; concoction 310/10.
decours *n.* downward flow 45/11.
decrepesie *n.* decrepitude 36/7, 182/28, 255/14, *etc.*
decretall *n.* decree 197/7.
dedely, dedialy *adj.* deadly 373/32, 36; mortal 7/24; intolerable 118/9.
deduce *v.* derive 311/4; *pp.* 20/9.
defatigate *pp.* exhausted 206/23.
defaulte, defawte *n.* lack 11/29, 42/5, 53/12, *etc.*; offence 106/25, 111/33, 164/16, *etc.*; *in* ~ guilty 113/18.
defecate *v.* purify from dregs 312/21.
defensable, defensible *adj.* defensive 327/30, 367/25.
defensed *pp.* protected 46/20.
defensive, diffensyve *adj.* of or pertaining to defence 196/33, 289/19, 302/35, 372/7, *etc.*
defensyf *n.* defence 367/20.
deformative *adj.* deformed 258/6.
deignous *adj.* disdainful 316/15, 323/29.

Glossary

delate *v.* report 358/29; *pt.* handed down or over 179/9. See dilate.
deliberative *adj.* carefully deliberated 191/11.
deluynge *vbl. n.* digging 394/6; doluen, dolvyn *pp.* dug 47/12, 74/17, 395/4; buried 375/14.
delyten *pr. pl.* delight 8/24.
delyuer *adj.* nimble 283/20, 388/27.
delyueraunce *n.* nimbleness 353/23.
demenaunce *n.* behaviour 95/12, 96/10.
demene, demeane *v. refl.* conduct (themselves) 214/16, 384/21; *pt.* became (as suitable conduct) 6/14; behaved 78/23, 82/26, 93/24, *etc.*; *shold be ~ pp.* should demean or conduct (herself) 25/30.
demonstrative *n.* interpretation 314/29; proof 320/7; *pl.* demonstrations 328/26.
denominacion *n.* name 23/15, 73/14, 86/13, *etc.*
depart *v.* share 217/7; *pr. 3 s.* separates 183/14; *pr. p.* going away 93/2, 169/28; departynge *vbl. n.* death 115/6; departed *pt.* shared 172/13, 271/6; divided 92/21; went away 144/26; *pp.* divided 100/12, 121/10; gone away 18/17, 182/11, 191/24, *etc.*; dead 155/25, 29.
depaynte *v.* depict 118/30, 350/1; *pt.* 117/2; *pp.* 69/11, 70/26, 91/15, *etc.*
dependeth *pr. 3 s.* is suspended 70/2.
deploracion *n.* lamentation 99/3.
depopulacion *n.* devastation 391/19.
depraue *v.* vilify 394/21.
depressyd *pt.* repressed 83/35.
deraynyd, dereyne, dereynyd. See darreyne.
derive *v.* engage (battle) 225/9; *pp.* 148/3, 215/14.
descence, discens *n.* descent 91/7, 188/10, 16, *etc.*; family descent 198/17; discentes *pl.* slopes 45/30.
descensive *adj.* downward, descending 186/26.
desidious *adj.* idle, slothful 1/15, 384/28, 391/8.

detected *pt.* revealed 107/7.
determynacion *n.* conclusion 54/9, 60/8, 175/15, *etc.*; (?) explanation 19/11, 60/8, 116/10, *etc.*; (?) certainty 16/19, 23/18.
determynate *adj.* definitive 53/21, 177/33.
determynatly *adv.* conclusively 369/12.
determyne *v.* conclude 72/30; *pt.* decided 90/35, 169/2, 24; *pp.* 32/32; determyned *ppl. a.* fated 171/35.
devyce *n.* archetype 58/27.
dictes *n. pl.* sayings 18/34; ~ *metrefyed* poems 24/13.
diffensyve. See defensive.
difference *v.* differ 357/11; *pr. p.* 20/11, 104/30, 178/25, *etc.*; differensyng *vbl. n.* distinction 192/16.
diffuse *adj.* difficult (to understand) 3/11, 9/33, 111/1, *etc.*; difficult 260/20, 336/33, 373/21, *etc.*
diffyne *v.* determine 103/25, 243/4, 8; *pp.* made evident 277/20; decreed 196/10.
diffynytive *adj.* final 69/31, 104/5, 173/9, *etc.*
digne *adj.* worthy 41/21, 65/20, 76/13, *etc.*
dilate *v.* amplify 322/21, 333/1; *pr. p.* 178/4; delated *pp.* 313/9; dilated *ppl. a.* 116/7, 138/16, 186/31.
dilectacion *n.* delight 166/11, 15, 314/37, *etc.*
directorye *n.* guide 341/8.
direned. See darreyne.
discence, discens, discentes, *etc.* See descence.
discepptacon *n.* disputation 357/13.
discouer *v.* make known 105/10, 155/9; *pt.* 167/25; *pp.* 160/4, 168/9, *etc.*
discretive *n.* discernment 285/30; means of discrimination 2/23.
discutions *n. pl.* arguments 303/8.
disdaynous *adj.* disdainful 12/11, 185/34, 314/8, *etc.*
disparsed *pp.* scattered 161/33; *ppl. a.* 43/20, 142/27.

Glossary

disperplid *pp.* scattered 8/5, 30/4.
dispitously *adv.* spitefully, 94/2.
dispositive *n.* arrangement 295/32; quality 328/29.
dispositive *adj.* well ordered 286/33, 360/14.
dispuciouns *n. pl.* disputations 320/19, 354/6, 356/15.
dispusitions, *n. pl.* disputations 183/7.
disputacions, disputicions *n. pl.* disputations 58/26, 336/32, 387/3.
dispytous *adj.* spiteful 365/2; pitiless 355/18.
dissipate *ppl. a.* dispersed 310/7.
dissymyll *v.* dissemble 159/28.
distemperate *adj.* intemperate 251/32.
disteyned *pp.* stained 108/8.
disvsed *pp.* unpractised 137/8.
divisively *adv.* by division 310/8.
divulgate *pp.* published 178/6, 290/14; proclaimed 11/27, 173/24, 292/32, *etc.*
doluen, dolvyn. See **deluynge.**
dommage *n.* harm, damage 8/30.
domycelles *n. pl.* damsels 314/11.
doubtous, dowttous *adj.* hazardous 373/20, 390/8.
doucette *adv.* sweetly 359/16.
doulcet *adj.* sweet 310/22.
douspieris, douze pieris *n. pl.* the twelve peers 91/23, 33, 92/13.
dowttous. See **doubtous.**
draaf *pt.* drove 119/27; **drave** 252/24, 262/7.
draftes *n. pl.* impurities 236/22.
dressed *pt.* equipped 158/33.
druggis *n. pl.* drachmas 110/5.
dryfte *n.* logical consequence 60/12; purpose 178/5.
drynkehayl *n.* drink-hail—a courteous reply to a drinking pledge 349/7.
dulcour *n.* sweetness 208/25, 276/27, 302/30.
dymmysshe *adj.* somewhat dim 334/11.
dysseuere *v.* separate 394/4.

edefye *v.* build, establish 90/36, 145/9, 209/31, *etc.*; *pt.* 20/22, 26/26, 65/23, *etc.*; *pp.* 7/2, 23/13, 20 *etc.*; **edefyenge** *vbl. n.* construction 5/9, 72/28, 195/6.
elate *adj.* haughty 75/28, 181/32, 335/21; high (as of uplands) 188/7; tall 210/21.
electe *pp.* chosen 389/17; *ppl. a.* choice 321/7, 342/32.
electuaries. See **allectuarye.**
elementaire *adj.* elemental 385/30.
eleuacions *n. pl.* rising grounds 55/33.
eleuate *adj.* raised up 57/20.
ellectuaryes. See **allectuarye.**
elurus *n.* cat. 113/10; **elures** *pl.* 114/14.
embacyate, embasiate *n.* embassy 127/35, 128/7, 167/35, *etc.*; **enbassiates** *pl.* 384/15.
embassiatours *n.* ambassadors 165/5.
embatelled, enbatayllyd *pp.* prepared for battle 168/8, 367/28.
embathed *pp.* bathed 276/30.
embeawtie *v.* beautify 187/35; *pt.* 141/1; **embeauted, enbeawted, enbowted,** *etc.*; *pp.* 69/18, 72/19, 150/2, *etc.*
embelisshid *pp.* gratified 35/25.
embesy, enbesye *v.* busy, occupy 84/25, 96/26, 115/1, *etc.*; *pr. p.* 40/4; **enbesyenge** *vbl. n.* 383/33; *pt.* 102/31, 171/30, 189/8, *etc.*; *pp.* 174/31, 194/1, 221/24, *etc.*
emblased *pt.* filled with flames 314/21; *pr. p.* **enblasynge** 345/18; *pp.* blazing 376/15; **emblasyd** *ppl. a.* 381/1.
emblemysh *v.* blemish 287/25, 380/28, *etc.*; **emblemysshynge** *vbl. n.* 334/21, 358/18, 380/11; *pt.* 315/32; *pp.* 3/25, 83/8, 139/35.
emblemysshement *n.* blemish 68/16, 90/21.
emboced, embosed *pp.* studded 325/10; stuffed 157/29.
embretheth *pr. 3 s.* breathes 276/28.
embrosed *pp.* bruised 200/29, 277/8.
embrosure *n.* mashing 312/33.
emoistureth. See **enmoisture.**
empecement, empeshement, enpeshement, *etc., n.* harm, dam-

Glossary

age, or injury 74/6, 81/6, 143/15, etc.; *pl.* 51/35.
empercyd *pp.* pierced 371/4, 378/12; *pt.* 344/24, 373/6.
empettious *adj.* ruthless 331/11.
empeysened. See empoisounde.
empituous. See impetuous.
emplowed *pp.* ploughed 185/21.
empoisounde *ppl. a.* poisoned 373/5; *pp.* 208/7, 317/8, 365/7, *etc.*
empoort, impoort *v.* signify, imply, or betoken 68/23, 177/5, 227/20, *etc.; pr. 3 s.* 20/11, 25/6, 36/19, *etc.*; *pr. p.* 38/27, 85/30, 182/22, *etc.*; deriving 9/14; importynge *ppl. a.* meaningful 123/31; *pt.* 39/30, 69/16, 110/28, *etc.*; emported *ppl. a.* significant 200/2; *pp.* 323/33.
emportune *adj.* importunate 329/13.
emporyens *n. pl.* merchants 91/24.
empregnant *adj.* made pregnant 306/8.
empressed *pp.* stamped with a quality or character 166/5, 356/17; *ppl. a.* 285/26.
empressions *n. pl.* influences 177/3, 212/5, 276/9, *etc.*; *n. sing.* 59/10.
empressive *n.* pressure 277/11.
empressure *n.* squeezing 312/33.
emprowed *pp.* improved 275/22; *pt.* 297/20.
empryse *n.* enterprise 90/33, 378/28; *pl.* 338/26, 383/10, 386/11.
empryse *v.* undertake 368/26, 369/3, 378/16; *pt.* 372/12.
empyres *n.* empress 154/13.
enaged *pp.* aged, mellowed 375/25.
enarmed *pp.* armed 332/28, 371/8, 373/14, *etc.*; *ppl. a.* 332/28; *pr. p.* 374/7.
enbareynd *pp.* made barren 395/13.
enbleryd *pp.* bleared 361/22.
enblynded *pp.* blinded 351/20, 383/8.
enbolne *v.* flood 27/28, 359/23; *pr. 3 s.* 51/5, 59/27; *pr. p.* 237/19; enbolnynge *vbl. n.* swelling 57/21; *pp.* 14/2, 45/14, 52/6, *etc.*; embolmed *ppl. a.* 312/20, 324/28.
enbrewe *v.* defile 392/12.
enbristild *ppl. a.* bristled 373/13.

enbroydrure *n.* embroidery 383/31.
enbullyond *ppl. a.* adorned with gold 387/24, 388/7.
enbybe *v.* swallow 57/11; make wet 352/9; *pr. 3 s.* soaks up 59/26.
enbyttred *pp.* made bitter 328/36, 353/28.
enchace *v.* pursue 194/24; *pt.* 289/34.
enchaced *pt.* 366/33; enchacyng *pr. p.* 285/28 (? errors for enchafed, enchafing from enchafe *v.* to heat).
enchaffyd *pp.* warmed 59/10.
encharge *v.* burden 10/4.
encheson *n.* reason 34/22, 211/25, 225/4.
encident *adj.* likely to happen 316/32.
enclensyd *pp.* cleansed 380/21.
enclereth *pr. 3 s.* lights up 213/8.
enclothyng *pr. p.* clothing 327/29.
encompanyed *ppl. a.* in companies 15/27.
encovered *pt.* covered 140/11; *pp.* 350/27.
encowched *pp.* studded 325/10.
encrassate *pp.* manured 186/3, 310/26, 312/18, *etc.*
encrowned *ppl. a.* crowned 383/5.
enderked *pp.* darkened 177/29, 235/11, 256/13, *etc.*; *ppl. a.* 31/9, 125/30, 268/8, *etc.*
endeuoirment *n.* effort, endeavour 1/13, 9/6, 53/10, *etc.*
endewed, endued *pp.* endowed 208/27, 277/26, 322/6, *etc.*; *pt.* 78/31.
endigged *pp.* dug 395/4.
endoubted *pp.* afflicted with doubt 341/6.
endoundynge, *pr. p.* resounding 379/24.
endronkynd *pp.* drunken 349/3.
endrowned *pp.* drowned 351/35, 361/18.
endryeth *pr. 3 s.* dries 256/30; endryed *pt.* 224/16; endreyed *pp.* 18/17, 42/23, 55/23, *etc.*; endryed *ppl. a.* 392/16.
enduce *v.* lead to 351/19.
endued. See endewed.

438   Glossary

endulleth *pr. 3 s.* dulls, blunts 269/
2; *pp.* 322/1; **endulled** *ppl. a.*
277/5, 286/13, 348/27, *etc.*
endunged *pp.* filled with dung
380/2.
endurate *pp.* hardened 212/4, 235/1,
256/4; **endurate** *ppl. a.* enduring
13/31; **endurate** *ppl. adv.* durably
86/30.
enduryng *prep.* during 37/27, 171/
28, 331/33.
endyched *pp.* moated 72/26.
endymmed *pp.* obscured 256/12;
ppl. a. dark 338/24, 371/12.
endyrked. See **enderked.**
enewrid. See **envre.**
enfamysshed *pp.* famished 114/3;
enfamyshyng *vbl. n.* starvation
329/21.
enfatteth *pr. 3 s.* fertilizes 47/15, 23,
50/19, *etc.*; **enfatted** *pp.* 186/3,
310/26, 391/30, *etc.*; **enfatted**
ppl. a. 270/21.
enfayntid *pt.* grew weak 372/2; *pp.*
59/32.
enfeble *v.* grow feeble 199/9.
enfeblish *v.* enfeeble 229/23; *pp.*
36/7, 59/32, 219/4, *etc.*
enfectionate *adj.* infectious 193/15.
enfesture *v.* fester 373/7; *pp.* 365/
8.
enfetured *pp.* featured 353/12.
enfilthed *ppl. a.* made filthy 278/8.
enfogged *pp.* made boggy or marshy
395/13.
enforced *pt.* compelled 52/14, 89/
31; *pp.* 3/4, 121/24, 206/7, *etc.*;
driven 235/17, 329/14; **enforcyd**
ppl. a. forced 104/11; compelling
212/3. See also **afforce.**
enforcement *n.* compulsion 44/33,
109/13, 114/5, *etc.*
enformacion *n.* instruction 8/31,
13/3, 38/8, *etc.*; *pl.* 358/22.
enformer *n.* teacher 126/25, 350/19.
enfourme *v.* instruct 326/15; *pr. 3 s.*
creates 212/35; *pr. p.* 38/25; *pt.*
110/9, 182/3; *pp.* 36/20, 314/35,
335/26, *etc.*
enfyred *pp.* inflamed 381/1.
engendrure *n.* the action or kind of
engendering 14/7, 196/21, 213/21,
etc.; the cause of engendering
252/2, 307/4.
engladeth *pr. 3 s.* gladdens 325/
21.
engluteth *pr. 3 s.* swallows up 188/
20; **engluttyng** *ppl. a.* 282/8;
engluttyd *pp.* 42/28, 273/16;
smothered 60/15; stuffed (from
over-eating) 239/3.
engowte *v.* cause to gush or flood
60/5.
engroce *v.* collect together, combine
342/14; *pt.* made big or pregnant
381/10; *pp.* combined 10/17, 11/16,
133/22, *etc.*; massed 56/25, 62/1;
summed up 43/33, 70/14; thickened, solidified 13/28, 14/10, 57/24,
etc.; **engroced** *ppl. a.* amassed
342/8.
engusshynge *pr. p.* gushing 380/17,
394/8.
engyn, engynes *n. pl.* implements
of war 142/15, 158/3, 171/25.
enharded *pp.* hardened 385/28; *ppl.
a.* 289/20, 327/31. See **harded.**
enhaunce *v.* extol 2/11; *pr. 3 s.*
inspires 360/2; raises 226/4; *pp.*
extolled 8/21; elevated 172/12,
297/35; raised 225/34, 338/6.
enhebryateth *pr. 3 s.* delights exceedingly 359/21.
enheped *pp.* heaped up 225/35.
enheuyd *pp.* made heavy or sluggish
80/34, 170/19; saddened 93/21.
enhybyte *v.* restrain 103/7; *pr. 3 s.*
243/6; *pt.* forbade 108/19; *pp.* prevented 100/2, 109/20, 200/25; forbidden 115/32, 367/21.
enionccyon, eniunction, iniunction, *etc., n.* injunction, command
107/33, 216/22, 283/14, *etc.*
enkancred *pp.* corrupted 207/33,
360/27.
enkyndled *pp.* kindled 385/26.
enladed *pp.* laden 325/15.
enlarge *v.* increase 298/7; ~ (*itself*)
bestow (itself) 4/11; *pr. p.* bestowing 336/6; *pp.* bestowed 30/26,
277/27, 308/12; increased 10/35,
142/7, 293/23; praised, magnified
8/7; set at large 277/2; discussed
at large 289/13.

enlengthened *pp.* lengthened 348/
25, 353/1, *etc.*; *ppl. a.* 342/7, 382/
17.
enleueld *pp.* levelled 361/22.
enlonged *pp.* made distant from
311/19.
enlumyned *pp.* illumined 346/1;
ppl. a. 338/24.
enlynked *ppl. a.* linked 386/20.
enmarcheth *pr. 3 s.* borders 280/4.
enmasked *ppl. a.* meshed 380/5.
enmesured *pp.* measured, meted
out 352/11.
enmixte *pp.* mixed, mingled 42/22,
336/32, 349/8; *pt.* 58/30.
enmoisteth *pr. 3 s.* waters, floods
50/15, 183/32; *pr. p.* 51/6; enmoistynge *vbl. n.* dilution 349/11;
enmoysted *pp.* irrigated 47/14,
59/25; flooded 47/21, 57/23.
enmoisture *v.* water, irrigate 47/17,
152/17, 232/24; *pr. 3 s.* waters,
irrigates 395/6, 269/22 (emoistureth); enmoisterynge *vbl. n.*
irrigation 101/35; *pt.* wet 373/5; *pp.*
50/30, 214/28, 271/28, *etc.*; soaked
43/3; *v. refl.* drink 277/22.
ennaked *pp.* made naked 310/21,
342/31, 379/5.
ennesteth *pr. 3 s.* nests 325/19.
ennestlyd *pt.* nested 379/11.
ennewed *pp.* embellished 147/13,
162/27, 296/4, *etc.*
ennewynge *vbl. n.* renewing 348/33.
ennorish *v.* nourish, rear 251/9,
288/5, 349/34; *pr. 3 s.* 213/15, 214/
30, 215/3, *etc.*; ennorishyng *vbl. n.*
287/28, 353/10; *pp.* 310/14, 314/
28, 324/17, *etc.*
ennoyaunce *n.* injury 354/11. See
anoiaunce.
ennoye *v.* pester 148/8; *pt.* afflicted
51/35, 79/14, 101/3; harmed 111/
18; *pp.* afflicted 35/2, 40/21, 117/
33, *etc.* See annoy.
ennoyesaunce *n.* mortification 364/
27, 370/22.
ennued. See ennewed.
ennuncion. See enionccyon.
ennured *pp.* tinted, coloured 69/18;
adorned 353/12 (cf. Fr. nuer to
shade or tint).

enombred *pp.* counted, numbered
12/1.
enourned *pt.* adorned 66/15, 78/31;
pp. 204/15, 226/25.
enpayned *pp.* in difficulty 376/27.
enpechid *pp.* blamed 372/18.
enpittee *v.* pity 193/7, 235/31, 267/
26; *pt.* 35/5, 173/29, 377/19; *pr. p.*
302/4, 305/27, 323/25, *etc.*
enplye *v.* employ 39/33; *pp.* 2/31.
enpouered *pp.* impoverished 391/
34.
enpregnated *pt.* made pregnant
381/10; enpregnate *pp.* 106/15,
328/7, 345/23, *etc.*
enpressyd *pp.* squeezed 352/24.
enpropred. See appropre.
enprosperyd *pt.* made prosperous
391/31.
enprowment *n.* improvement, benefit 16/8, 28, 27/21, *etc.*; *pl.* 5/17.
enprynted *pt.* printed, recorded
128/24.
enquycked, enquyckend *ppl. a.*
quickened 349/31, 384/10.
enrypynge *vbl. n.* ripening 343/28,
349/35; *pp.* 218/6; enriped *ppl. a.*
328/23, 336/25.
enscribed *pt.* recorded 18/33, 21/
14; *pp.* 11/6, 12/13, 38/18, *etc.*;
inscribed 205/2; ascribed 27/4,
34/26, 381/13.
enscriblid *pp.* scribbled 8/5.
enseignementes *n. pl.* instructions
296/14, 301/3, 318/8, *etc.*
enserche *v.* seek 54/29; investigate
71/23, 175/17, 240/19, *etc.*; *pr. 3 s.*
searches, surveys 18/29; *pr. p.* investigating 52/32, 175/28; *pp.* investigated, canvassed 145/4, 176/8,
344/9, *etc.*
ensereth *pr. 3 s.* sears 282/1; ensered *pp.* burnt, seared 268/3,
276/35.
enshadowed *pp.* obscured 382/3.
enshamed *pp.* ashamed 380/5.
ensharped *pp.* sharpened 384/4.
enshrynkyng *pr. p.* shrinking 213/6.
ensigned *pt.* appointed 103/14; *pp.*
assigned 307/4.
ensignementes. See enseignementes.

440 Glossary

enslyderyd *pt.* made slippery 376/24.
ensommed. See **ensummed.**
ensondred *pp.* separated 6/1, 312/12.
ensparkled *pp.* made sparkling 376/16.
enstaunce *n.* plea 290/23.
enstaunce *v.* plead with 314/13; *pt.* 93/9, 163/1, 298/33, *etc.*
enstoppid *pp.* stopped 373/2.
enstraite *v.* restrict 315/35; **enstraytynge** *vbl. n.* 341/18; *pt.* 365/22, 366/3, 393/31; *pp.* 182/20, 349/13, 376/4; **enstraited**, *etc.*, *ppl. a.* narrow, restricted 324/15, 325/3, 367/34.
enstraunge *v.* depart from 17/6; *pp.* separated from 193/21, 311/19; made stranger to 342/33; gone astray 351/14.
enstrength *v.* strengthen 169/4; **enstrengthyng**, *etc.*; *vbl. n.* 302/34, 348/34; *pt.* 332/7, 367/16; *pp.* 48/27, 181/13, 186/34, *etc.*; **enstrengthed**, *etc.*, *ppl. a.* 327/25, 365/22, 375/25.
enstrewed *pp.* strewn 326/1.
enstuffed *pp.* stuffed 325/26, 371/21.
ensummed *pp.* summed up 178/13; combined 14/11, 342/9.
ensured *pp.* assured 54/4; **ensuryd** *ppl. a.* 382/13.
entailed *pp.* carved, sculptured 91/10, 14, 133/10, *etc.*; **entaylled** *ppl. a.* 133/6; **entailyng** *vbl. n.* 129/24, 304/7; *pp.* involved 85/1.
entamed *pt.* tamed 387/11; *pp.* 378/36, 386/34.
entende *v.* plan 118/25, 128/7; *pr. p.* 185/25; *pt.* 28/34, 80/32, 91/30, *etc.*; **entended** *ppl. a.* 104/30, 139/24, 199/30; *pp.* occupied 10/26.
entere *v.* inter 89/18.
enteres, enterest *n.* entry 226/5, 325/1.
entexturid *pp.* textured 383/31.
enthickyth, enthikketh *pr. 3 s.* thickens 55/9, 213/5; **enthikked, enthycked** *pp.* thickened 14/1, 42/22, 245/31, *etc.*; overgrown 183/28, 324/35.

entincture *n.* tint 221/13.
entreate *v.* treat, deal with 128/8; petition 144/10; *pt.* dealt with, treated 128/5, 330/7, 364/27; petitioned 149/31; *pp.* dealt with 119/11; petitioned 128/14.
entree *n.* entrance 80/10.
entriked, *etc.*, *pp.* interwoven 69/30, 244/30, *etc.*; entangled 206/24, 373/20; obscured 309/3; *ppl. a.* obscured 125/33, 128/3, 307/3; interwoven 262/35.
entroductive *n.* introduction 295/27.
entronanysed *pp.* enthroned 342/27; *pt.* 317/35.
entrowbled *pt.* troubled 375/27.
entrynge *vbl. n.* entrance 99/24.
entykled *pp.* tickled 381/3.
enuyrid *pp.* (?) smeared 122/19.
enuyron, *etc.*, *v.* encircle, surround 19/12, 45/30, 146/4, *etc.*; *pr. 3 s.* 45/21, 53/20, 87/9, *etc.*; *pt.* 71/1, 170/21, 171/21, *etc.*; *pp.* 29/7, 42/7, 47/13, *etc.*; made circular 58/25.
enuyron *adv.* around, about 6/9, 10/35, 13/13, *etc.*
envased *pt.* invaded 294/28.
envasyf *adj.* offensive 377/7; invading 186/13, 375/32.
enverdured *pp.* clothed in verdure 325/16, 359/11, 378/5; **enverdured** *ppl. a.* 342/28.
enviliatyve *adj.* diligent 374/29.
envre *n.* practice 220/12.
envre *v.* practise 181/26, 194/32, 200/22; *pt.* trained 200/7; educated 76/12; wrought 86/30; *pp.* trained 27/13, 75/14, *etc.*; experienced 5/25, 250/28; practised 17/10, 102/2, 110/24, *etc.*; accomplished 11/11; performed, wrought 390/3.
enwaketh *pr. 3 s.* weakens 282/2; **enweked**, *etc.*, *pp.* 249/1, 278/5, 372/27.
enwasteth *pr. 3 s.* wastes 8/8.
enwellyng *pr. p.* welling up 324/25.
enwepened *pt.* armed with weapons 376/13.
enwerieth *pr. 3 s.* wearies or wears out 259/10; **enweryd, enweried**

Glossary 441

pp. 79/17, 206/23, 250/12, etc.;
enweried *ppl. a.* 262/16, 277/3.
enwrethed, enwrythen *pp.*
wreathed 316/12, 350/11.
enwrotynge *pr. p.* writhing 373/14.
erable *adj.* arable 57/31.
ered, eryd *pp.* cultivated 50/31, 313/
19, 391/26.
erraunt *adj.* arrant 106/27.
erst *adv.* formerly, first, or at first
51/20, 267/9; earlier 170/21, 281/
31, 314/25, *etc.*
erthequave *n.* earthquake 292/15;
pl. 110/33, 176/14.
esbatementis *n. pl.* diversions 381/
28.
eschaunge *n.* alteration 196/11.
eschaunged *pp.* changed 234/35.
eschewe *v.* escape 53/25; eschewynge *vbl. n.* avoidance 352/7, 355/
1; *pp.* avoided 9/19.
espies *n. pl.* spies 326/13, 333/35.
essenciall *n.* life, being 177/23,
375/4.
estate. See astate.
estemyd. See exteme.
estraungere *n.* stranger, foreigner
136/27, 283/31, 317/13; *pl.* 216/5
217/5, 225/7, *etc.*
estraungiere *adj.* foreign 225/5.
estuacion *n.* heating 59/9, 189/24,
212/8, *etc.*
estudye *n.* study 1/26, 2/3, 5/16, *etc.*
estudyentis *n. pl.* students 2/19.
estyuale *adj.* of or pertaining to
summer or the summer solstice
56/18, 253/3, 268/8.
ethymologisation *n.* etymological
procedure 210/17.
ewthe, yougthe *n.* youth 296/28,
310/11, 366/1.
excersyue *adj.* disciplinary 75/17.
exclusive *n.* excluding agent 163/
23.
excusyves *n. pl.* excuses 373/12.
exemplare *n.* sampler 200/19.
exemplefye *v.* follow the example
of 82/18; *pr. p.* 39/11, 75/1, 97/29,
etc.; exemplefyenge *vbl. n.* 338/
2; *pt.* 201/13, 338/26.
exhybyte *v.* provide 20/15; *pr. 3 s.*
18/13; *pp.* solemnized 24/27, 26/24.

exorted *pp.* expelled 14/4.
explosed *ppl. a.* investigated 314/
29; *pp.* 342/32.
exposed *pp.* expounded 308/32,
388/5.
exposityf *adj.* of the nature of exposition 382/2.
exposytyve *n.* exposition 375/14.
expowneth *pr. 3 s.* expounds, explains 339/22; expownynge *pr. p.*
35/27; expowned *pp.* 17/4, 61/5,
341/18, *etc.*
expresse *v.* press out, extract 312/
19 (exspresse); expressed *pp.*
310/16, 328/23.
expressyue *adj.* exact 10/12.
exquysite, exquesite *adj.* carefully ascertained 103/4; meticulous
3/18, 83/33; accurate 184/30; carefully adjusted or appropriate 106/7,
126/14; careful 285/30, 302/32,
etc.; distinctive 52/16, 310/29.
exquysitely, exquesitely *adv.*
meticulously 175/17, 193/24, 215/
28, *etc.*
exteme *v.* hold, consider, believe, or
judge 64/21, 73/6, 196/21; *pr. p.*
229/32; extemyd, estemyd *pt.*
13/18, 108/1, *etc.*; *pp.* 3/16, 7/17,
81/5, *etc.*
extolled *pp.* magnified, praised 8/1;
pt. raised in dignity or rank 180/28.
eyen, ien, yen *n. pl.* eyes 18/29,
70/3, 144/17, 258/27, *etc.*

faccion, faction *n.* shape 151/19,
258/17, 304/8; *pl.* 285/11.
facounde *n.* fluency 10/33.
facounde, faconde, facunde *adj.*
fluent 189/8, 295/32, 346/1.
factes *n. pl.* deeds 164/11, 179/22.
facultees *n. pl.* branches or departments of knowledge 8/28, 30,
95/29, *etc.*
fadom *v.* encircle or measure with
outstretched arms 158/26.
fallace *n.* trickery 329/4.
falle *v.* happen 118/12; *pr. 3 s.* 56/19.
fallible *adj.* unreliable 54/4, 259/34,
353/25.
famylier *n.* intimate associate 65/4.
fantyme *n.* fantasy 310/12.

Glossary

fastidious *adj.* wearisome 4/1, 184/ 29, 206/25, *etc.*
fawteth *pr. 3 s.* lacks 325/12.
fayne *v.* feign, invent 85/28; *pr. p.* 96/6.
fayt *n.* art, skill, knack, or contrivance 157/6, 340/10; *pl.* 7/5, 24/29, 157/32, *etc.*; deeds or accomplishments 5/20, 6/9, 31, *etc.*; ~ *of marchandyse* mercantile business 40/4, 127/21, 207/14, *etc.*; ~ *of warre* warfare 215/20.
feces *n. pl.* lees 312/21.
feles, felis *n.* cat 112/9, 117/29.
femyny *n.* woman-kind 330/31.
fensyd *pt.* buttressed 28/14; *pp.* protected 42/3.
fercibille. See **forcyble.**
ferde *pt.* fared, acted 367/6.
(so) ferforth *adv.* to such a degree or extent 42/23.
(thus) ferfortly *adv.* (thus) far forth 380/31.
ferme *v.* cleanse 380/1.
fet *ppl. a.* fetched 311/19.
fete, fetes. See **fayt.**
figure *n.* shape 157/23; symbol 313/ 35, 323/33; figure of speech 85/31; *pl.* shapes 15/26; statues or sculptures 147/21.
firyng *vbl. n.* fuel 209/4.
flagraunt *adj.* fragrant 113/7, 123/ 20, 209/3, *etc.*
flauour *n.* fragrance 185/6, 225/1, 375/23; *pl.* 276/7.
fleed *pt.* flayed 303/12.
flete *v.* float 152/9.
fletes *n. pl.* small channels 28/16, 245/5.
flewes *n. pl.* fixed nets 84/22.
flok-mele *adv.* by troops or companies 237/26.
florysshyd *pp.* flowered 346/4.
foison *n.* plenty 50/31, 156/31, 184/ 34, *etc.*
fome of the se sea-weed 236/18, 241/28, 266/12. See **see-fome.**
fonde *pt.* established 354/5; **founde, founden** *pp.* 21/34, 26/6, 71/14.
fonned *pp.* made or become foolish 155/9; *ppl. a.* 361/23.
fonned *pt.* fawned 352/21.

fonnes *n. pl.* idiots 255/1.
fonnysh *adj.* idiotic 254/27, 303/24.
foole *n.* foal 196/27; *pl.* 50/2.
foon *n. pl.* foes 80/12.
forcyble *adj.* severe 16/3; vigorous 80/13; forceful 372/30; sturdy 75/ 18,147/3; impetuous 57/12,110/15.
forcybly *adv.* strongly 42/13, 169/5, *etc.*; with force or powerful effect 45/8, 113/12, *etc.*; inextricably 152/7.
forefaders, forn-fadres, fornefader, *etc., n. pl.* fore-fathers 20/ 15, 26/12, 41/12, *etc.*
foreyne *n.* foreigner 136/28; *pl.* 92/ 27, 30, 225/7.
forfayttes *n. pl.* infractions of law 346/27.
forfayture *n.* infringement of law 105/32.
forgyd *pp.* fashioned 87/6.
forisfacture *n.* infringement of law 173/17; *pl.* 173/22, 195/21, 308/17 (cf. **forfayttes** and **forfayture** above).
former *adj.* fore 17/27, 28, 85/29; first 95/29, 116/16, 256/17.
formest, formmyste *adj.* first 88/ 14, 171/13; foremost 375/2, *etc.*
fort *adj.* strong, powerful 308/3, 326/30.
fortrassed *pp.* protected as with a fortress 229/11.
fostrure *adj.* foster 20/16.
fother, fudder *n.* talent 74/26, 122/26.
founde, founden. See **fonde.**
frame *v.* construct 157/19; fashion 209/20; *pr. 3 s.* disposes 7/19; *pr. p.* fashioning 147/29, 195/1; *pp.* constructed 31/15; manufactured 24/5; made 67/27; fashioned 182/ 17.
franke *adj.* enfranchised 346/36.
frauncheis *n.* freedom 167/32, 171/ 2, 180/17.
fraunchised *pp.* granted political liberty 319/18.
frenesye, fronesye *n.* frenzy 254/2, 299/12, 349/10, *etc.*
frette *pp.* studded 67/22, 351/7, 358/11.

Glossary 443

fretted *pp.* eaten (metaphorically) 168/31; *pr. p.* 365/9.
fretyng, frotyng *pr. p.* scratching 251/24, 256/11.
fronesye. See frenesye.
fructefye *v.* bear fruit 392/18; make fruitful 187/34; *pr. 3 s.* 204/2; *pt.* 74/2.
fructuous *adj.* profitable 4/3, 25/17, 29/9, *etc.*
fructuously *adv.* fruitfully 358/28.
fudder *n.* fodder 51/31. See fother.
fudders *n. pl.* cart-loads 86/9.
fulfilled *pp.* filled 83/22, 325/26, 326/13, *etc.*
fumous *adj.* full of fumes 351/32, 375/24.
fusible *adj.* capable of being fused or melted 67/1, 2, 275/27.
fuskish *adj.* dusky 257/23.
fyaunsed *pp.* betrothed 37/33.
fygured *pp.* represented 28/4.
fynaunced *pt.* put to ransom 77/15.
fyned *pp.* refined 234/16.
fysycion *n.* physician 98/5.

gaaf *pt.* gave 27/15, 29/28, 32/1.
gan *pt.* began 52/7.
garnyshed *pt.* furnished 289/15; *pp.* 143/2, 157/13, 390/11; decorated 279/17.
garnyson *n.* defence 7/9.
gastely *adj.* horrible 33/34.
gastful *adj.* horrifying 56/26.
gate *pt.* begot 22/10; *pl. refl.* went 16/2; goten *pp.* 161/17, 297/15, *etc.*
geneolagye, geonealogye, geonelogye, *etc., n.* genealogy 295/16, 308/33, 362/8, *etc.*
generative *n.* begetting 310/6.
gentylles *n. pl.* gentle-folk 27/22.
gere *n.* matter 236/9, 16.
gestes *n. pl.* deeds 6/9, 9/18, 25, *etc.*
gewesse. See iewes.
gibbosities *n. pl.* protuberances 215/6.
glasyng *ppl. a.* glaring 260/36.
gleves *n. pl.* lances 283/22.
gobet *n.* lump 235/20; *pl.* 235/23.
golet, golette, gullette, *etc., n.* reservoir 74/3; pit 188/23; gullet 392/12; canal 395/11; *pl.* throats 365/22; gullets 239/17; gulleys 28/16.
good *n.* wealth 66/25.
goolis *n. pl.* gulleys 45/18.
goor, gore *n.* mud 42/32; slime 57/26.
gouen, goven *pp.* given 83/15, 134/18.
gouernall, gouernayl, *etc., n.* government 11/1, 26/1, 192/7, *etc.*
graffe *v.* plant 391/27; graffyng *vbl. n.* 312/23; *pp.* 150/1.
grauynge *vbl. n.* engraving 68/6; graued *pt.* sculptured 152/20; grauen grauyn *etc., pp.* engraved 38/5, 27, 79/14, *etc.*; sculptured 66/17, 67/27, 68/25, *etc.*
grevelingges, grovelyng *adv.* face downward 243/28, 248/24.
groos *n.* sum 64/17, 71/20.
ground *n.* foundation 9/23, 23/12.
grounded *pt.* established 126/14; *pp.* 7/3, 8/35, 98/4, *etc.*; *ppl. a.* 89/28, 95/30, 192/27, *etc.*
groundly *adv.* thoroughly 54/30, 69/29, 328/26; firmly 96/2, 103/4, 127/19, *etc.*
grudge (vpon) *v.* complain about 341/25; grugged *pt.* grumbled 180/9; grudchynge *vbl. n.* 79/18.
grypes *n. pl.* vultures 112/20.
guerdoned *pp.* rewarded 29/16, 168/22; *pr. p.* 383/26.
gullette, *etc.* See golet.
guyde *v.* govern 27/25, 163/3, *etc.*; guydynge *vbl. n.* management 2/17, 6/13, 25/35, *etc.*; *pp.* 308/24; *v. refl.* behave 197/18; *pp.* 100/1.
guydere *n.* governor 326/9.
guyse *n.* fashion 32/5, 109/21, 219/7, *etc.*; custom 216/7, 226/33, 228/10 (gyse), *etc.*
gyggyng *pr. p.* giggling 255/1.
gynne *n.* trap 362/17.
gyse. See guyse.

habituation *n.* clothing 257/17.
habytacle *n.* canopied space or structure on the deck of a ship 115/27; *pl.* canopied niches in the wall of a building 70/25.

Glossary

habytuate *v.* accustom 126/9; *pp.* clothed 123/31.
hacches *n. pl.* cramps for reinforcing stone-work 146/16.
halve *n.* side 161/9.
halynge *pr. p.* tossing off 349/5.
hanope *n.* goblet or bumper 349/6.
harded, hardyd *pp.* hardened 247/17, 384/3.
hardy *adj.* presumptuous 75/16, 102/30.
hares *n.* travelling harem 315/28 (cf. **haras** an enclosure or establishment in which horses and mares are kept for breeding).
haskard *n.* a base, vulgar fellow 125/35; *pl.* 8/36.
haunsyd *pp.* raised 52/6.
hauoir, havour, *etc., n.* behaviour 6/28, 114/25, 195/29; class or caste 105/30, 196/6, 7.
hawt *adj.* high (as of uplands) 188/11.
hawtly *adv.* haughtily 145/3.
haynnardes *n. pl.* wretches 220/19.
haynous, haynnows *adj.* shameful 78/19, 84/17, 111/18; odious 88/25, 96/21, *etc.*
haynously *adv.* shamefully 106/30, 121/12, 128/5, *etc.*
hechforthis *n. pl.* heifers 117/15.
heldyng *pr. p.* sloping 236/9.
hemycicle *n.* a semi-circular structure 124/6.
hente *pt.* seized 371/35.
her *pron. adj.* their 156/24.
hesperyan *adj.* western 56/16.
hight(e), hyght(e) *pr. 3 s.* is named 264/25, 359/4; *pt.* 21/31, 26/16, 39/24, *etc.*
historiall *n.* history 281/22.
historyal(l) *adj.* historical 52/15, 30, *etc.*
historyous *adj.* historical 394/1.
historyously *adv.* historically 53/2.
holdes *n. pl.* strongholds 189/22.
holpen *pp.* helped 83/6.
hostryes *n. pl.* hostelries 73/3.
hountesse, hownties, howteis *n.* shame 166/13, 229/24, 355/16.
humbres. See **vmbre.**
humerous *adj.* moist 213/6.

humour *n.* moisture 14/9; *pl.* 13/29, 14/3, *etc.*
huples, hupplys *n. pl.* hillocks 51/11, 12, 18.
husbondis *n. pl.* husbandmen 74/11.
hynde *n.* deer 113/27; *pl.* 112/23 (Skelton's error for **cat**).
hyndermer *comp. adj.* hinder, more to the rear 17/29.
hynge *pt.* hung 69/26.

iape *n.* jest or trifle 113/37, 284/31; *pl.* 11/7, 27/6, 35/31, *etc.*
iawlyng *vbl. n.* scolding 235/16.
ichneumon *n.* Pharaoh's rat 49/14, 117/31; **ichumonys, iehuemones,** *etc., pl.* 112/9, 23.
iconomy *n.* agriculture 346/11.
iconomycall, icanomycal, *etc., adj.* agricultural 184/37, 185/27, 190/7, *etc.*
ideal *n.* an implicit pattern or archetype 13/22.
ideottis *n. pl.* uncouth persons 65/8.
idole *n.* 'a visible but unsubstantial appearance . . . an incorporeal phantom' (*O.E.D.*) 285/22, 26.
iehuemones. See **ichneumon.**
iemowes *n.* a double ring 275/31.
ien. See **eyen.**
ieobarde, ieoparde *v.* place in jeopardy 101/9, 366/21; **ieoparted** *pp.* 3/11.
iewes, iewesse, gewesse, iuesse, iue, *etc., n.* punishment 7/14, 90/5, 106/7, 197/19, 228/17, *etc.*
illumynarye *n.* illumination 212/22.
imbuted *pp.* imbued 346/30.
immoble *adj.* immovable 240/26; motionless 260/25, 285/4.
immyxt *pp.* mixed, mingled 13/22, 272/13, 277/1.
impetuous, impituous, empituous *adj.* swift, violent 56/30, 146/18, 188/22, *etc.*
importune *adj.* grievous 22/29; exacting, burdensome 83/25, 88/3, 232/16, *etc.*
improued *pp.* disproved 54/25, 56/20, 58/32, *etc.*; *pr. 3 s.* 155/19.

Glossary 445

incombent *adj.* threatened or threatening, imminent 116/33, 171/35, 180/33, *etc.*
incommoditie *n.* inconvenience 256/34; *pl.* 163/23.
inconstaunce *n.* inconstancy 353/32.
incorrupt *adj.* uncorrupted 239/14.
indyfferently *adv.* fairly 101/11; justly 192/29; impartially 202/3.
inexpugnable *adj.* impregnable 136/27.
inferre *v.* confer or bestow 8/28; bring forward as an argument 361/2; imply or betoken 15/3, 314/29; *pr. 3 s.* adduces 295/27; confers 212/8; *pt.* conferred 198/7; *pp.* brought forward 192/9, 310/32, 320/9, *etc.*; alleged 224/30.
inflative *adj.* overbearing 192/17, 320/29; filled or blown up with air 303/3.
infused *pp.* poured in 146/16.
ingenye *n.* ingenuity 379/13.
inhabitable *adj.* uninhabitable 38/20, 58/5, 31, *etc.*
iniunction *n.* union 187/26. See **enionccyon.**
inmyxtion *n.* mixture 356/19; **immixtions** *pl.* 277/29.
inopynable *adj.* excessive 42/12, 178/2, 183/7; unbelievable 228/26, 277/3, 360/33.
instynction *n.* instinct 49/19, 122/10, 136/13, *etc.*; *pl.* 303/17.
intellective *n.* understanding 174/35, 296/15, 297/8, *etc.*
intensive *adj.* intent 170/17, 193/31, 296/16, *etc.*
intensively *adv.* intently 143/29, 360/17.
intentive *adj.* intent 125/24, 146/9, 345/32.
intentively *adv.* diligently 228/29.
intercysed *pp.* interrupted 101/31, 386/7.
interiectyf *adj.* interposed 177/30, 281/16, 366/13.
intermyssyf *adj.* of the nature of intermission 391/5.
intrusour, intruyser *n.* interloper 94/21, 330/3.

inuencion, *etc., n.* inventive faculty 326/25; use of inventive faculty 306/16, 312/2, 343/8; origination 313/35, 339/3; *pl.* originations 349/17; graces of rhetoric 323/11.
inuentyf, *etc., n.* inventive faculty 22/8, 212/29; use of inventive faculty 158/17, 300/21; origination 22/22, 226/17; invention, thing originated 95/28; *pl.* inventions, things originated 190/17.
inuentyf *adj.* inventive 23/32, 35/22, 63/20, *etc.*
irous *adj.* angry 255/4, 329/8, 365/28, *etc.*
irously *adv.* angrily 377/12.
irriguous *adj.* of or pertaining to irrigation 150/26, 156/24, 184/24, *etc.*
irriguously *adv.* in the manner of irrigating or watering 271/28, 274/25, 324/24, *etc.*
iudicial *n.* decision 175/26; judgement 3/18, 9/35, 42/24, *etc.*; opinion 56/12, 79/36, 118/11, *etc.*; *pl.* 177/31, 243/4; legal verdicts 190/15.
iue, iuesse. See **iewes.**
iuppartowrs *adj.* hazardous 372/32.
iupparty *n.* jeopardy 371/15, 373/23.

kalendes *n. pl.* first days or beginnings 301/15.
kantyd *pp.* shared 355/13.
kennyng *n.* landmark 266/30.
knackis *n. pl.* tricks 27/5.
kyndely *adj.* natural 14/30.
kynnysbeest *n.* kind of beast 115/3.
kyste. See **cast.**
kytte *pp.* cut 84/9, 107/27.

langour *n.* languishment 197/4.
langoure *v.* languish 36/1.
largeis *n.* largess 213/4, 260/17, 272/12.
largely *adv.* freely 82/13.
latyn *n.* latten 184/19.
lawers *n. pl.* courses (as of bricks) 150/18.
lay *n.* song 217/29, 301/30, 325/25, *etc.*

446   Glossary

layd. See leye.
lecture *n.* reading aloud 6/24.
leefful *adj.* lawful 37/24, 303/4.
lefte *pt.* gave over, abandoned 14/23.
legated *pp.* left as a legacy 197/11.
legister, legyste *n.* lawgiver 95/26, 108/10.
legytyme *adj.* lawful 23/12.
lenger *comp. adv.* longer 246/17; lengest *superl.* longest 251/13.
leres *n. pl.* cheeks 300/19.
lesse *conj.* lest 74/3, 7.
lesynge *n.* untruth 8/31, 57/25.
let *pp.* stopped 329/6.
leye *v.* adduce 59/8; *pr. 3 s.* 59/18; *pr. p.* 53/21; layd *pp.* 59/16; ~ (*vnto*) *pp.* granted 63/19.
leyser, leisoure, leyzer, *etc., n.* opportunity 1/12, 83/27, 85/10, *etc.* intermission 101/31, 235/18; rest 234/29, 249/3, 391/5.
liegeaunce *n.* allegiance 137/29, 292/30.
lies *n. pl.* lees (of wine) 312/21.
lieuest *superl. adj.* most preferred 30/17.
listeth *pr. pl.* desire, choose 151/10.
lofe *n.* luff 276/26.
looveth *pr. 3 s.* makes use of 226/18.
lote, lotum *n.* lotus 47/32, 63/11.
louynge *vbl. n.* praising 124/27, 221/27; *pl.* 26/23, 83/15, 117/8, *etc.*
loyng *vbl. n.* lowing (as of oxen) 239/10.
lustre, luster *n.* period of five years 63/28, 67/11, 95/5, *etc.*
lusty *adj.* pleasant 60/30, 104/16.
lute *v.* seal (with clay) 236/20.
lycorous *adj.* greedy 356/7.
lygnee *n.* lineage 385/1.
lymyted *pp.* assigned 32/3; allotted 81/14, 87/18; appointed 96/24; *pt.* 25/36, 200/16.
lyteratyf *adj.* literary 357/16, 360/23.
lytteral *adj.* literary 63/15.
lyuely *adj.* living 18/2, 4, 10, *etc.*

magry. See maugree.
male-talente *n.* malevolence 6/36, 96/21.

malyncolyous. See melancolious.
mancipate *pp.* enslaved 192/1.
marche *v.* border 206/19; *pr. 3 s.* 210/9, 282/6; marchen *pr. pl.* extend 203/23; *pr. p.* 24/10, 60/23, 84/12, *etc.; pt.* 138/4.
marches *n. pl.* borders 26/1.
mareis, mares, maryse, mareys, *etc., n.* marsh 42/16, 19, 44/24, *etc.; pl.* 146/4, 231/2, 24, *etc.*
mareis, maris *adj.* marshy 92/7, 232/14.
mased *pp.* confounded 142/27; *ppl. a.* foolish, confused 163/22, 296/34, 356/10, *etc.;* demented 299/12.
masked *pp.* enmeshed 144/14, 262/9, 303/22.
matratyve *adj.* full of pus 373/6.
matriculate *adj.* admitted to, registered or enrolled in special honour 11/22, 299/24, 337/23, *etc.*
matural *adj.* maturing 349/35.
maugree, magry, mawgre, *etc., prep.* in spite of 290/3, 366/5, 390/33, *etc.*
mawe *n.* liver 28/5, 118/3, 385/33.
mayne *adj.* solid 42/30; ~ see chief or principal sea, open sea 44/17, 267/8, 274/14.
mayne, mayny *n.* multitude 161/5, 239/1.
med(e)ly *n.* conflict 283/24, 373/25.
melancolious, malyncolyous *adj.* melancholy 307/32; malevolent 185/19, 330/10.
meleagrides *n. pl.* guinea fowl 213/16; mistakenly called 'trees' 264/19 (maleagridis).
memorative *n.* memory 10/23, 227/11, 375/20; record 187/31; memorial 172/25, 299/2; recorded history 25/25.
memorative *adj.* commemorative 1/6, 191/27, 203/19, *etc.*
memorial, *etc. n.* record 7/25, 11/7, 14, *etc.* memory 6/20.
menour *n.* thief 109/15.
menyall *adj.* middle 303/17.
mercuriall *adj.* commercial 102/27, 182/8.
meridiane *n.* south 18/6, 41/23, 42/7, *etc.*

Glossary

meridionall *adj.* southern 186/30.
mete *n.* food (*hard* ~ dry grain) 51/31, 195/15; *pl.* 47/29, 62/29, 64/29, *etc.*
metely *adj.* meet, fitting 6/7, 183/3, 192/8, *etc.*
metely *adv.* suitably 229/11.
mette *pt.* dreamed 90/9.
meuyngis *vbl. n. pl.* motions 110/23.
mo(e)ble *adj.* movable 132/23, 205/18, 21, *etc.*
moderative *adj.* moderate 194/4.
moeuyd *pt.* moved 17/29; influenced 85/34, 91/30; instigated 79/19; *pp.* influenced 33/18 *bis*, 36/1, 96/18, *etc.*
monstruous *n. pl.* monsters 282/16.
montuous *adj.* mountainous 22/2, 31/12, 141/7, *etc.*
monycion *n.* admonition 369/8.
monysh *v.* warn, admonish 267/29; *pt.* 144/16; *pp.* 126/2.
moo *comp. adj.* more 6/21, 22/11, 43/32, *etc.*; **more** larger 258/21.
morous *adj.* dilatory 265/27.
mortal *adj.* deadly 48/32, 274/33, 287/7, *etc.*
mortally *adv.* fatally 291/8.
mote *n.* (?) middle 207/20. Cf. **motes**.
motelyes, motles *n. pl.* variegated patches 187/35, 324/22.
motes *n. pl.* courses 177/19.
motive, moetyf, *etc., n.* movement 13/25, 19/14, 176/3, *etc.*; *pl.* 148/24, 175/31, 176/31.
motive *n.* inspiration 3/5, 7/1, 32, *etc.*
motles. See **motelyes**.
mountenaunce *n.* extent 171/33.
movere *n.* (*primum mobile* first moving) 296/32.
mowe *v.* be able 10/5, 11, 71/33, *etc.*
moyen *n.* means 49/13, 52/2, 109/15, *etc.*; *pl.* 105/20, 343/15, 349/32, *etc.*
moyte *n.* half, moiety 276/25.
musid *pp.* bemused 368/12.
mynded *ppl. a.* disposed 86/4, 145/3.
myng *v.* mix 238/14; *pr. 3 s.* 253/29.
mynyssheth *pr. 3 s.* diminishes 55/15; **mynyshed** *pp.* 236/24.

mysaduenture, mysauenture *n.* misfortune 193/21, 299/8, 352/4.
myscontent *adj.* ill-pleased 32/33, 128/19, 144/21, *etc.*
myscreaunce *n.* false belief 386/30.
mysdoers *n. pl.* evil-doers 129/22.
myseracion *n.* compassion 32/2, 140/6, 300/7.
mysguydyng *vbl. n.* mismanagement 103/7, 164/16.
myslyuers *n. pl.* ill-conducted persons 97/15.
mysprisyng *pr. p.* contemning 231/25.
mysterye *n.* ceremony 63/22, 65/15; *pl.* 29/21, 32/17, 40/27, *etc.*; (?) arcana 311/10, 361/30.
natyue *adj.* by birth 96/16.
nega(r)denes *n.* niggardliness 227/23.
nepe *n.* dry channel 59/23.
nerehande *adj.* close by 22/3.
neuewis *n. pl.* nephews 340/12.
(of) new anew 372/28; for the first time 23/3, 6, 338/19, *etc.*; the new 64/1.
newfanglenes *n.* novelty 76/25.
nobles, noblesse noblys *n.* nobleness 5/24, 306/19, 357/27, *etc.*
nomos *n.* administrative district 100/10.
non-aduenture *adv.* without doubt 141/17.
(for the) nones for the time being 142/19.
norises *n. pl.* nurses 219/17.
notabylite *n.* ability to be noted or known or understood 104/20; *pl.* significations 227/29.
notice *n.* knowledge 9/10, 10/14, 12/10, *etc.*; intimation 56/15; advance knowledge 76/5.
nott *n.* nut 210/2.
noyous *adj.* injurious 8/30, 15/17, 143/15, *etc.*
nutritive *n.* nourishment 253/31, 326/7; *pl.* 166/10, 184/27, 220/39.
nutritive, nutratyf *adj.* nourishing 15/32, 19/13, 22, *etc.*
nygardship *n.* niggardliness 86/6.
nys *v.* is not 73/32, 86/11, 111/38, *etc.*

448   Glossary

obeyssaunt *adj.* subjected 78/3.
obfuscate *pp.* obscured 256/12.
obiect *n.* opposite 58/23; 'something placed before the eyes, or presented to the sight or other sense' (*O.E.D.*) 224/19.
obiecture *n.* (?) opposition 269/2.
oblivion *n.* forgetfulness 53/3, 299/14, 338/24.
obloquy *n.* calumny 3/12, 33/4.
oblyviously *adv.* remissly 191/14.
obsequy *n.* ritual services 62/8.
obsidion *n.* siege 171/18, 28.
obtused *pp.* obscured 311/12; dulled, deafened 328/37; **obtused** *ppl. a.* dulled 286/14, 358/23.
obtusively *adv.* thickly 285/10.
obyte *n.* death 31/20.
occasion *n.* reason 80/28.
occasionarye *adj.* causative 254/1.
occident *n.* west 44/15, 148/23, 183/16.
occision *n.* slaughter 352/8.
occupy *v.* consume 65/12; expend 74/14; use 48/14, 151/28; employ 184/7; 287/22; practise 196/15; *pr. p.* filling 287/32; *pt.* employed 79/12; held 100/33; *pp.* consumed 120/28; used 157/34; employed 100/30; disturbed 171/30.
ocupacion *n.* practice 52/8; use 244/8; labour 89/31, 109/3; occupation 124/31.
odoure *n.* savour 29/12.
of excepte *prep.* except 45/4.
of new. See **new.**
oies *n.* noise 273/13.
omyssyf *adj.* neglectful 383/20.
operacion *n.* construction 89/6, 7.
oppoyntement. See **appoyntement.**
opynable *adj.* conjectural 53/18, 56/12, 304/36, *etc.*
ordynate *adj.* regulated 25/20, 35/24, 296/6.
ordynaunce *n.* military gear or weapons 42/29, 158/12, *etc.*; preparation, esp. military 158/18, 261/35.
oriente *n.* east 44/15, 80/15, 92/17, *etc.*
original *n.* beginning, origin 4/8,
5/3, 6, *etc.*; originator 311/24; *pl.* beginnings 237/1.
origynal *adj.* first, initial 32/19, 24, 53/15, *etc.*
orisaunt *n.* (?) horizon 213/18.
ornacy(e) *n.* ornateness 85/33, 147/30, 363/14.
orygynally *adv.* from the beginning 342/6.
oueral *adv.* universally 65/32.
ouerfroren *pp.* frozen over 256/4.
ouerly *adv.* excessively 2/9.
ouersee *v.* peruse 96/28, 354/22; inspect 140/29; look over 149/30; examine 243/11; **ouerseen, ouersene** *pp.* perused 336/35; examined 339/29, 394/2; in error 32/13, 59/33, 233/25; neglectful 383/8.
ouersight *n.* supervision 195/20; miscalculation 193/24.
ought *pt.* owed 330/22.
ougly *adj.* ugly 33/34.
oute-marchis *n. pl.* remote districts 53/26.
outlandyssh *adj.* foreign 119/10, 342/32.
outrance. See **vtteraunce.**
outray *v.* vanquish utterly 248/8, 249/7; *pr. p.* 28/5, 180/30; *pt.* 77/15, 92/12, 179/11, 374/26 (**awtraijd**), *etc.*; *pp*, 137/20, 182/34, 202/26, *etc.*
owhere, *adv.* anywhere 91/9, 115/4, 116/18.
oynementis *n. pl.* ointments 74/24, 85/32, 99/17, *etc.*

paile *n.* enclosure 253/28.
pampred *pp.* stuffed (with food) 239/3; filled (with water) 247/15.
pane *n.* panel 69/17, 23, 86/26, *etc.*; *pl.* 86/25, 26, *etc.*
parage *n.* lineage 362/20, 376/7.
paramours *adv.* as a lover 89/20.
parifye *v.* liken 177/33; *pp.* made equal 133/27.
pariurye *n.* perjury 104/35.
party *n.* part 40/14, 124/13; *pl.* parts 44/21, 46/10; districts 38/21, 42/9, 43/8, *etc.*
passe *v.* surpass 68/19, 89/4; *pr. 3 s.*

Glossary 449

45/18; *pr. p.* 25/30, 36/11, 49/25, *etc.*; **passynge** *ppl. a.* 58/16; **passynge** *ppl. adv.* 18/6, 42/16, 47/30, *etc.*; *pt.* 43/26, 71/10, 74/31, *etc.*; *pp.* 91/20.
passyngly *adv.* surpassingly 10/16, 48/28, 66/2, *etc.*
patasshed, patesshid, patessyd *pp.* conquered 80/11, 81/13, 198/30, *etc.*; **patished** *pt.* 288/29.
paumys *n. pl.* flat pieces of wood for striking the hands of children in punishment, ferules 352/15.
paves *n.* shield 320/30, 374/8.
payment *n.* pavement 150/16, 21.
payne *n.* penalty 76/27, 106/7, 117/10.
payned *pt.* punished 89/29.
pedegrew *n.* pedigree 33/2, 14, 23.
perdure *v.* endure, last 347/16.
peregal *adj.* equal 6/25, 26/15, 34/21, *etc.*
perliously *adv.* perilously 46/3 (? a scribal error).
persecution *n.* pursuit 162/3.
perspectyf *n.* proof, evidence 17/31; mirror 374/21.
persuasion *n.* argument 56/23.
persuasive *n.* persuasion 229/4, 314/12, 329/13; system of beliefs 186/14.
picture *n.* representation 258/1; carved representation 117/22, 304/28, *etc.*; *pl.* representations 147/21; carved representations 91/15, 120/22.
pietous *adj.* piteous 99/11, 20, 34, *etc.*; pitiful 90/8.
pight *pt.* pitched 152/14, 180/20, 387/30; placed 152/18, 392/30, 393/24, *etc.*; *pp.* pitched 154/22, 168/33, 215/15, *etc.*
pike *v.* throw (pikes or darts) 247/31; *pr. p.* 247/29; *pt.* 261/36.
pirry *n.* squall 272/22.
pittevous, pietyuous, *etc.*, *adj.* pitiful 290/14, 21, 299/16, *etc.*
pittevously *adv.* pitifully 295/2.
placarde *n.* breastplate 384/2.
plage, plaige *n.* region 183/13, 186/30, 241/21, *etc.*
plaige *n.* plague 189/25, 32, 303/27, *etc.*

plaistre *n.* gypsum 151/24; ~ of *Parys,* Skelton's error for asphalt 207/12.
plasshes *n. pl.* puddles 14/5, 232/23.
plenare *adj.* complete 259/2, 263/12.
plenarly *adv.* completely 3/20, 36/8, 57/2, *etc.*
plentevous *adj.* plentiful 184/34; rich or fertile 210/9, 244/25, *etc.*
plentevously *adv.* plentifully 20/14, 184/6.
pocokkes *n. pl.* peacocks 213/13.
pole artik *n.* north star 55/15, 56/16, 220/27, *etc.*; north pole 183/14, 187/22, 203/24, *etc.*
porte, poort *n.* bodily carriage 277/16, 287/13, 323/21.
porte *n.* harbour 274/10; ~ *salew* safe harbour 43/10, 13, 273/27.
popped *pt.* (?) smeared 166/4.
popyngiayes *n. pl.* parrots 213/15.
portentuous *adj.* portending 71/24, 100/23, 176/5, *etc.*
posicion *n.* belief 95/26.
potestates *n. pl.* potentates 21/13.
pourchace *v.* seize 367/32; *pt.* acquired 76/19, 79/7; *pp.* provided 5/16.
poyntment *n.* agreement 283/30 (cf. **appoyntement**).
poyntyd *pt.* equipped 367/17; *pp.* 207/1, 350/9.
poysed *pt.* hung balanced or undecided 369/27.
practive *n.* practice 322/32, 328/17.
practyke *n.* practice 24/29, 133/3, 338/10, *etc.*
practyke *v.* practise 335/30.
preace, prees *n.* press 161/14, 28, 354/18, *etc.*
preace *v.* press 215/18, 261/32; *pr. p.* **presinge** 373/30, **precynge** 375/32, 388/23; *pt.* 160/28, 367/36, 371/23, *etc.*
prebendare *n.* fodder 195/17.
preced, *etc.* See **preace.**
precedentes *n. pl.* presiding officers 39/9.
precedentes, presedentis, procedentes, *etc.*, *n. pl.* precedents 8/22, 44/4, 75/2, *etc.*; procedures 111/30, 178/10, 190/12, *etc.*;

G

documents which serve as guides 375/15, 385/26, 394/28; *s.* precedent 318/2.
precellence *n.* pre-eminence 8/14.
precognysate *pp.* made known beforehand 123/34.
preiudiced *pp.* damaged 74/6.
premordial *n.* beginning 13/21.
prenosticacion, pronosticacion, *etc., n.* prophecy 35/27, 71/5, 24, *etc.*
prenosticate, pronosticate *v.* prophesy 110/30, 35, 167/2, *etc.*; *pt.* 172/16; **prenosticate, pronostycate** *ppl. a.* prophetic 36/21, 356/30.
preparative *n.* refining (of gold) 223/5.
presagious *adj.* prophetic 133/9, 169/27.
presidentis, *etc.* See **precedentes.**
presinge, *etc.* See **preace.**
pressure *n.* wine-press 352/23.
pretence *n.* purpose 70/4.
pretende *v.* exhibit 392/9; *pr. 3 s.* 47/18; *pr. p.* 155/24, 353/24; *pt.* 331/6.
pretensyuely *adv.* extensively 353/9.
preu *adj.* doughty 367/36, 383/19, 384/28.
preued, prevyd *pp.* proved 79/4, 105/22.
preuenewes. See **prouenew.**
preuydyng *pr. p.* foreseeing 142/1.
probate *n.* proof 7/2, 77/31, *etc.*; *pl.* 40/19, 212/22, 313/11, *etc.*
probatyf *n.* proof 33/2.
procedentes. See **precedentes.**
processe *n.* discourse, literary composition 4/1, 12, 6/19, *etc.*; by ~ by degrees, in course of time 16/8.
procure *v.* stimulate 2/34, 7/15.
profres *n. pl.* offers 93/18.
progeny *n.* ancestry 6/29; generation 375/20.
prohemy *n.* foreword 3/21, 4/19, 5/1, *etc.*
prolacion *n.* utterance 358/3.
proloyned *pp.* purloined 265/15.
prompte *adj.* expert 24/4.
promptly *adv.* expertly, skilfully 133/17.

promyscuate *adj.* promiscuous 196/22.
prone *adj.* prepared, eager 76/21, 96/22, 101/8.
pronosticacion, pronosticate, *etc.* See **prenosticacion, prenosticate.**
proprety, proprietie *n.* quality 275/28, 288/9.
propynque *adj.* neighbouring 213/12.
prosecute *v.* proceed with 271/3; treat of 44/5, 360/25; *pr. p.* 16/34; *pt.* took advantage of 96/12.
protensyd *pp.* extended 342/6.
prouenew *n.* profit 9/11; **preuenewes** *pl.* 50/29.
proues, prowesse *n.* prowess 34/20, 73/17.
prouffytable *adj.* useful 118/6.
prouydence *n.* foresight 15/33.
prymordiall *adj.* original 15/9, 17/32, 224/12, *etc.*
pryncipall, pryncypal, *etc., adj.* beginning 11/5; of highest rank 176/27.
prynciple *n.* beginning 13/9, 17/1, 18/13, *etc.*; *pl.* 326/27.
pryses *n. pl.* booty 78/28.
puissaunce *n.* number, power 79/26, 92/29, *etc.*
purphirians *n. pl.* purple coots 213/16.
purueyaunce, pourueyaunce, *etc., n.* provision 27/25, 42/13, 190/14.
purvey, pourueye *v.* provide 115/2, 157/6, 169/5, *etc.*; *pt.* 63/21, 65/30, 108/10, *etc.*; *pp.* 80/35, 158/33, 160/6, *etc.*
pylar, pyller, *etc., n.* pillar 33/30; stela 38/4, 5, 17, *etc.*; pyramid 73/25, 87/26, 28, *etc.*; *pl.* stelae 33/26, 67/26; pyramids 61/14, 74/19, 86/19, *etc.*; columns 69/26, 91/12, 92/19, *etc.*; caissons 146/12, 17.
pynot *n.* pine cone, especially one containing an edible seed 209/19.

quadrant *n.* square (for a pool) 148/7.
qualifijd *pp.* given or bearing a specific quality 13/30, 328/29.

Glossary

quarellis *n. pl.* legal pleas or disputes 103/26.
quasi *adv.* virtually 51/3.
quenne *n.* wench 239/2; queynes *pl.* 317/19, 318/20.
querely *adj.* choirly 315/8.
quernes *n. pl.* mills for grinding or crushing 235/25.
questis *n. pl.* public inquiries 102/28.
quoke *pt.* quaked 331/7.
quyck, *etc., adj.* living 106/10, 112/6, 249/5, *etc.*; swift 276/35; lively 323/11, 328/19; teeming 276/3; quycker *comp.* more vigorous or lively 56/22.
quycketh *pr. 3 s.* quickens 212/26.
quykly *adv.* vigorously 330/24; firmly 127/24.
quyknes *n.* life 224/17, 311/17, 336/5.
quyse *v.* squeeze 236/14.
quyte *adj.* acquitted 104/17; unencumbered 271/4.

racemes, rasemes *n. pl.* clusters (of grapes) 310/2, 15, 312/34.
rapely *adv.* hastily 239/22, 291/24.
rappe & rynde pillage 375/34.
raryte *n.* openness or looseness of texture 57/24.
rase *v.* erase 231/33; *pr. 3 s.* tears, slashes 49/1, 251/26; *pt.* scratched 373/6; *pp.* erased 7/23, 136/11 (raced), 286/21, *etc.*; torn 301/1.
rather *comp. adv.* more quickly 266/28, 278/9.
rauayne, raven *n.* pillage 206/8, 379/15.
rauenours *n. pl.* pillagers 356/7.
rauenous *adj.* pertaining to robbery or pillage 282/27; fierce 300/6, 370/28, 371/18, *etc.*
rauenously *adv.* fiercely 291/25, 332/28.
raught *pt.* reached 261/7; seized 291/24, 364/25, *etc.*; picked up 374/10, 387/5.
raylled *pp.* roamed 344/11.
rayne *n.* scum 14/4; *pl.* 14/13.
rayseines *n. pl.* resins 209/16.
reboyllynge *pr. p.* boiling up or over 56/29.

receptive *n.* receptive capacity 188/19.
recheles *adj.* reckless 96/10.
rechelesnes *n.* negligence 291/32, 383/21.
recognysaunce, reconysaunce *n.* formal pledge of fealty or submission 78/26, 348/22; acknowledgement 112/27, 173/8.
recomfort *v.* recreate, gain recreation 150/24; assist 82/28; *pr. 3 s.* refreshes 276/12, 277/4, 281/29; *pr. pl.* nourish 47/27; *pr. p.* comforting 298/32; soothing 27/18, 334/5; recomfortynge *vbl. n.* healing 35/23.
recomfortably *adv.* refreshingly 325/26.
recompt *v.* record 165/26, 192/10, *etc.*; *pr. 3 s.* tells, recounts 321/8; *pr. p.* telling, relating 286/9, 299/7; *pp.* 153/20, 171/11, 36, *etc.*
recomptre, recountre *n.* encounter 283/25, 316/20, 378/7.
recomptre *v.* encounter 260/34; *pt.* 291/7, 317/26 (recompted), 337/2.
recrayed *ppl. a.* craven 355/20.
rectifucuge *n.* rectification 195/21.
redoundynge *pr. p.* abounding 45/10, 274/7.
reedsperis, redesperes *n. pl.* rushes 63/9, 221/34.
referrynge *pr. p.* carrying back 33/2; referred *pp.* carried back logically 310/12.
reflaire *n.* redolence 208/30, 212/31, 276/35.
reflaire *v.* give forth or emit fragrance 123/22, 185/7, 209/24; *pr. p.* 155/7, 324/24, *etc.*; reflairyng *vbl. n.* 276/23.
regalitie *n.* realm 163/2, 166/33.
regaly *n.* rule, realm 22/20, 25/32, 29/3, *etc.*
regement, regy- *n.* rule. administration 2/17, 81/15, 94/18, *etc.*
reheytyng *pr. p.* scolding 159/6; *vbl. n.* 235/16.
reightes, rightes *n. pl.* rites 197/9, 304/10.

452 Glossary

relentyng *pr. p.* melting 256/7; *vbl. n.* 269/22; **relented** *pp.* 54/31, 34, 55/32.
releuement *n.* relief 189/13, 218/25, 294/22, *etc.*
relucent *adj.* gleaming 210/3; sparkling 212/1, 19, *etc.*
reme *n.* realm 84/27.
remembrauncer *n.* recorder 320/12, 342/9; one who remembers (gratefully) 377/31.
remocion *n.* remoteness 53/26.
remorde *v.* reproach 164/15; *pp.* filled with remorse 140/4, 169/18, 360/25.
remotyue *adj.* remote 13/11, 24/16, 54/4, *etc.*
remyssyue *adj.* remiss 1/17, 51/32, 53/3, *etc.*; characterized by remission or abatement 276/35.
remyssively *adv.* remissly 307/16.
renommee *n.* renown 63/24, 333/10, 338/29, *etc.*
renomynge *pr. p.* giving renown 79/7; **renomed** *pp.* renowned 21/25, 27/16, 33/8, *etc.*
renyed *pt.* denied 144/14; *pp.* abjured 370/27.
repentyne *adj.* sudden 225/19, 292/14.
replevished *pp.* replenished 214/18, 244/25, 251/35, *etc.* (Skelton uses **replenish** also; see 208/24, 276/6, 283/34, *etc.*).
reporture *n.* reporting 372/20; report 359/3, 387/20.
repressure *n.* relief 184/15.
reprisyd *pt.* captured 372/4.
repugnaunce *n.* refutation 54/35, 58/28, *etc.*; objection 32/32; contradictoriness 175/18; resistance 372/30.
repugnaunt *adj.* contradictory 96/7, 234/6.
rescouse *n.* succour 40/1.
rescrybe *v.* reply in writing 103/34.
resemblaund *n.* resemblance 374/33.
resemblaunt *adj.* resembling 274/9.
reserued *prep.* except 30/5, 40/21, 72/9, *etc.*

reserueth *pr. 3 s.* retains 207/19; **reserued** *pp.* excepted 12/7, 31/27; preserved 123/25, 155/23, 185/11.
resoluyd *pp.* melted 87/14.
respected *pt.* respited 138/20.
responsion *n.* response 369/11.
responsive *n.* response 155/2; *pl.* 228/33.
retroublous *adj.* troubled 216/30.
reuerberate *v.* dissipate 325/1; dazzle 262/38.
reuers *v.* turn back 245/7; *pr. 3 s.* 237/23; *pr. p.* 327/13; *pt.* 216/29, 371/26; *pp.* 167/29, 178/19, 201/30, *etc.*
reuestrye *n.* vestry 92/17, 131/22.
reve *v.* pillage 216/1; *pr. p.* 206/8.
reveilyng *vbl. n.* revelling 291/19.
rexnyd *pt.* reigned (perhaps a scribal confusion with Lat. *rex*) 94/5.
ridde *v.* separate 255/11; **ryddyd** *pt.* bereft of life 390/34; *pp.* destroyed 389/20.
rode *n.* anchor 273/5, 280/11.
roialme. See **royame.**
rome, rowme *n.* position 72/11, 75/6, 82/21, *etc.*; *at rome* at large 239/29.
rore *n.* tumult 90/27.
rowhnes *n.* roughness 45/4.
rowte *n.* horde 237/26, 330/18.
royame, roialme *n.* realm 25/27, 35, 90/13, *etc.*
ruddes *n.* complexion 300/19.
ruddes *n. pl.* rods, poles 266/24.
ruskeled *pt.* rustled 261/1.
rygorous *adj.* rough 27/28, 88/5.
rynde. See **rappe & rynde.**

saciable *adj.* satisfying 185/2.
sacred *pt.* consecrated 293/31.
sad *adj.* serious 6/18, 27/35, 96/10, *etc.*
sadly *adv.* soberly 97/28, 333/20.
sadnes *n.* seriousness 2/30, 89/29, 126/17.
sailyng, salyenge *pr. p.* leaping 324/25, 367/32.
salares *n. pl.* salaries 193/9.
salew, salu. See **porte salew.**
saluage *adj.* savage 369/35.

Glossary

sanatyf *adj.* healing 35/23, 36/5, 49/12, *etc.*
sanxiouns *n. pl.* enactments 8/26.
sauacion *n.* preservation 272/8, 383/11.
saueconduyt *n.* safe conduct 93/31.
sauete, saulftie, *etc.*, *n.* safety 43/23, 100/32, 194/28, *etc.*
saulf *adj.* safe 216/26.
saulfgard, savegarde, *etc.*, *n.* safety 144/5; protection 147/4, 159/33, 253/11, *etc.*
savage, savaige *n.* savagery 182/3; impetuousness 146/18; rage 180/25, 258/20.
sawcerye *n.* sauces 220/39.
scarmysshe *n.* skirmish 377/21.
scissure *n.* crack 68/16; *pl.* fissures 15/7, 56/25, 57/14.
scorkynd, skorkened, squarkend, skorkyd, *pp.* scorched 58/5, 238/8, 244/2, 251/3, *etc.*
screpulous. See scrupulous.
scrowes *n. pl.* scrolls 8/4.
scrupulous, screpulous *adj.* doubtful 3/22, 16/26, 53/22, *etc.*
se *v.* see 324/30, *etc.*; sye *pt.* 160/3; sawe *pt.* 161/29, *etc.*
sectes *n. pl.* ceremonies 39/22, 41/6, 304/23.
sedicion, seducion *n.* strife 348/9; wrangling 110/16, 219/21, *etc.*
sedicyous, seducious, *etc.*, *adj.* factious 113/25, 127/34, 131/13, *etc.*
see *n.* throne 168/6.
see-fome *n.* sea-weed 244/20. See fome of the se.
seell *n.* throne seat 149/5.
selde, silde *adv.* seldom 57/34, 233/16, 239/25, *etc.*
semblably *adv.* similarly 15/11, 57/28.
sendale *n.* silk 99/9.
senowes. See synewes.
sensitive *n.* faculty of sensation 277/5.
sentence *n.* meaning 3/24, 286/33, *etc.*; significance 95/30; opinion 71/6; record 78/11.
sentencyous *adj.* meaningful 360/12.

senture *n.* fragrance 47/25, 58/20, 277/12, *etc.*
septentrione *adj.* north 186/30.
sepulture, sepulturis *n. pl.* tombs 67/4, 7, 18, *etc.*
sequestrid *pt.* appropriated 337/25; *pp.* separated 56/23; hidden 310/8.
serious, ceryous *adj.* continuous 17/9, 296/30, 304/12, *etc.*
seriously, ceryously *adv.* in order, or seriatim 11/14, 41/19, 67/19, *etc.*
seriousnes *n.* continuity 9/17.
seruoyse *n.* ale 346/24.
seruyture *n.* servant 172/27, 369/23; *pl.* 96/15, 22, 100/20, *etc.*
servaige *n.* slavery 225/7.
sette (by) *v.* value 63/7; *pr. 3 s.* fears 259/5; sette (by) *pt.* valued 88/28.
shed *pp.* poured 146/16.
shetteth, shitteth *pr. 3 s.* shuts 244/37, 245/9; shette, shytte *pp.* 51/30, 74/12, 99/6.
sheuall *n.* horse (*on* ~ mounted) 289/19.
shirle *adj.* shrill 230/20.
showre *n.* skirmish or attack 318/28, 372/8, 385/18; *pl.* 184/12, 335/36; pangs 197/6.
shrewdnes *n.* depravity 6/37.
shrynyd *pt.* enshrined 32/35.
sighment *n.* cement (Skelton's error for asphalt) 278/6.
signefyaunce *n.* significance 32/9.
signyfycatyf *adj.* meaningful 35/26.
silde. See selde.
sillibication *n.* syllabification 227/9.
singuler *adj.* personal 86/11; unusual 150/2.
sith *adv.* since 7/13, 16/22, 36/34, *etc.*
sittynge *adj.* fitting 6/7, 58/33, 81/25, *etc.*
skifill *v.* scuffle 255/10.
sklaunderous, sclaunderous *adj.* slanderous 3/12, 6/37, 12/12, *etc.*
skorkend, skorkyd. See scorkynd.
skry *n.* outcry 170/25.
slaughter, slawhter *n.* cannibalism 22/21, 28.
slaven *n.* an over-all garment 143/14.

slee *v.* slay 155/1; slow *pt.* 153/15; slayne *pp.* 250/15.
slope *n.* an over-all garment 143/14.
slow. See slee.
slowpe-wise *adj.* sloping 236/9.
slypper *adj.* slippery 341/4, 376/25.
smelle *n.* (?) fire (possibly a scribal error for smeek, a Scottish word for smoke from smouldering matter) 22/4.
snytes *n. pl.* snipes 112/9.
so as because 83/29, 88/15, 91/24, *etc.*
sociated *pp.* associated 179/7.
soden, sothen *pp.* boiled 99/15, 114/26, 27, *etc.*
soisceth *pr. 3 s.* throws (possibly from dial. *soss* to throw heavily) 248/26.
solacious *adj.* full of solace or recreation 150/24, 170/17, 274/9, *etc.*
solaciously *adv.* with solace or recreation 300/24.
sote *adj.* sweet 212/31.
sothen. See soden.
sourdeth *pr. 3 s.* arises 49/10; springs 56/30, 359/2; sourded *pp.* 185/33, 189/1 (surded).
sowes *n. pl.* movable structures 'having a strong roof, used to cover men advancing to the walls of a besieged town or fortress, and to protect them while engaged in sapping and mining or other operations' (*O.E.D.*) 171/22.
sowght *adj.* soft 276/31.
sowndeth *pr. 3 s.* tends 227/17; sownynge *pr. p.* sounding 345/17; sownded *pt.* tended 94/1; *pp.* sounded 227/8.
spack *pt.* spoke 15/24, 82/13.
specialitie, specyalte *n.* legal instrument 104/18, 107/34, 108/18; explanation 205/17; *pl.* documents 204/13, 342/13.
speculative *n.* body of theoretical knowledge 322/32.
spede *v.* succeed 259/10; sped *pt.* 141/9; sped *pp.* 170/14; proficient 54/30, 61/23, 95/17, *etc.*
speer *n.* range 268/9.

speres *n. pl.* spear-men, spear-women 289/18, 19.
sprynge *n.* flood 50/13, 51/3, 52/11, *etc.*; spring or source 44/9, 53/14, 33; *pl.* floods 54/14.
sprynge *adj.* source 44/10.
sprynge *v.* flood 57/3; *pr. p.* 27/28.
spyre *n.* peristyle 67/24, 69/21.
squarkend. See scorkynd.
stablysshe *v.* make firm 50/23; *pp.* established 96/2.
stande *v.* consist 291/33; ~yng *with* consistent with 106/2, 285/1, 322/20; *stondeth vppon* consists of 194/19; depends upon 346/32, 350/20.
stang *pt.* stung 252/25, 261/10.
stature *n.* statue 182/21, 304/27.
stirte (vnto) *pt.* leaped (at) 371/35, 261/7 (stert).
stirttinge place *n.* starting hole, way of escape 371/29.
stole *n.* weaving or embroidery frame 200/19.
stoppen *pr. pl.* stop 51/13.
stowres *n. pl.* staves 247/18.
strength *v.* reinforce 171/10, 19; strengthynge *vbl. n.* strengthening 109/26; *pt.* made strong 80/9, 91/27, 136/19; *pp.* 41/24, 42/14, *etc.*
strete *n.* village or town 30/3, 94/29, 288/31, *etc.*; *pl.* 51/25, 189/18, 257/8, *etc.*
strikle *v.* sprinkle 218/19.
sturdely *adv.* savagely 161/1, 329/20.
sturdy *adj.* severe 16/4; tempestuous 60/31, 216/19; impetuous 28/1; tough 34/9; strong 34/12, 89/22; *sturdye stones* jagged rocks 273/14.
styf *adj.* strong 89/22.
stythe *n.* stithy 360/27.
subgette *adj.* subject 83/31.
subsidious *adj.* helpful 328/11.
subsidye *n.* assistance 15/30, 23/2, 82/28, *etc.*; *pl.* taxes or moneys levied by a ruler 366/30.
subtilitie *n.* sleight 142/18.
suffrage *n.* help 15/32, 31/21; *funeral suffragyes* funeral tributes or prayers 100/3.

Glossary 455

suffumigation *n.* generation of fumes by burning from below 208/31, 225/1.
suffysaunce *n.* sufficiency 3/27, 341/17.
superflue *adj.* superfluous 64/21, 96/4, 111/22.
supplyeth *pr. 3 s.* supplicates 36/7; **supplyed** *pt.* 323/26; **suppleed** *pp.* 172/26.
supportacion *n.* support 92/28, 108/26.
supposail, supposell, *etc., n.* supposition or belief 19/28, 53/18, 72/30, *etc.; pl.* 231/11.
surded. See **sourdeth.**
surfeture *n.* surfeit 111/25; *pl.* 166/9.
surquedous, surquydous *adj.* overbearing 41/8, 159/3, 322/10, *etc.*
surquidous *adv.* overbearingly 75/29, 181/32, *etc.*
(in) suspence in question 53/18.
suspensive *adj.* sustained 9/17, 322/22.
suspensively *adv.* in a sustained manner 295/10, 342/6.
swalow *n.* pit 151/31; abyss 43/7, 188/19; *pl.* 56/26, 57/10, 14, *etc.*
sydre *n.* cedar 113/6.
sye *pt.* See **se.**
synewes, senowes, synowes *n. pl.* sinews 217/12, 248/16, 22.
syssures. See **scissure.**

tacches, tatches *n. pl.* blemishes 287/24; immoral habits 222/8.
talaunt *n.* disposition 25/20.
tapetes *n. pl.* (?) limits or restrictions 394/19.
taskes *n. pl.* taxes or tribute 76/34, 101/4, 195/9, *etc.*
tassailes *n. pl.* cress (i.e. **tassels,** Skelton's translation of **cardamonium,** cress) 268/15.
tasture *n.* taste and smell 62/20, 84/15, 184/38, *etc.; pl.* 212/32.
tatches. See **tacches.**
taxed workes *n.* piece-work 221/26.
tayllagis *n.* forced tribute 101/4.
temerary *adj.* foolhardy 42/27; presumptuous 196/16, 307/16, *etc.*

tentre-hoke *n.* tenter-hook 261/2.
tenure *n.* tenor 197/17, 317/5, 344/17, *etc.*
terce *n.* the third hour of the day; more loosely, before noon 237/18.
terrestre *adj.* terrestrial 209/25, 324/20.
theatrial *adj.* theatrical 354/2.
therebinthus *n.* turpentine 209/18.
thithe *n.* thigh 311/22.
tho, thoo *pron. adj.* those 33/18, 34/2, 11, *etc.*
threst, thurst *v.* thrust 144/16, 254/29; **thristeth** *pr. 3 s.* 248/27; **thristyng** *pr. p.* 161/25; **threste** *pt.* 80/37.
thronge *pt.* thrust 376/20.
thryllyd *pt.* penetrated 351/32.
thurst. See **threst.**
(all) to-brekyth *pr. 3 s.* breaks in pieces 49/16, 117/32.
(all) to-brosed *pp.* severely bruised 262/13, 310/8.
(alle) to-flappe *v.* flap vigorously 386/31.
to-fore *adv.* heretofore 27/17, 52/33, 57/14, *etc.*
to-fore *prep.* before 10/31, 43/19, 65/11, *etc.*
to-raggyd *pp.* torn to rags 122/23.
(all) to-rent *pt.* tore to pieces 161/6; *pp.* 386/27.
(al)to-reveth *pr. 3 s.* tears to pieces 251/26.
(all) to-stongen *pp.* stung all over 106/9.
totehill *n.* look-out hill 153/2.
(alle) to-tere *v.* tear to pieces 113/13; *pr. 3 s.* 332/28; **to-torne** *pp.* 387/8.
towche *n.* black marble 88/19.
towgh, towhe *adj.* tough 34/13, 50/7.
trace *n.* dance 359/32.
traditoriously *adv.* treacherously 317/10.
traditory *n.* treason 165/23, 308/18.
traditory *adj.* treasonable 331/18.
traite *adj.* tardy 265/27.
traitory, trayterye *n.* treason 29/35, 317/22, 331/3.

456   Glossary

transfused *pp.* caused to transmigrate 116/1.
transgresse *n.* transgression 331/15.
transuerted *pp.* converted 173/36.
trauers *n.* dispute 302/14; legal case 69/31, 104/2.
trauers *v.* dispute 178/2; oppose 373/26; disagree 320/19, 341/21; **trauersen** *pr. pl.* turn away 52/24; *pr. p.* trying (legally) 97/30; **trauersynge** *vbl. n.* conflict (of theories) 336/32; *pp.* fought out 347/21; competed in 354/6.
trayne *n.* orderly sequence or argument 363/8.
traytte *n.* treaty 387/32.
tree *n.* wood 69/28, 116/4, 131/24.
trewage, truage *n.* forced payment 27/25, 74/23, 91/26, *etc.*; royal income 90/2; *pl.* 80/24, 366/30.
trews, triews, trieux *n.* truce 128/4, 9, 181/1, *etc.*
tropik estyuale *n.* southern solstice 183/21, 253/3.
truage, *etc.* See **trewage**.
trye *v.* test 59/2; ~ *out* extract (juice from grapes) 312/33; extract or refine (gold) 234/20, 275/5, 7; deduce 10/11, 104/26; *tryed out pt.* learned by investigation 54/7; extracted (gold) 173/32, 234/16, 236/25.
tryme *v.* span with the arms 68/2.
trymes *n. pl.* fathoms 266/9.
trypudacions *n. pl.* dancing steps 353/22, 358/4.
tunsions *n. pl.* incisions 113/5, 277/10.
tyldyd *pp.* covered with an awning or canopy 115/26.
tymbre *n.* timbrel 299/13, 301/30.
tymbryng *pr. p.* timbrelling 299/26.
tyre *v.* tear flesh in feeding 385/32; *pt.* 28/4.

variacion *n.* disagreement 177/31, 320/19, 336/12.
veer, vere *n.* springtime 19/15, 21/1, 25/3, *etc.*
vegetal *adj.* 'characterized by, exhibiting or producing, the phenomena of physical life and growth' (*O.E.D.*) 14/14, 23, 17/23, *etc.*
vengeable *adj.* revengeful 88/25, 144/35.
verdure *n.* savour 48/13, 58/19, 155/7, *etc.*; vegetation 187/35; *pl.* viridities 212/32, 269/23.
verdured *pp.* having a specified flavour or taste 59/10.
vere. See **veer**.
vertue *n.* strength, power 211/21, 213/3, 23; (?) pursuit 1/20.
vertuous *adj.* strength-giving 211/32.
very *adj.* true 79/36.
virydary *n.* viridarium 359/13.
vmbeset *pp.* surrounded 267/1.
vmbre *n.* shadow 177/30; **humbres** *pl.* 183/26.
vmbrous *adj.* shadowy 130/8.
vnaduenture *adv.* doubtlessly 9/30; by bad luck 114/7, 193/23, 361/2, 373/36 (**vnaventur**), *etc.*
vnconnynge *n.* lack of skill 12/15.
vndisposed *ppl. a.* ill disposed 7/11, 128/20.
vnfasshend *ppl. a.* mis-fashioned 327/10.
vnfeyned *pp.* true 155/12.
vnhabitable *adj.* uninhabitable 252/1.
vnkowthe *n.* strangeness 255/30.
vnmetely *adj.* improper 203/18, 280/3.
vnnethe *adv.* hardly 161/17, 206/23, 239/18, *etc.*
vnquyete *v.* disturb 193/34.
vnrecompted *pp.* unrecounted 280/18.
vnresonable *adj.* incapable of reason 230/16, 237/8, 238/32.
vnrestely *adj.* restless 369/32.
vnshappen *adj.* mis-shapen 258/6.
vnsittyng, *etc., adj.* unfitting 2/7, 197/23, 229/27, *etc.*
vntemporat *adj.* intemperate 44/11, 55/1.
vnwarely *adv.* at unawares 365/3, 373/36.
volluble *adj.* rotating 176/3, 296/23.
volunte *n.* will 394/17.

Glossary 457

vprist *n.* ascension 19/6, 281/2, 3, *etc.*
vre *n.* use 185/27.
vre *n.* ore 235/5.
(well) vred *pp.* possessed of good fortune 270/1, 278/15.
vryd *pp.* put into use 385/30.
vtteraunce, outraunce *n.* extreme vanquishment 37/12, 318/21, 327/29, *etc.*
vttre *v.* sell 24/20, 245/3.
vulgary *adj.* vulgar 288/33.
vylayne, villane *n.* villein 96/16, 194/15, 209/13, *etc.*; *pl.* 356/4, 376/7.
vytaylled *pt.* provided with victuals 51/32.

waftynges *n. pl.* signal flags 267/29.
wage *v.* engage 157/4.
(laid in) wait guarded 234/31; *hauynge in a ~* holding under guard 21/17.
wake-fyres *n. pl.* watch-fires 291/17.
want (of) *v.* lack 247/22.
warely *adj.* watchful 374/9.
warke *v.* work 236/2.
warly, warrely *adj.* warlike 187/3, 332/21, 333/17, *etc.*
warrye *v.* curse 97/15; *pr. p.* 231/25; *pt.* 180/34.
wayenge *pr. p.* weighing, considering 105/30.
wayne *n.* wagons 67/25, 69/27, 86/27.
wedde *n.* pledge 108/18.
weder *n.* weather 60/30.
wele in comyn, wele encomyne, *etc.*, communal welfare 2/17, 6/11, 7/6, *etc.*
wele publik public welfare 103/1, 186/10, 191/35, *etc.*
welkes *n. pl.* whelks 219/25.
wellis *n. pl.* freshets 60/5.
welnyh *adv.* closely 24/16.
welth *n.* felicity 5/27, 7/7, 8/29, *etc.*

welthfull *adj.* happy 216/27.
welthy *adj.* felicitous 27/21, 95/34, 98/26, *etc.*
where-so *adv.* wheresoever 27/10.
whulyng *pr. p.* whining 230/20.
widdreth *pr. 3 s.* withers 282/2.
withinforth *adv.* inside 80/19, 279/18.
withsayde *pt.* gainsaid 82/9; *pp.* 228/35.
wode *adj.* savage 46/8, 375/29.
wodenes *n.* violence 72/2; madness 369/36.
wodewoses *n. pl.* wild men of the woods 253/1.
woose, wose *n.* ooze 18/17, 42/29, 47/15, *etc.*
worme *n.* serpent 260/31, 34, 261/15, *etc.*; *pl.* 117/30, 118/8, 265/6, *etc.*
wortes *n. pl.* vegetables 47/26, 62/19, 87/30.
wose. See **woose.**
wosy *adj.* oozy 15/6.
wote *v.* know 54/2.
wymmen *n. pl.* female animals 115/3.

yate *n.* gate 67/22; *pl.* 66/1.
ycomonycall. See **iconomycall.**
yeftys *n. pl.* gifts 29/14.
yen. See **eyen.**
yerthe *n.* earth 236/11, 15.
yerthen *adj.* earthen 236/17.
yet *adv.* still 87/1.
yette *v.* gush forth 57/21; *pr. 3 s.* 56/28.
ymages *n. pl.* mummy cases 155/24, 26.
ymagynative *n.* imagination 182/21, 202/5, 228/20, *etc.*
ymagynative *adj.* artificial 161/2.
ymagyned *ppl. a.* artificial 160/2.
ymnes, ympnes *n. pl.* hymns or poems 129/17, 204/10, 22, *etc.*
yougthe. See **ewthe.**
ypocrace *n.* hippocras 353/27.
yrke *adj.* tired, weary 79/16.

H

INDEX OF PROPER NAMES

THE main entries in the following index use standard modern spellings, mostly as in Oldfather. Cross-references are given from Skeltonic spellings which vary greatly from the standard form—e.g. *Abactians*. See *Nabataeans*. When the Skeltonic spelling does not vary so much as to require a cross-reference, but might still be confusing, it is added in parentheses after the main entry—e.g. *Alcmenê (Alcumena)*. Minor differences in spelling, as between *i* and *y*, and the Latin spellings of Poggio, many of which appear in footnotes to the text, are disregarded.

Abactians. See *Nabataeans.*
Abaris 205/5.
Abaterians. See *Nabataeans.*
Abileians. See *Alilaei.*
Acanthi 131/3.
Acarnania (Acanarina) 57/29.
Acesinus 187/29.
Achathartus Gulf 264/21.
Achelous 57/29.
Acherousia 130/12, 18.
Achilles 203/11.
Acridophagi 250/20.
Acrisius 362/12.
Actisanes 83/27, 32.
Adippa. See *Alcippe.*
Aeacus 340/19.
Aegis 327/2, 35.
Aella 388/26.
Agamemnon 164/34.
Agatharchides of Cnidus 59/34; 233/27; 240/16; 281/21.
Agave (Agathus) 344/21.
Agyrium 11/1.
Alcaeus 34/17; 365/30.
Alcida. See *Aegis.*
Alcinois. See *Alcyone.*
Alciones. See *Halcyonê.*
Alcippe 389/10, 12.
Alcman 357/7.
Alcmenê (Alcumena) 34/16; 339/7; 362/14, 28; 364/14.
Alcyone 377/8.
Alexander the Great 9/26; 11/17; 32/10; 36/25; 72/15; 77/22, 23; 115/9; 145/20; 148/17; 177/9; 178/13; 187/6, 17; 192/4; 280/9; 387/15.

Alexandria 32/11; 72/16; 257/11; 260/5, 19; 262/17; 263/4; 271/22.
Alibrota. See *Palibothra.*
Alilaei 275/16.
Almeon. See *Alcman.*
Alpheius 380/16; 383/4.
Amaltheia 323/25, 31; 324/4, 6; 337/31.
Amasis 61/13; 62/16; 83/21; 92/24; 94/20, 30; 95/9; 127/26; 128/9.
Amasus. See *Amosis.*
Amazons 135/4; freq. pp. 199-203; 223/14; freq. pp. 286-95; 330/21, 27; 338/13; 387/25 *bis*; 388/4, 19; 389/18, 22.
Ammon 21/29; 23/28; 35/18; 223/14; 323/15, 18; 324/8; 326/8; 329/4, 8, 14, 17, 22, 25, 28; 330/4, 16; 331/3; 333/27; 334/23, 26; 335/7; 336/29; 337/2, 9, 21, 31.
Amosis 89/17.
Amphion 377/1.
Amphitryon 363/21; 366/7, 14.
Anaxagoras 14/26; 54/29; 55/29.
Andromeda 362/13.
Antaeus (governor of Egypt) 26/1.
Antaeus (giant) 30/3; 390/31; 391/2 392/3.
Antaeus (village) 30/2.
Antigone. See *Autonoe.*
Antigonus 177/12.
Antimachus 318/16.
Antris, Antrus. See *Antaeus.*
Anubis 26/16, 18; 117/22.
Apanda. See *Aspandas.*
Aphrodite's Harbour 264/15.

Index of Proper Names 459

Apis 30/32; 114/17; 115/19; 116/6; 119/1.
Apollo 20/23; 22/16; 26/4, 14; 27/15; 32/6, 17; 36/20; 126/26; 204/4, 6, 8, 21; 302/11, 14, 17, 22, 24, 28, 37; 303/7, 10, 20; 369/10; 384/18. Cf. also *Pythian Apollo.*
Apollodorus 11/31.
Apries 94/5, 25, 30.
Apys (a mis-translation) 116/2.
Arabia 28/19; 30/2; 38/2; 39/18; 44/15, 24; 45/30; 65/5; 75/22; 80/16; 84/10; 87/5; 92/11; 120/3; 135/5; 137/3; 139/1; 205/32; 206/1, 4; 208/19; 209/37; 210/6; 211/15; 213/30; 214/17, 24; 215/21, 31; 223/6; 230/11, 12; 234/15; 236/32; 237/4; 263/4, 17, 20; 264/1; 266/6; 269/7, 11; 270/9; 292/23; 314/27; 318/18, 20; 320/15.
Arabia Felix 24/10; 208/21; 214/4, 10, 25; 237/5; 276/4.
Arabians 137/4; 167/34; 206/26; 209/12; 213/1; 271/14; 272/26; 273/21; 274/29; 275/15; 276/3; 281/34.
Araxes 197/33.
Arbaces (*Arbacus*) 134/22; 166/27; 167/3, 29; 168/22, 34; 169/17; 170/6, 18, 20; 171/3; 172/9, 12, 30; 173/30; 179/26.
Arbianes 179/31.
Arcadia (*Archady*) 373/16; 377/9.
Archemidorus Ephesius. See *Artemidorus.*
Archerusia. See *Acherousia.*
Archimedes 47/18.
Arcturus 280/23.
Argeius 376/38.
Argire. See *Agyrium.*
Argolians (*Argyens*) 368/21, 34.
Argos 35/11; 39/15.
Arianans (*Arianes*) 188/7.
Arians 126/30.
Arimaspi (*Armaspeans*) 198/29.
Arione. See *Orion.*
Aristaeus 326/9 bis; 331/38; 332/4; 340/25. See *Artaeus.*
Aristeus. See *Aristaeus* and *Artaeus.*
Ariston 269/8, 10.
Armaeus 89/16.

Armenia 137/10; 151/3, 13.
Armonia. See *Harmonia.*
Arsinoē 47/8; 264/7.
Artaeus 179/31; 180/22; 181/10.
Artaxerxes 179/16.
Artemidorus of Ephesus 233/28.
Artemis (*Artena*) 389/8.
Artibanus. See *Astibaras.*
Artycas (*Arteranus*) 179/31.
Artynes (*Artenes*) 181/10.
Asa 245/15.
Ascalon 139/26.
Ascapon. See *Astapus.*
Ascij. See *Asty.*
Asia 28/32; 36/25; 39/18; 57/27; 60/14; 66/29; 77/21, 28; 78/3; 134/7; 136/7, 9; 137/24, 31, 32; 141/19; 142/6; 143/18; 145/20; 151/2; 154/13, 24, 32; 156/10; 165/3; 178/27; 179/26; 199/27; 202/8; 203/23; 205/31; 224/1; 316/26.
Asians 162/23; 179/30; 187/8; 233/28.
Asopus 340/19.
Aspandas (*Apanda*) 182/30.
Assyrians 134/2, 20; 136/8, 11, 26; 139/15; 145/2; 160/8; 161/5, 10, 23, 35; 162/26; 164/25, 26, 30; 165/2, 6, 29; 166/25, 33; 167/31, 33; 169/20; 170/16; 172/26; 173/36; 178/27; 179/25; 183/5; 198/34.
Astapus 53/35.
Asteria 389/10.
Asteropes. See *Steropē.*
Astibaras 181/11; 182/28.
Asty 39/24.
Astyages 179/10; 182/33.
Athenians 40/32.
Athens (city) 11/28, 31; freq. pp. 39–40; 93/24; 103/17; 105/27; 108/34; 129/8; 162/25; 204/29.
Athens (state) 29/6.
Athesis. See *Etesius.*
Athesius. See *Etesian.*
Athyrtis (*Athircia*) 75/32.
Atlantians 304/32; 306/2.
Atlantides 305/7.
Atlas (son of Uranus) 305/2, 3; 306/1, 34.
Atlas (mountain) 223/.15; 224/5; 288/20; 289/7, 30; 291/3; 295/12, 18; 305/9, 23.

460   *Index of Proper Names*

Attis 301/15, 24; 304/1, 4.
Augeas 380/1.
Auschisae 282/14.
Autariatae (*Attariotans*) 252/18.
Autonoe 344/21.

Babylon (city of Egypt) 79/22.
Babylon (city of Mesopotamia) 39/7,
    9; 134/14; 137/5; 145/9; 149/17,
    22; 151/7, 17, 23; 166/34; 168/22;
    169/8; 172/16, 22, 32, 35.
Babylonia 79/16; 111/4; 134/18;
    169/17; 172/18; 173/19; 210/13;
    213/13, 31; 244/24.
Babylonian (adj.) 149/4.
Babylonians 137/4; 148/2; 166/31;
    167/6, 23, 32; 174/5, 7.
Bacchus 18/35; 32/6; 129/18; 312/8;
    318/3; 338/15; 347/31; 349/4;
    352/20.
Bachorides. See *Bocchoris*.
Bactra 142/13, 30, 31; 143/22.
Bactriana 142/12.
Bactrians 68/27; 137/33; 138/17;
    139/21; 141/6; 142/10, 16, 25;
    144/22; 156/10; 157/9, 21; 158/
    5; 162/4; 170/4, 9; 188/6.
Bagistanus 152/13.
Banizomenes 272/24.
Barathra 42/15, 43/6.
Barbarye (a Skeltonic nation) 138/9.
Barce 94/14.
Barzanes 137/11, 16.
Basileia 297/25, 28, 33.
Belues 395/23.
Belus 39/6; 148/2.
Belysys 166/31; 167/19, 32; 168/22;
    169/7, 26; 172/16, 34; 173/8, 16,
    20.
Bithynia 138/8.
Bocchoris 89/21; 107/31; 127/18.
Boeotia 57/29; 344/14; 346/35; 347/
    11; 395/10.
Boeotians 275/7; 347/15; 395/18.
Bolbitine (mouth of the Nile) 46/16.
Bolgii 53/27.
Borcanii 138/12.
Boreades 205/26.
Boreas 205/26.
Bousiris 116/5.
Britain 11/25; 263/8, 15.
Britons 263/12.

Bromius 352/24.
Bubastus 38/14.
Bucchoris. See *Bocchoris*.
Busiris 25/36; 65/22, 23; 93/35; 119/
    12; 392/6, 14.

Cadmus 32/26, 33; 33/6; 52/25; 314/
    2; 321/17; 339/25; 344/2.
Cadusii 138/11; 180/1, 12, 16, 21,
    27; 181/2, 6, 7.
Caesar (*Julius*) 11/21; 263/14.
Caïcus 293/7.
Caire. See *Caria*.
Caldees, etc. See *Chaldaeans*.
Calliopê 357/27; 360/6.
Callisthenes 342/1.
Cambyses 45/23; 48/4; 64/7; 66/28;
    71/7; 95/3; 128/19; 225/12.
Campê 332/31.
Canaus. See *Tanäis*.
Canicular (days) 27/27.
Canopic (mouth of the Nile) 46/16.
Cappadocia 138/8.
Caproans. See *Cypriots*.
Carbae (*Carbosyns*) 276/2.
Caria 92/11; 138/6.
Carioti (people of Syria—a mistranslation of *caryoti*, meaning dates) 213/28.
Carmania 237/3.
Carmanii 138/11.
Caron. See *Charon*.
Carthage 274/10; 392/24.
Caspiana 138/13.
Caspian Gates 138/14.
Caspian Hills 198/25.
Cayre. See *Caria*.
Caucasus 60/15; 197/37.
Celaeno (an Amazon) 389/6.
Celaeno (one of the Atlantides) 306/4.
Celinus. See *Uranus*.
Celtis 203/26.
Celum. See *Uranus*.
Cenocephali 46/4.
Centaurs 374/25, 28; 375/8, 10, 17,
    26; 376/11, 28; 377/6; 378/14;
    384/23.
Cepheus 362/13.
Cephisus 57/30.
Cephren (*Cephis*) 87/21.
Ceraunia 327/18.
Cerberus 129/29.

Index of Proper Names 461

Ceres 22/18; 35/15; 40/27; 41/2; 129/20; 310/7, 9, 14, 20, 28; 313/16; 349/16, 20; 384/20.
Cernê (Cercena) 289/31.
Ceteno. See *Celaeno*.
Cetes 85/16.
Chabinus 274/28.
Chabryes 87/24.
Chaldaeans 39/10; 111/4; 134/26; 166/34; 167/19; 174/6; 175/3, 20; 178/7, 19.
Charmuthas 273/29.
Charon 124/9; 130/24.
Charops 317/14, 31.
Chauon (Chaonas) 153/1.
Cheiron 378/6, 9.
Chelonophagi 243/12.
Chemmis 86/18.
Chemmo (Chenvium) 26/27.
Cherinus. See *Mencherinus*.
Cheronessus (a mistranslation) 264/23; 273/27.
Cherronesus 289/4.
Choromnaei 138/12.
Chrysaor 390/13, 15.
Chrysauri 393/2.
Chyron. See *Cheiron*.
Cifissus. See *Cephisus*.
Cilicia 138/6.
Cilicians 292/26, 32, 34.
City of the Crocodiles 120/14.
Cleio 357/24; 359/1.
Cleitarchus 145/19.
Cocalus 340/24.
Cocodrylla. See *City of the Crocodiles*.
Cocytus (Cochitus) 130/26.
Colchis 39/17; 77/30; 387/17.
Collisthenes. See *Callisthenes*.
Conobitum. See *Canopic*.
Continence (a mistranslation) 244/4; 264/8.
Coromnes. See *Choromnaei*.
Corybantes 294/14.
Cotfloditians (a Skeltonic tribe) 266/2.
Cotta 171/8.
Courte of Fame 7/26.
Creon 367/6; 368/11.
Crete 85/6, 8; 126/23; 307/7, 10, 14; 329/23; 330/1; 336/30; 337/7; 339/1; 380/34; 381/15; 390/21, 24.
Cretê 329/27.
Crisauri. See *Chrysauri*.

Criseus. See *Chrysaor*.
Crito. See *Triton*.
Ctesias of Cnidus 79/30; 138/2; 141/13; 144/28; 145/17, 25; 147/15; 155/19; 158/5; 162/24; 164/27; 179/16.
Curetes 307/11; 329/23.
Cyaxares 179/6, 14.
Cybelê 300/15; 301/11, 26; 303/23; 304/1, 18, 31.
Cybelus 300/5, 16.
Cyclades 51/27; 78/4.
Cymê 293/16.
Cynamolgi (Cynamynyans) 252/36.
Cynegi (Cynecians) 247/4.
Cypriots 157/11.
Cyprus 94/6, 10; 95/1.
Cyrenê 94/14; 282/9; 283/33.
Cyrus 179/10, 17; 181/9; 182/35; 199/19.
Cyte of Fame 21/25.
Cyte of Nilus. See *Nilopolis*.
Cyte of the Sonne. See *Heliopolis*.
Cyte wyth the Hondred Yates. See *Hecatompylon*.

Daedalus 85/4; 129/6; 131/15, 20, 21; 132/2; 340/23; 381/6.
Danaê 362/11.
Danaus 39/14.
Daphnis (son of Hermes) 340/25.
Daphnis (centaur) 376/38.
Darcietus. See *Zarcaeus*.
Dardanus 340/21.
Darius 46/26; 82/7, 12; 128/17, 21; 141/21; 177/10.
Debae (Debeans) 274/29.
Dedalus. See *Daedalus*.
Deianeira (Dianyra) 389/10.
Delians 205/9.
Delos 204/30.
Delphi 369/9.
Delta (of the Nile) 45/34; 47/9.
Demeter 20/10.
Democritus of Abdera 55/28; 129/9; 132/33.
Denmark 38/22.
Denyse the Sircusane. See *Dionysius of Sicily*.
Derbici (Deruices) 138/11.
Derceto 139/28.
Derpos. See *Doupon*.

Deucalion 18/4; 311/14.
Diana 201/21.
Dimetor 351/9.
Dindymê 300/1.
Diodorus Siculus 3/8; 4/18; 5/15.
Diomedes 386/14, 28, 37; 387/4.
Dionisius of Newe 64/1.
Dionysius (historian) 286/32.
Dionysius (of Sicily) 141/26.
Dionysus 18/33, 35; 19/1; 22/17; 24/13; 26/7; 33/16; 35/17; 38/3; 129/20; 131/11; 189/18; 190/1, 3, 34; 223/17; 225/21; 286/35; freq. on pp. 302–56; 375/16, 21; 385/21; Tetyas 319/23, 28.
Dipites. See Petes.
Dirreta. See Derceto.
Dorectice (a mistranslation) 293/12.
Doupon 377/2.
Drangi (Drances) 138/11.

Eacus. See Aeacus.
Ecatius. See Hecataeus.
Ecbatana (Echatans) 153/17, 26; 173/34.
Echinades 273/24.
Egeus. See Augeas.
Egipcyan (the Nile). See Egyptus.
Egipte (son of Nilus). See Egyptus.
Egypt 5/5, 10; 15/4; freq. pp. 17–134; 141/24; 154/26; 165/17; 198/22; 211/25; 223/5; 224/1; 225/29, 33; 226/7, 9; 233/29, 32; 234/14; 236/26; 245/14; 264/29; 282/15; 284/15; 292/19; 327/15; 335/22; 337/5, 34; 338/32; 392/5.
Egyptian (adj.) 23/18; 26/8; 31/17; 39/1, 31; 41/8, 19; 53/19; 61/12; 67/13; 74/33; 82/1; 85/22, 25, 28; 90/18; 95/14; 96/9; 104/31; 116/12; 126/13, 15; 128/22; 129/3; 130/9; 132/10; 133/2, 29; 136/2; 226/19; 234/1, 21; 240/10; 274/18; 346/7.
Egyptian (n. s.) 33/28; 40/10, 17; 94/19.
Egyptians 5/2, 4; freq. pp. 17–138, 225–34; 156/7; 174/9; 206/2; 282/7; 292/22; 308/33; 335/30; 355/8, 37.
Egyptus (the Nile) 28/9, 10; 86/14.
Egyptus (son of Nilus) 73/16, 18.

Elanicus. See Hellanicus.
Electra 306/3.
Electryon 362/12.
Elephantine 119/27.
Eleusis 41/5.
Eleutherae. See Libera.
Eliconyes Well. See Helicon's Well.
Elienses 127/33; 128/2; 319/17.
Eliopolis. See Heliopolis.
Ellespontus. See Hellespont.
Elysian (Fields), Elisius 129/23.
Emodus 183/14.
Emyneus (king of Egypt, a mistranslation) 70/11.
English (language) 46/12; 211/18; 298/11.
Epasus 391/11.
Ephesians 133/12.
Ephorians 195/18.
Ephorus 17/3; 52/32; 56/22; 341/26.
Epirians (a mistranslation) 237/4; Epire 263/23; 294/10; Iles Epirian 263/26; Mount Epirian 270/4.
Eraclidaris. See Heracleidae.
Erato 357/26; 359/25.
Erechtheus 40/17, 23, 32.
Ergamenes 229/7.
Erginus (Erigynus) 366/27; 367/5, 28.
Eriboea (Erubia) 389/5.
Eridanus 298/23.
Eristeus. See Aristaeus.
Eritheus. See Erechtheus.
Erodotus. See Herodotus.
Erotone. See Tretus.
Erutheus. See Hecataeus.
Erymanthus 373/13.
Erytheus. See Erechtheus.
Eryx 340/26.
Esucane (a mistranslation) 45/1.
Etesian (winds) 54/19; 56/2, 15, 17.
Etesias. See Ctesias of Cnidus.
Etesius 54/19.
Ethemasians Iles. See Echinades.
Ethesie, Ethesius. See Etesian.
Ethiocles 11/28.
Ethiopia 26/1; 27/3; 28/14; 31/12; freq. pp. 42–60, 89–93; 123/2; 132/20, 25; 134/16; 155/2, 14; 156/3, 7; 211/26; 213/19; 216/27; 224/31; 225/18; 226/7, 9, 19; 234/2, 14; 236/33; 240/20; 245/14; 257/12; 288/18.

Index of Proper Names 463

Ethiopian (n. s.) 248/25.
Ethiopians 27/23; 46/3; 64/3, 5; 77/14; 83/31; 119/25; 165/6, 17, 24; 216/4, 31; freq. pp. 223-50; 257/32; 259/21; 262/26; 281/33.
Eudoxus 129/9.
Eumolpidae (Eumelipede) 41/7.
Eumolpus 18/34.
Euphrates 39/8; 139/5; 144/31; 145/12; 147/4; 150/29; 151/2; 170/34; 172/25.
Euridice. See Eryx.
Euripides (Euripules) 14/26; 54/32; 55/29.
Europe 10/28; 28/33; 77/28; 78/5; 199/27; 316/26; 339/14; 344/5.
Eurus 281/28.
Eurybia 389/8.
Eurydicê 362/13.
Eurystheus 202/17; 339/11; 363/32; 364/6, 11; 368/20, 29, 33; 369/4, 6, 15; 370/30; 372/12; 373/18; 374/12; 377/9; 378/15, 20; 379/34; 380/14, 34; 381/23; 386/12; 387/12, 22; 390/1, 18.
Euterpê 357/25; 359/3.
Euxeinus 387/27.
Excerces. See Xerxes.
Exion. See Ixion.

Feminy 387/23.
Femur. See Meros.
Fenyce. See Palm Grove.
Fortune 187/6; 202/24; 277/27.

Gabyne. See Chabinus.
Gadeira (Gades) 392/32.
Galaemenes 170/27, 31.
Gallia Comata 11/20.
Gandaridae 186/33; 187/10, 13.
Ganges 77/25; 151/2; 186/28; 187/21.
Garindanes (Garundaneans) 270/14, 28.
Garnade. See Granada.
Gasandi 275/16.
Gedrosia 237/3.
Gerrhaeans 270/10.
Geryones 361/27; 390/4, 13; 393/1.
Getae (Getyans) 126/31.
Glaucopis (Glaropis) 21/1.
Gnefactus Vecoridis. See Tnephachthus.

Gnidius Etesias See Ctesias of Cnidus.
God 2/20; 6/3; 97/19; 127/2; Goddis of counsaill 176/19.
Gorgons 223/14; 287/7; 291/2, 7, 34, 36.
Granada 358/14.
Grecian (adj.) 33/19; 35/31; 224/28.
Greece 28/2; 32/22; 129/5; 132/5, 8; 141/23; 222/22; 345/37; 347/25; 368/9.
Greek (language) 18/27; 46/11; 93/27; 100/10; 229/8; 321/19; 351/9; Grew 205/2.
Greek (n. s.) 166/18; 287/9; 316/22; 336/14.
Greeks, Grecians 3/23; 8/13; freq. pp. 11-40; 53-74; 85/16, 27; 91/25; 93/24, 26, 35; 94/1; 95/16; 100/28; 106/16; 109/2, 32; freq. pp. 118-33; 165/22; 174/23, 25, 34; 175/7, 33; 177/28; 179/24; 182/32; 189/2, 35; 191/3; 204/28, 32; 205/4, 20; 222/18; 252/36; 253/23; 255/5; 260/16; 266/5; 274/23; 288/9, 20, 36; 289/10; 295/13, 25; 306/23; 308/35; 319/2, 15, 28; 320/27; 321/1, 6, 15, 26; 338/1; 343/22, 37; 347/15; 365/27; 394/32; 395/18, 20.
Grew. See Greek (language).

Halcyonê 306/4.
Hannibal 142/1.
Hanochite. See Auschisae.
Happy Island 216/25.
Harmonia 344/18.
Hebrew (language) 127/2.
Hecacembas (a mistranslation) 270/22.
Hecataeus 52/25; 67/14; 203/25.
Hecatompylon 392/23.
Hector 203/9.
Helen 132/5, 8.
Helicon's Well 321/4.
Heliofagians. See Hylophagi.
Heliopolis 80/16; 83/1; 103/14; 114/18; 130/11; 132/12 bis.
Hell 7/15; 35/20; 43/7; 73/7; 119/21; 124/13; 129/30; 130/26; 193/5.
Hellanicus 52/25.
Hellespont 28/32; 138/7; 316/29.
Heracleidae (Heraclydarians) 11/32; 342/1.

Index of Proper Names

Heracleotic (mouth of the Nile) 46/17.
Hercules 7/30; 25/31; 27/35; 28/4; 30/3; freq. pp. 33–35; 191/2, 23; 202/17; 203/2; 225/20; 231/19; 252/21; 275/10, 11; 292/3; 321/31 bis; freq. pp. 338–95.
Hercules Felde 364/18.
Herculeum. See Heracleotic.
Hermaphroditus 340/5; 356/15, 24.
Hermes 25/5.
Herodotus 52/26; 54/5; 55/10; 96/5; 155/18; 178/25; 179/14, 16.
Hesiod 357/15, 22.
Hespera 288/12, 13.
Hesperus 305/21.
Hiberia. See Iberia.
Hippolyté 202/20; 388/3; 389/24.
Hippotion 377/1.
Hister. See Ister.
Homadus 377/7, 13.
Homer 20/3, 17; 21/12; 95/24; 129/6; 132/3, 8; 295/25; 320/11; 321/3; 322/15, 29, 32; 345/37; 357/15, 17.
Horus (Kyng Crosies sonne) 292/21.
Horus (son of Isis) 29/32; 36/13, 19; 38/12; 63/26; 119/19.
Hyapetes 140/33.
Hyberia, Hyberus. See Iberia.
Hydaspes (son of Semiramis) 140/34.
Hydaspes (river of India) 60/19; 187/28.
Hylophagi 246/14, 19.
Hypanis 187/28.
Hyperboreans 135/4; 203/20, 30; 204/25, 33; 205/3, 9; 303/25.
Hyperion 298/8, 10, 16; 304/35.

Iambulus (Iammilus) 215/28; 222/4, 14.
Iao 127/2.
Iapetes. See Hyapetes.
Iason. See Jason.
Iberia 390/6; 392/34, 35.
Iberians (Spaynardis) 395/24.
Ichthyophagi 237/2; 241/16 242/4, 26; 244/22; 266/2; 267/32; 288/31.
Idaea (island of Crete) 307/12; 329/34.
Idaea (wife of Zeus, King of Crete) 307/12.
Idapses, Idaspes. See Hydaspes.

Iithiophagians. See Ichthyophagi.
Ilienses. See Elienses.
Iliopolys. See Heliopolis.
Iliophagians. See Hylophagi.
Ilium 79/25. See Troy.
Inachus 337/34.
Inaros 89/17.
India 28/20, 24, 25, 28; 38/20; 60/17; 77/20, 25; 134/17; 135/1; 156/16, 19 bis, 22; 157/15, 25; freq. 183–97; 211/28; 213/19; 222/12, 24; 223/8; 253/4; 316/22; 347/8, 14, 17.
Indian (adj.) 358/12.
Indian (n. s.) 312/17, 29; 313/12.
Indians 137/33; freq. pp. 157–62; pp. 183–97; 312/26; 313/2; 318/32; 327/13; 343/31; 352/30.
Indus 157/14; 158/24 bis; 159/16; 183/17; 187/21; 280/10.
Ino 344/21.
Inopides. See Oenopides.
Io 35/12; 337/33.
Iolaüs 370/2, 10; 372/34.
Iona (a mistranslation) 58/7.
Ionia 92/12.
Ioppe. See Joppa.
Iperion. See Hyperion.
Iradeum 365/28.
Isis freq. pp. 18–38; 63/12, 26; 117/24 bis; 119/19; 129/20; 231/19; 272/32, 355/17.
Isocrates 341/26.
Isoples 377/1.
Ister 38/21.
Italians 113/24.
Italy 142/2; 252/10, 307/21.
Ithyphallus 355/38.
Iubiter, etc. See Jupiter.
Iulius Cezar. See Caesar.
Iuno. See Juno.
Iupiter, etc. See Jupiter.
Ixion 374/30, 34.

Jason 387/17.
Jews 39/17, 78/2; 127/1.
Joppa 43/12.
Juno 21/29; 22/11; 23/24; 34/19; 35/16; 70/24; 132/20; 149/2, 8; 295/28; 314/7, 16; 345/15; freq. pp. 363–6; 369/33; 374/31, 35; 387/13.

Index of Proper Names 465

Jupiter freq. pp. 11–12; 20–24; 32–35; 63/28; 65/16; 67/12, 19; 70/23; 95/6; 118/20; 126/25; 132/19, 23, 25; 148/2, 19; 149/1, 3, 16; 152/14; 154/28; 162/12; 172/19; 179/13; 190/1; 202/17; 224/29; 231/20; 287/9; 292/1; freq. pp. 307–14; 328/11; 334/14; 335/23, 28; 337/4, 25, 29, 33, 37; 339/5, 7, 23; 344/21, 25; 345/1, 10, 15, 25, 36; 349/9, 11, 25; 357/5; 362/11, 24; 363/7, 9, 24, 33; 365/7; 368/32; 369/1, 8, 30; 374/32; 382/11; 384/31; 385/17, 21, 26; 386/3; 390/29.
Jupiter (planet) 176/1.

Krete. See *Crete.*
Kyng of Marcedony. See *Perseus.*

Labyrinth 84/32; 120/20; 131/16.
Lacedaemon 12/2; 126/24; 316/23.
Lacedaemonians 103/18.
Laeanites (gulf) 271/12.
Latin 11/3; 20/11.
Latona 204/6.
Launtes. See *Laeanites.*
Lebanon 327/15.
Lectrie. See *Electryon.*
Lenaeus 352/23.
Leofera. See *Memnonian.*
Leontopolis (*Leontes*) 114/20.
Lernae 372/16.
Lesbos 293/19.
Letheofagians. See *Ichthyophagi.*
Libany. See *Lebanon.*
Libera 347/3.
Liber Pater 347/4.
Libicus 281/28.
Libya (mother of Belus by Neptune) 39/7; 391/10.
Libya (country) 26/2; 33/30; freq. pp. 42–45; 54/6; 55/12, 22; 59/29; 66/11; 75/25; 86/21; 91/6; 92/14; 120/3; 131/3; 132/23; 154/26; 156/31; 158/15; 184/6; 210/13; 211/27; 213/19, 25; 223/2; 232/11; 250/23; 252/26; 286/3, 8, 16; 287/4; 289/2, 22; 292/7, 19; 295/7; 307/21; 320/17; 323/3, 16; 327/16; 332/22; 339/1; 390/31; 391/9, 12, 32; 392/16, 29.

Libyan (adj.) 330/21.
Libyans 54/11; 223/13; 224/5; 232/18; 282/6, 11, 21, 24; 283/5; 320/35; 333/18; 334/24; 337/31; 339/29; 391/7.
Linus 303/18; 321/14, 18, 27; 322/5, 24.
Lolaus. See *Iolaüs.*
Lombardy 11/19, 23; 12/4.
Lucina 20/23; 363/30.
Luna 298/11, 24.
Lycia 138/6.
Lycopolis 119/28.
Lycurgus (of Sparta) 126/23, 25; 129/7; 132/28.
Lycurgus (King of Thrace) 28/33; 294/26; 316/23, 27; 317/6, 19, 26; 318/17; 348/18.
Lydia 138/6.
Lydians 299/31.
Lyneuer. See *Lenaeus.*

Macae 282/19.
Macedon 26/16, 19; 29/3.
Macedonia 29/4; 64/4; 136/24; 158/12; 206/34.
Macedonians 9/24; 64/11; 128/33.
Maea 306/3, 11.
Maenads 347/36.
Maeotis 77/29; 198/1, 26.
Magaverians. See *Megabari.*
Magna Mater. See *Basileia.*
Mandanes. See *Maudaces.*
Maranitae (*Maraneans*) 270/13, 26.
Marcedony. See *Macedonia.*
Marcias. See *Marsyas.*
Marcury. See *Mercury.*
Maria (*Mariage*) 94/28.
Marmaridae 282/15.
Maro. See *Marrus.*
Maron 26/30; 29/1, 2.
Maronea 29/3.
Marpé 389/10.
Marrus 84/30; 131/18.
Mars 142/24; 160/24; 198/13; 200/15; 201/21; 203/5; 306/12; 331/10; 369/21; 376/20.
Mars (planet) 176/1.
Marsyas the Phrygian 300/32; 302/3, 14, 18, 22, 26, 27; 303/2, 9, 11.
Marus. See *Inaros.*
Massagetae 198/29.

466 Index of Proper Names

Maudaces 179/29.
Meander 57/25.
Mede (n. s.) 166/27.
Medea 340/10.
Medes 143/18; 144/35; 164/26; 166/29; 167/20, 30; 173/37; 178/22, 28; 179/7, 14, 25; 180/22; 181/2, 7, 11, 12, 16, 19, 20; 182/28; 183/1, 6; 199/1.
Media 66/33; 134/22, 24; 137/18, 30; 150/31; 151/5; 152/13, 26; 154/12; 168/26; 173/35; 180/29; 206/32; 252/13.
Medusa (Medrusa) 292/1.
Megabari 254/23.
Megara 368/18; 370/11.
Meïon 300/1.
Melampus (Melampedes) 129/6; 131/10.
Melanchaetes 377/1.
Melanippê 387/24; 389/16, 26.
Melpomenê 357/25; 359/14.
Memnon 164/31; 165/8, 10, 18.
Memnonian (highway) 165/16, 17.
Memnonian (palace of Memno in Susa) 165/15.
Memory. See Mnemosyne.
Memphis (sacred bull) 30/32.
Memphis (city) 31/8; 52/2; 57/35; 66/10; 71/27; 72/13, 15, 25; 73/12, 25; 80/4, 25; 82/8; 86/18, 22; 90/31; 92/1, 13, 18, 24; 103/14; 114/17; 115/11, 19, 28; 130/13; 131/4, 23; 132/1, 17.
Menadyens. See Maenads.
Menalyppe. See Melanippê.
Menas 63/13; 64/26; 120/7; 126/16.
Mencherinus 88/13.
Mendes (city of Egypt) (Mideta) 114/18.
Mendes (king of Egypt) (Mendetus) 84/29, 131/17.
Mendesian (mouth of the Nile) 46/15.
Menê (island) 288/34.
Menê (the moon) 299/6.
Menelaus 79/25.
Menestheus 40/9.
Mennenia. See Memnonian.
Menno (a mistranslation) 68/7.
Mennon, Mennona. See Memnon.
Menoes. See Meïon.
Menones. See Onnes.

Meotidas, Meotis. See Maeotis.
Mercuriall (stars) 176/2.
Mercury (god) 20/23; 21/30; 24/20; 25/4, 29; 29/19; 38/8; 63/14; 126/21; 129/26; 130/2; 306/14; 345/27; 356/21; 384/13.
Mercury (planet) 176/1.
Merina. See Myrina.
Meroë (city) 45/22, 28.
Meroë (island) 44/19; 45/22; 53/32; 230/5.
Meropê 306/4.
Meros ('thigh' hills of India) 189/33.
Merres. See Meroë.
Mesopotamia 151/5.
Messagetians. See Massagetae.
Metrophorus. See Mitrephorus.
Metroplite. See Napata.
Micerynus. See Mencherinus.
Midas 304/24.
Mideta. See Mendes.
Minaeans 270/10.
Minerva 25/11; 327/24; 328/12; 330/28; 337/5; 364/19, 22, 29.
Mineus 395/11.
Mingades 395/20.
Minos 85/6; 126/23, 24; 340/23; 381/20.
Minotaur 85/7; 340/23; 361/24; 381/13.
Minyans (Mynyeris) 366/28; 368/5.
Mirida, Mirides, Miris. See Moeris.
Mirrenys. See Mnevis.
Misra. See Phrygia.
Mitrephorus 351/2.
Mitylenê 293/20.
Mnemosynê 357/6; 359/14.
Mnevis 114/18; 119/2.
Moeris (the Fayûm) 74/16; 114/19; 120/9.
Moeris (lake in Libya) 91/7.
Moeris (King of Egypt), Miris 73/24; 74/30.
Moon (as goddess) 35/16.
Mopides Chius. See Oenopides.
Mopsus the Thracian 294/24, 34.
Moses 127/1.
Mount of Taurus. See Tauri.
Musaeus 129/6.
Muses 27/14; 303/16; 322/11; 325/35; 340/6; 353/31; 357/1, 5, 19; 358/14, 26; 360/13.

Index of Proper Names

Mycenaeans 371/8.
Mycerinus 88/12, 24.
Mynas. See Menas.
Mynyans, Mynyeris, Mynyons. See Minyans.
Myrina (Queen of the Amazons) 289/14; 291/4, 8, 12, 27; 292/18; 295/1.
Myrina (city) 290/27; 293/13.
Myrrhanus 316/22.

Nabataeans 206/5; 207/4; 271/14.
Nalanchetes. See Melanchaetes.
Napae 198/16.
Napata 230/4.
Napes 198/12.
Nasamones 54/7; 282/12.
Nature 49/12; 58/26; 162/27; 166/5; 233/17; 246/5; 256/17; 272/11; 276/8, 20; 300/17; 344/32; 356/17; 357/20; 364/33; 371/21.
Naxians (Naxiences) 319/17.
Necho (Nechaus) 46/25.
Neleus 340/17.
Nemea 371/1, 9.
Nemphes, etc. See Nymphs.
Neptune 39/7; 269/9; 384/9. See Posidium.
Nicator Sileucus. See Seleucus Nicator.
Nile 5/10, 12; 15/5; 17/16; 18/15; 20/20; 27/26; 28/10, 12, 15; 41/21; 42/7; freq. pp. 44–49; 51–63; 71–73; 79–82; 86/13, 22; 87/14; 93/8; 110/12; 112/25; 120/1; freq. pp. 130–7; 151/1; 183/18; 198/22; 225/32; 230/9; 232/11; 345/31; 346/6.
Nilopolis 115/25.
Nilus (King of Egypt) 73/13; 86/13.
Nilus Portus 31/13.
Nina 293/15.
Ninus, Nina (city) 139/17; 140/33; 144/34; 166/30; 168/1, 7, 15; 171/13; 172/33.
Ninus (son of Semiramis) 144/25; 154/33; 162/7.
Ninus (King of Asia) freq. pp. 134–7; 141–7; 164–5; 174/1.
Ninus (Kyng of Ynde), Skelton's error for Myrrhanus 316/22.
Niobé 340/20; 384/31, 33.

Nymphs 306/30; 314/29; 325/35; 345/33; 346/9.
Nysa (daughter of Aristaeus) 326/8.
Nysa (city of Arabia) 24/9, 14, 18; 38/2; 302/11; 314/27; 318/20; 320/15, 21; 323/4; 324/10; 330/14, 18; 331/4; 345/30, 35; 346/3.
Nysa (city of India) 28/21, 24.
Nysaean Gates 324/16.
Nysium 317/21.

Oabreus. See Chabryes.
Ocean (the Nile) 28/7; 130/9.
Oceané 20/16, 17, 18, 20; 38/23; 53/20; 77/26; 130/5, 10; 135/7; 183/13; 186/31; 187/23; 198/23; 203/27; 215/23; 223/7; 243/13; 263/18; 269/11; 288/16, 21; 289/11; 295/20; 28, 304/33; 305/6; 320/18; 323/3; 390/7; freq. pp. 392–4.
Oeagrus 318/5.
Oenomaus 340/20.
Oenopides of Chios 59/18; 129/9; 132/34.
Ogdous (a mistranslation) 71/25.
Olympiad 11/27; 63/29; 67/12; 95/5; 179/13.
Olympic Games 127/34; 382/1, 6, 8, 27.
Olympian (gods) 339/26; 385/20.
Olympus 335/26.
Omades, Omados. See Homadus.
Omer. See Homer.
Onnes 140/30; 144/19.
Ophiodes 264/26.
Opis 149/2, 5.
Orchomenians 368/4.
Oreius 377/1.
Orion 340/26.
Orographia 37/7.
Orontes 154/2.
Oros. See Horus.
Orpheus 19/1; 20/12; 32/15, 23; 33/7, 19; 95/24; 124/11; 129/6, 16; 130/1, 2; 303/18; 310/30; 318/9, 12; 321/31; 322/17, 27.
Orus. See Horus.
Osiris 18/26, 27; freq. pp. 22–38; 70/19; 115/35; 117/24, 25, 27; 119/2, 6, 7, 13, 20; 129/20; 225/27; 343/21; 355/11.
Osymandyas 67/21; 68/18; 71/9.

468 Index of Proper Names

Out yles. See Cyclades.
Oxyartes 142/16.

Palenes. See Pallenê.
Palestine 270/9.
Pali 198/16.
Palibothra (Palicotra) 191/20; 222/16.
Pallas 20/25; 326/19; 327/23; 383/29; 384/7.
Pallenê 385/15.
Palm Grove 269/13; 270/3, 18.
Palus 198/12.
Pamphylia 138/6.
Pan 20/23; 26/22, 28; 35/19; 231/19.
Paniticum. See Tanitic.
Panormus 263/22.
Pantasilea. See Penthesileia.
Paphlagonia 171/6, 198/34.
Paraetacenê (Paratrynes, Paretans) 150/31; 151/5.
Paraetonium (Paretony) 43/11.
Paris 207/12.
Parmenides of Camarina 95/6.
Parsean. See Persian.
Parsondes (Parsodes) 180/3.
Parthyaei (Parthes) 138/12.
Pasiphaê 380/35, 36.
Pastophori 41/10.
Pelasgian (letters) 322/26, 33; Pelasgians 321/25.
Pelasgians ('theym of Pelasgye') 321/25.
Pelias (Peleus) 340/11.
Peloponnesians 275/8.
Peloponnesus 381/22.
Pelops 340/20.
Pelusiac (mouth of the Nile) 46/14, 22.
Pelusium 80/16, 30; 92/23.
Peneius 395/7.
Penthesileia 203/4.
Pentheus 316/22; 348/18.
Permedies Camarineus. See Parmenides of Camarina.
Persephonê. See Proserpina.
Perseus 287/7; 292/1; 362/11; 'Kyng of Marcedony' 158/12.
Persia 46/26; 64/4; 66/33; 78/5; 136/24; 148/17; 149/18; 182/35; 199/20; 206/32; 222/20.

Persian (n. s.) 149/29; 180/3.
Persians 48/3; 64/6; 66/28; 71/8; 82/6; 95/4; 165/9, 14; 167/21, 31; 179/11, 21; 181/9, 12, 19; 183/1; 363/27.
Persis (people of), Persians 138/13; 154/12.
Persius 35/10.
Pessynute. See Pisinus.
Petes 40/9.
Petra 270/9.
Phallus (Phalon) 32/8.
Pharnus 137/18.
Pharos 43/13.
Phatnitic (Pheniticum, mouth of the Nile) 46/15.
Phenyce. See Phoenicia and Palm Grove.
Philip of Macedon 9/25.
Philippis 388/31.
Phirigians. See Phrygians.
Phocae 270/4.
Phoceans 57/30.
Phoebê 389/8.
Phoebus 19/1; 321/5; 324/26.
Phoenicia 24/16; 25/36; 94/7, 9; 123/15; 321/24; 327/14; 344/4, 7; 345/32; 346/6.
Phoenician (letters) 321/24.
Phoenicians 91/25; 94/11; 138/5; 157/11; 321/17.
Pholoê (Mount Pholus) 375/10; 378/4.
Pholus 375/8, 20, 32, 34; 377/17, 18.
Phoroneus (Phroroneus) 384/31.
Phrixus 377/2.
Phrygia 138/6, 7; 327/7, 9.
(the) Phrygian (poem) 323/13.
Phrygians 293/5; 299/30, 31; 303/26; 304/16, 20, 32.
Phrynya. See Prienê.
Picthogoras. See Pythagoras.
Pingenius. See Pyrigenes.
Pirhius. See Pythian Apollo.
Pisinus 304/20.
Pitana 293/16.
Plato 129/8; 132/28.
Pleiades 306/29.
Pliopoli. See Heliopolis.
Pluto 35/18, 20. See also Palus.
Plutons. See Pali.
Poggius 4/19.

Index of Proper Names

Polimina, Polinnya. See *Polymnia*.
Polimnia. See *Polydamna*.
Polusio. See *Pelusium*.
Polycrates 128/4, 11, 16.
Polydamna 132/9.
Polydorus 344/21.
Polymnia 357/26; 359/34.
Pontus 198/34.
Poort Nisian. See *Nysaean Gates*.
Posidium 269/7.
Potana 280/9.
Priam 165/3; 340/22.
Priapus 340/5; 354/18, 23; 355/4, 10, 34; 356/1.
Prienê 293/16.
Prometheus (*Promothe*) 27/30, 32; 28/5; 385/28.
Pronapides 322/28.
Propontis 138/8.
Proserpina 313/15, 17; 349/25.
Proteus 85/17, 36.
Prothoê 388/33.
Prudence 331/13.
Psammetichus of Sais (*Psammichus Sactes*) 46/26; 91/23; 92/2, 10, 16; 93/21; 94/4.
Psebaean (*Pseuerans*) 268/12; 269/5.
Ptolemaïs 268/6.
Ptolemy I 43/31; 67/8, 15; 115/9, 13.
Ptolemy II 47/2; 53/5, 8; 229/6; 260/7, 20; 262/21.
Ptolemy III 240/12; 269/10.
Ptolemy XI 64/1; 113/21.
Ptolemy (stream) 47/6.
Pygion. See *Alpheius*.
Pyrigenes 352/27.
Pythagoras of Samos 95/25; 129/8; 132/30.
Pythian Apollo (mistranslated to *Pirhius, the ymage of Apollo*) 133/9.

Rarofagians. See *Rhizophagi*.
Rea Pandoxa. See *Rhea*.
Red Sea 28/19; 46/24; 47/2; 77/17; 151/8; 213/19; 234/11; 240/10.
Regina. See *Basileia*.
Rhea (i.e. *Pandora*) 21/28; 22/10; 297/26; 307/1; 323/16; 324/8; 326/13; 328/35; 329/13; 333/33; 334/7, 13; 335/23.
Rhicius. See *Rhoecus*.
Rhinocolura 84/8.

Rhizophagi 245/16.
Rhodes 257/10.
Rhodopis 89/18.
Rhoecus 133/8.
Rinocera. See *Rhinocolura*.
Rodosude. See *Rhodopis*.
Romans 11/1, 20, 24; 113/26, 30; 141/29; 158/14.
Rombes (a mistranslation) 138/12.
Rome (city) 10/34.
Rome (empire) 11/24; 113/22; 263/14.
Roodes. See *Rhodes*.

Sabaco (*Sabacus*) 89/24.
Sabae 278/11; 279/5.
Sabaeans 276/2.
Sebazius (*Sabasis*) 349/26.
Sacae (*Saceans*) 181/16, 19, 22; 198/28.
Sacra Gleba 83/14.
Sagans. See *Sacae*.
Sagrus. See *Oeagrus*.
Salamenus. See *Galaemenes*.
Samathicus. See *Psammetichus*.
Samians 128/3.
Samius Pichthogaras. See *Pythagoras*.
Samos 133/26; 294/6.
Samothrace 294/3, 7.
Saortes. See *Oxyartes*.
Sapience 2/19.
Sarapis 35/17, 19.
Sardanapallus 134/20; 164/22, 24; 165/28; 167/14, 22; 168/5, 10, 19, 30; 170/13, 26; 172/19, 28, 31; 179/28.
Sasychis (*Sasochis*) 127/10.
Saturn (planet) 175/34.
Saturn (god) 21/28; 22/9; 38/10, 18, 24; 131/13, 18; 305/2; 306/34; 307/20, 30; 308/2; 323/17; 329/12; 330/3, 17, 36; 331/35; 333/27; 334/10, 12; 335/23.
Saturnes Places 307/29.
Satyrs 27/5, 17; 353/21, 29, 34.
Sauromatae 109/2.
Scicyle, Scissill. See *Sicily*.
Scrotophagians. See *Struthophagi*.
Scythes (*Scitha*) 198/7.
Scythia 60/15; 183/15; 199/16.
Scythians 77/27; 135/4; 141/22; 183/15; 188/6; 197/23, 25; 198/3, 8;

Index of Proper Names

199/4, 8; 202/8; 255/34; 257/8; 294/28, 31.
(*the*) *Se.* See *Pontus*.
Sebennytic (mouth of the Nile) 46/16.
Seileni (*Sylenes*) 332/11.
Seilenus 332/12, 14; 350/18.
Seisachtheia (*Sisacertheam*) 108/34.
Seleucus Nicator 177/12.
Semelê 32/14, 26; 33/6, 17; 202/17; 311/4, 5, 8; 314/2, 11, 13, 22; 338/1; 339/24; 344/21, 23, 31; 345/8; 350/4; 384/32; 385/1.
Semiramis 79/32; freq. pp. 134–64; 225/15.
Semiramis Way 153/25.
Serapis. See *Sarapis*.
Serbonis 42/16.
Sesoösis 74/30; 75/20; 76/8; 78/11; 79/37; 82/8, 10, 20; 127/16.
Seven Sages 54/18.
Shitio. See *Scythia*.
Sichthiophagians. See *Ichthyophagi*.
Sicily 11/1; 141/26; 203/28; 307/21, 28.
Sidon 94/8.
Silenus. See *Seilenus*.
Silice. See *Cilicia*.
Silla (river of India) 188/16.
Silla (a mistranslation) 188/17.
Simandius. See *Osymandyas*.
Simi (Simyans) 249/27; 250/11.
Simmas (*Sinma*) 140/22, 31.
Simmias 240/15.
Sipylus 294/28, 34.
Sirces. See *Syrtes*.
Sirënes. See *Cyrenê*.
Sisacertheam. See *Seisachtheia*.
Skelton 12/19.
Socrates. See *Isocrates*.
Sol 21/31; 298/11, 22, 31.
Solon 95/25; 105/25; 108/33; 129/8; 132/28.
Sosanê 144/13.
Sosarmus (*Sosarmones*) 179/30.
Sotiras (a mistranslation) 266/4.
Spain 393/4, 7.
Spaniards (i.e. Iberians) 395/24.
Spartan 129/7.
Spermatophagi (*Spermacophagians*) 246/15.
Stabrobates (*Staurobates*) 156/20; 158/18; 160/21.

Steropê (*Asteropes*) 306/4.
Sterres in nombre vij. See *Pleiades*.
Stimphalidas. See *Stymphalian Lake*.
(*the*) *Stone.* See *Petra*.
Struthophagi 249/28.
Stymphalian Lake 252/23; 379/11.
Suberniticum. See *Sebennytic*.
(*the*) *Sun* 20/23; 21/28; 36/24.
Susa (*Susis*) 165/12.
Susianans (*Suasions*, etc.) 138/13; 165/7.
Sylenes. See *Seileni*.
Symandius. See *Osymandyas*.
Syphalus. See *Ithyphallus*.
Syracusan 47/18; 141/26.
Syria 42/15; 43/12; 80/15; 92/30; 138/5, 21; 139/26; 206/32; 210/9; 213/15, 27; 214/18.
Syrian (adj.) 152/22.
Syrians 140/7, 25; 149/27; 157/11; 162/21; 206/2; 292/25.
Syrinthe. See *Tiryns*.
Syrtes (*Sirces*) 282/10, 20; 284/19.

Tamyris, etc. See *Thamyras*.
Tanäis 77/27; 137/24; 198/2, 19; 199/1; 201/6, 27.
Tanitic (mouth of the Nile) 46/15.
Tantalus 340/20.
Tapyri 138/11.
Tauri 268/6; 271/23; 293/1; 323/20; 327/11.
Tauropolian (festival) 201/24.
Taÿgetê 306/4.
Teans 319/17.
Tebans. See *Thebans*.
Tecmessa 389/10.
Telecles (*Teledeus*) 133/8, 11.
Telemachus 132/5.
Tempê 394/33.
Tereus. See *Thereus*.
Termodons. See *Thermodon*.
Terpsichorê 357/25; 359/20.
Terra 297/23; 357/9.
Tethys 20/19; 295/27.
Tetians. See *Teans*.
Tetyas. See *Dionysus*.
Teutamus 164/33; 165/5.
Thaleia 357/25; 359/7.
Thales 54/17.
Thamudeni (*Thamodomans*) 273/22.
Thamyras 303/18; 321/31; 322/5.

Index of Proper Names

Thanais, Thanaus. See *Tanäis.*
Tharopes. See *Charops.*
Thebaid 17/25; 23/14; 26/26; 68/2; 88/18. See *Thebes.*
Thebans 32/18; 33/10, 15; 118/18; 366/22, 26.
Thebas (mistranslated as a person) 118/15.
Thebes (city of Boeotia) 318/32; 340/14; 344/17; 366/9; 367/3, 7; 368/11.
Thebes (city of Egypt) 15/4; 23/17, 21; 24/3; 31/23; 32/14, 26; 65/16, 25, 33; 66/10; 67/15; 71/12; 72/12, 14; 80/20; 90/11; 103/14; 132/10, 12; 314/3.
Theledius. See *Telecles.*
Themiscyra (*Themestria*) 201/1; 387/29.
Thenijs. See *Thon.*
Theodorus 133/8, 12.
Theomodons. See *Thermodon.*
Theonis. See *Thonis.*
Theopompus 52/32; 342/1.
Thereus 377/1.
Thermodon 200/1, 35; 286/5; 387/28.
Thermyssa. See *Tecmessa.*
Theseus 340/13; 389/25.
Thesmophorus 35/15.
Thessalians 165/23.
Thessaly 395/7, 16.
Thetis, etc. See *Tethys.*
Thion, Thion Semeles. See *Semelê.*
Thiphon, etc. See *Typhon.*
Tholomache. See *Telemachus.*
Tholomaeus Lagus. See *Ptolemy I.*
Thon 132/9.
Thonis 28/11.
Thrace 28/34; 78/8; 198/20; 201/29; 294/27; 316/23; 317/37; 318/18; 386/32.
Thracians 294/6, 32; 295/5; 316/28; 317/3, 4; 347/15; 386/14.
Thucydides 52/30.
Thymoetes 322/34.
Thyonê. See *Semelê.*
Thyphone. See *Typhon.*
Tigris 150/29; 151/3.
Tiphones. See *Tychon.*
Tiritus. See *Tyrcaeus.*
Tiryns 366/8.
Titaea (*Titana*) 297/16, 18.

Titans (*Titians*) 36/14; 131/13; 223/17; 297/18; 308/3; 323/17; 329/10, 16; 330/17, 34; 331/1, 19; 333/11; 336/28; 337/2, 18, 27; 339/22, 24; 355/10, 20.
Tithonus (Titan, *Titanas*) 164/31; 165/8, 26.
Tnephachthus 65/4.
Togloditica. See *Trogodyta.*
Trace. See *Thrace.*
Tracians, etc. See *Thracians.*
Tretus 371/11.
Triathericum 347/19.
Tridonidas. See *Tritonis.*
Triptolemus 26/31; 29/5.
Triton (*Tritoma*) 288/17; 324/13; 326/18, 19.
Tritonis 288/16; 289/5; 292/13.
Troad 138/6.
Trogodyta 237/6.
Trogodytes (*Trogloditians*) 42/9; 53/25; 236/33; 253/22; 254/19, 23; 255/26, 34; 256/22; 257/32; 259/16; 263/20; 264/5; 269/3; 281/34.
Trojans 34/27; 79/27; 164/31; 165/1, 20; 203/8; 321/11.
Trojans 34/27; 79/27; 164/31; 165/1, 20; 203/8; 321/11.
Troy (see also *Ilium*) 3/10; 4/8; 11/12, 17, 29; 12/8; 34/3, 6; 40/10; 85/18; 165/3, 6; 203/3; 224/29; 339/9; 340/22.
Troy (city of Egypt) 79/24, 30.
Tucidides. See *Thucydides.*
Tychon 356/1.
Typhon 22/16; 29/27, 33; 31/29; 116/2; 119/5, 7, 20, 22.
Tyrcaeus 263/25.

Uchoreus 71/26.
Urania 357/26; 359/38.
Uranus 295/31; 297/6, 14, 24; 304/36; 307/6; 323/16; 357/8.

Valaus. See *Iolaüs.*
Varon. See *Marrus.*
Vchoreus. See *Uchoreus.*
Venicians. See *Phoenicians.*
Venus (goddess) 22/16; 26/13; 132/15; 139/30; 277/16; 323/24; 354/24; 356/21.
Venus (planet) 176/1.

Index of Proper Names

Venyce. See *Phoenicia.*
Venycians. See *Phoenicians.*
Vesta 21/30; 126/32.
Volgios. See *Bolgii.*
Vorcanes. See *Borcanii.*
Vrania. See *Urania.*
Vulcan 20/5; 21/29, 33; 22/5; 31/9; 76/7; 80/25; 81/7, 8; 115/29; 131/22; 383/34; 384/8.

Watre of Ynde. See *Indus.*
Welthy Ireland. See *Happy Island.*
Wilde Lande. See *Phocae.*
Wulcan, etc. See *Vulcan.*

Xenophon 3/5, 22; 52/29.
Xerxes 82/7; 128/17; 141/23; 178/26.
Xiaxares. See *Cyaxares.*

Ypolite, &c. See *Hippolytê.*

Zabirna (*Zambirea*) 332/22.
Zalmoxis (*Zamolxis*) 126/31.
Zarcaeus 153/18.
Zarina 181/23.
Zathraustes (*Zotrastes*) 126/30.
Zenophontes. See *Xenophon.*
Zepherus 250/23; 281/28.

EARLY ENGLISH TEXT SOCIETY

OFFICERS AND COUNCIL

Honorary Director
Professor NORMAN DAVIS, F.B.A., Merton College, Oxford

Professor J. A. W. BENNETT
R. W. BURCHFIELD
Professor BRUCE DICKINS, F.B.A.
Professor E. J. DOBSON
A. I. DOYLE
Professor P. HODGSON

Professor G. KANE, F.B.A.
Miss P. M. KEAN
N. R. KER, F.B.A.
Professor J. R. R. TOLKIEN
Professor D. WHITELOCK, F.B.A.
Professor R. M. WILSON

Editorial Secretary
Dr. P. O. E. GRADON, St. Hugh's College, Oxford

Executive Secretary
Dr. A. M. HUDSON, Lady Margaret Hall, Oxford

Bankers
THE NATIONAL WESTMINSTER BANK LTD., Cornmarket Street, Oxford

---

THE Subscription to the Society, which constitutes full membership for private members and libraries, is £3·15 (U.S. members $9.00, Canadian members Can. $9.50) a year for the annual publications in the Original Series, due in advance on the 1st of JANUARY, and should be paid by Cheque, Postal Order, or Money Order made out to 'The Early English Text Society', to Dr. A. M. Hudson, Executive Secretary, Early English Text Society, Lady Margaret Hall, Oxford.

The payment of the annual subscription is the only prerequisite of membership.

Private members of the Society (but not libraries) may select other volumes of the Society's publications instead of those for the current year. The value of texts allowed against one annual subscription is £5·00, and all such transactions must be made through the Executive Secretary.

Members of the Society (including institutional members) may also, through the Executive Secretary, purchase copies of past E.E.T.S. publications and reprints for their own use at a discount of 30% of the listed prices.

The Society's texts are also available to non-members at listed prices through any bookseller.

The Society's texts are published by the Oxford University Press.

The Early English Text Society was founded in 1864 by Frederick James Furnivall, with the help of Richard Morris, Walter Skeat, and others, to bring the mass of unprinted Early English literature within the reach of students and provide sound texts from which the New English Dictionary could quote. In 1867 an Extra Series was started of texts already printed but not in satisfactory or readily obtainable editions.

In 1921 the Extra Series was discontinued and all the publications of 1921 and subsequent years have since been listed and numbered as part of the Original Series. Since 1921 just over a hundred new volumes have been issued; and since 1957 alone more than a hundred and thirty volumes have been reprinted at a cost of £65,000. In 1970 the first of a new Supplementary Series was published; books in this series will be issued as funds allow.

In this prospectus the Original Series and Extra Series for the years 1867–1920 are amalgamated, so as to show all the publications of the Society in a single list.

LIST OF PUBLICATIONS
Original Series, 1864–1971. Extra Series, 1867–1920

O.S. 1. Early English Alliterative Poems, ed. R. Morris. *(Reprinted 1965.)* £2·70 — 1864
2. Arthur, ed. F. J. Furnivall. *(Reprinted 1965.)* 50p — ,,
3. Lauder on the Dewtie of Kyngis, &c., 1556, ed. F. Hall. *(Reprinted 1965.)* 90p — ,,
4. Sir Gawayne and the Green Knight, ed. R. Morris. *(Out of print, see O.S. 210.)* — ,,
5. Hume's Orthographie and Congruitie of the Britan Tongue, ed. H. B. Wheatley. *(Reprinted 1965.)* 90p — 1865
6. Lancelot of the Laik, ed. W. W. Skeat. *(Reprinted 1965.)* £2·10 — ,,
7. Genesis & Exodus, ed. R. Morris. *(Out of print.)* — ,,
8. Morte Arthure, ed. E. Brock. *(Reprinted 1967.)* £1·25 — ,,
9. Thynne on Speght's ed. of Chaucer, A.D. 1599 ed. G. Kingsley and F. J. Furnivall. *(Reprinted 1965.)* £2·75 — ,
10. Merlin, Part I, ed. H. B. Wheatley. *(Out of print.)* — ,,
11. Lyndesay's Monarche, &c., ed. J. Small. Part I. *(Out of print.)* — ,,
12. The Wright's Chaste Wife, ed. F. J. Furnivall. *(Reprinted 1965.)* 50p — ,,
13. Seinte Marherete, ed. O. Cockayne. *(Out of print, see O.S. 193.)* — 1866
14. King Horn, Floriz and Blauncheflur, &c., ed. J. R. Lumby, re-ed. G. H. McKnight. *(Reprinted 1962.)* £2·50 — ,,
15. Political, Religious, and Love Poems, ed. F. J. Furnivall. *(Reprinted 1965.)* £3·15 — ,,
16. The Book of Quinte Essence, ed. F. J. Furnivall. *(Reprinted 1965.)* 50p — ,,
17. Parallel Extracts from 45 MSS. of Piers the Plowman, ed. W. W. Skeat. *(Out of print.)* — ,,
18. Hali Meidenhad, ed. O. Cockayne, re-ed. F. J. Furnivall. *(Out of print.)* — ,,
19. Lyndesay's Monarche, &c., ed. J. Small. Part II. *(Out of print.)* — ,,
20. Richard Rolle de Hampole, English Prose Treatises of, ed. G. G. Perry. *(Out of print.)* — ,,
21. Merlin, ed. H. B. Wheatley. Part II. *(Out of print.)* — ,,
22. Partenay or Lusignen, ed. W. W. Skeat. *(Out of print.)* — ,,
23. Dan Michel's Ayenbite of Inwyt, ed. R. Morris and P. Gradon. Vol. I, Text. *(Reissued 1965.)* £2·70 — ,,
24. Hymns to the Virgin and Christ; The Parliament of Devils, &c., ed. F. J. Furnivall. *(Out of print.)* — 1867
25. The Stacions of Rome, the Pilgrims' Sea-voyage, with Clene Maydenhod, ed. F. J. Furnivall. *(Out of print.)* — ,,
26. Religious Pieces in Prose and Verse, from R. Thornton's MS., ed. G. G. Perry. *(See under 1913.) (Out of print.)* — ,,
27. Levins' Manipulus Vocabulorum, a rhyming Dictionary, ed. H. B. Wheatley. *(Out of print.)* — ,,
28. William's Vision of Piers the Plowman, ed. W. W. Skeat. A–Text. *(Reprinted 1968.)* £1·75 — ,,
29. Old English Homilies (1220–30), ed. R. Morris. Series I, Part I. *(Out of print.)* — ,,
30. Pierce the Ploughmans Crede, ed. W. W. Skeat. *(Out of print.)* — ,,
E.S. 1. William of Palerne or William and the Werwolf, re-ed. W. W. Skeat. *(Out of print.)* — ,,
2. Early English Pronunciation, by A. J. Ellis. Part I. *(Out of print.)* — ,,
O.S. 31. Myrc's Duties of a Parish Priest, in Verse, ed. E. Peacock. *(Out of print.)* — 1868
32. Early English Meals and Manners: the Boke of Norture of John Russell, the Bokes of Keruynge, Curtasye, and Demeanor, the Babees Book, Urbanitatis, &c., ed. F. J. Furnivall. *(Out of print.)* — ,,
33. The Book of the Knight of La Tour-Landry, ed. T. Wright. *(Out of print.)* — ,,
34. Old English Homilies (before 1300), ed. R. Morris. Series I, Part II. *(Out of print.)* — ,,
35. Lyndesay's Works, Part III: The Historie and Testament of Squyer Meldrum, ed. F. Hall. *(Reprinted 1965.)* 90p — ,,
E.S. 3. Caxton's Book of Curtesye, in Three Versions, ed. F. J. Furnivall. *(Out of print.)* — ,,
4. Havelok the Dane, re-ed. W. W. Skeat. *(Out of print.)* — ,,
5. Chaucer's Boethius, ed. R. Morris. *(Reprinted 1969.)* £2·00 — ,,
6. Chevelere Assigne, re-ed. Lord Aldenham. *(Out of print.)* — ,,
O.S. 36. Merlin, ed. H. B. Wheatley. Part III. On Arthurian Localities, by J. S. Stuart Glennie. *(Out of print.)* — 1869
37. Sir David Lyndesay's Works, Part IV, Ane Satyre of the thrie Estaits, ed. F. Hall. *(Out of print.)* — ,,
38. William's Vision of Piers the Plowman, ed. W. W. Skeat. Part II. Text B. *(Reprinted 1964.)* £2·10 — ,,
39, 56. The Gest Hystoriale of the Destruction of Troy, ed. D. Donaldson and G. A. Panton. Parts I and II. *(Reprinted as one volume 1968.)* £5·50 — ,,
E.S. 7. Early English Pronunciation, by A. J. Ellis. Part II. *(Out of print.)* — ,,
8. Queene Elizabethes Achademy, &c., ed. F. J. Furnivall. Essays on early Italian and German Books of Courtesy, by W. M. Rossetti and E. Oswald. *(Out of print.)* — ,,
9. Awdeley's Fraternitye of Vacabondes, Harman's Caveat, &c., ed. E. Viles and F. J. Furnivall. *(Out of print.)* — ,,
O.S. 40. English Gilds, their Statutes and Customs, A.D. 1389, ed. Toulmin Smith and Lucy T. Smith, with an Essay on Gilds and Trades-Unions, by L. Brentano. *(Reprinted 1963.)* £5·00 — 1870
41. William Lauder's Minor Poems, ed. F. J. Furnivall. *(Out of print.)* — ,,
42. Bernardus De Cura Rei Famuliaris, Early Scottish Prophecies, &c., ed. J. R. Lumby. *(Reprinted 1965.)* 90p — ,,
43. Ratis Raving, and other Moral and Religious Pieces, ed. J. R. Lumby. *(Out of print.)* — ,,
E.S. 10. Andrew Boorde's Introduction of Knowledge, 1547, Dyetary of Helth, 1542, Barnes in Defence of the Berde, 1542–3, ed. F. J. Furnivall. *(Out of print.)* — ,,
11, 55. Barbour's Bruce, ed. W. W. Skeat. Parts I and IV. *(Reprinted as Volume I 1968.)* £3·15 — ,,
O.S. 44. The Alliterative Romance of Joseph of Arimathie, or The Holy Grail: from the Vernon MS.; with W. de Worde's and Pynson's Lives of Joseph: ed. W. W. Skeat. *(Out of print.)* — 1871
45. King Alfred's West-Saxon Version of Gregory's Pastoral Care, ed., with an English translation, by Henry Sweet. Part I. *(Reprinted 1958.)* £2·75. — ,,
46. Legends of the Holy Rood, Symbols of the Passion and Cross Poems, ed. R. Morris. *(Out of print.)* — ,,

		1871
O.S. 47.	Sir David Lyndesay's Works, ed. J. A. H. Murray. Part V. (*Out of print*.)	
48.	The Times' Whistle, and other Poems, by R. C., 1616; ed. J. M. Cowper. (*Out of print*.)	,,
E.S. 12.	England in Henry VIII's Time : a Dialogue between Cardinal Pole and Lupset, by Thom. Starkey, Chaplain to Henry VIII, ed. J. M. Cowper. Part II. (*Out of print*, Part I is E.S. 32, 1878.)	,,
13.	A Supplicacyon of the Beggers, by Simon Fish, A.D. 1528–9, ed. F. J. Furnivall, with A Supplication to our Moste Soueraigne Lorde, A Supplication of the Poore Commons, and The Decaye of England by the Great Multitude of Sheep, ed. J. M. Cowper. (*Out of print*.)	,,
14.	Early English Pronunciation, by A. J. Ellis. Part III. (*Out of print*.)	,,
O.S. 49.	An Old English Miscellany, containing a Bestiary, Kentish Sermons, Proverbs of Alfred, and Religious Poems of the 13th cent., ed. R. Morris. (*Out of print*.)	1872
50.	King Alfred's West-Saxon Version of Gregory's Pastoral Care, ed. H. Sweet. Part II. (*Reprinted* 1958.) £2·50	,,
51.	Þe Liflade of St. Juliana, 2 versions, with translations, ed. O. Cockayne and E. Brock. (*Reprinted* 1957.) £1·90	,,
52.	Palladius on Husbondrie, englisht, ed. Barton Lodge. Part I. (*Out of print*.)	,,
E.S. 15.	Robert Crowley's Thirty-One Epigrams, Voyce of the Last Trumpet, Way to Wealth, &c., ed. J. M. Cowper. (*Out of print*.)	,,
16.	Chaucer's Treatise on the Astrolabe, ed. W. W. Skeat. (*Reprinted* 1969.) £2·00	,,
17.	The Complaynt of Scotlande, with 4 Tracts, ed. J. A. H. Murray. Part I.(*Out of print*.)	,,
O.S. 53.	Old-English Homilies, Series II, and three Hymns to the Virgin and God, 13th-century, with the music to two of them, in old and modern notation, ed. R. Morris. (*Out of print*.)	1873
54.	The Vision of Piers Plowman, ed. W. W. Skeat. Part III. Text C. (*Reprinted* 1959.) £2·75	,,
55.	Generydes, a Romance, ed. W. Aldis Wright. Part I. (*Out of print*.)	,,
E.S. 18.	The Complaynt of Scotlande, ed. J. A. H. Murray. Part II. (*Out of print*.)	,,
19.	The Myroure of oure Ladye, ed. J. H. Blunt. (*Out of print*.)	,,
O.S. 56.	The Gest Hystoriale of the Destruction of Troy, in alliterative verse, ed. D. Donaldson and G. A. Panton. Part II. (*See* O.S. 39.)	1874
57.	Cursor Mundi, in four Texts, ed. R. Morris. Part I. (*Reprinted* 1961.) £2·00	,,
58, 63, 73.	The Blickling Homilies, ed. R. Morris. Parts I, II, and III. (*Reprinted as one volume* 1967.) £3·50	,,
E.S. 20.	Lovelich's History of the Holy Grail, ed. F. J. Furnivall. Part I. (*Out of print*.)	,,
21, 29.	Barbour's Bruce, ed. W. W. Skeat. Parts II and III. (*Reprinted as Volume II* 1968.) £4·50	,,
22.	Henry Brinklow's Complaynt of Roderyck Mors and The Lamentacyon of a Christen Agaynst the Cytye of London, made by Roderigo Mors, ed. J. M. Cowper. (*Out of print*.)	,,
23.	Early English Pronunciation, by A. J. Ellis. Part IV. (*Out of print*.)	,,
O.S. 59.	Cursor Mundi, in four Texts, ed. R. Morris. Part II. (*Reprinted* 1966.) £2·50	1875
60.	Meditacyuns on the Soper of our Lorde, by Robert of Brunne, ed. J. M. Cowper. (*Out of print*.)	,,
61.	The Romance and Prophecies of Thomas of Erceldoune, ed. J. A. H. Murray. (*Out of print*.)	,,
E.S. 24.	Lovelich's History of the Holy Grail, ed. F. J. Furnivall. Part II. (*Out of print*.)	,,
25, 26.	Guy of Warwick, 15th-century Version, ed. J. Zupitza. Pts. I and II. (*Reprinted as one volume* 1966.) £3·75	,,
O.S. 62.	Cursor Mundi, in four Texts, ed. R. Morris. Part III. (*Reprinted* 1966.) £2·00	1876
63.	The Blickling Homilies, ed. R. Morris. Part II. (*See* O.S. 58.)	,,
64.	Francis Thynne's Embleames and Epigrams, ed. F. J. Furnivall. (*Out of print*.)	,,
65.	Be Domes Dæge (Bede's *De Die Judicii*), &c., ed. J. R. Lumby. (*Reprinted* 1964.) £1·50	,,
E.S. 25.	Guy of Warwick, 15th-century Version, ed. J. Zupitza. Part II. (*See* E.S. 25)	,,
27.	The English Works of John Fisher, ed. J. E. B. Mayor. Part I. (*Out of print*.)	,,
O.S. 66.	Cursor Mundi, in four Texts, ed. R. Morris. Part IV. (*Reprinted* 1966.) £2·00	1877
67.	Notes on Piers Plowman, by W. W. Skeat. Part I. (*Out of print*.)	,,
E.S. 28.	Lovelich's Holy Grail, ed. F. J. Furnivall. Part III. (*Out of print*.)	,,
29.	Barbour's Bruce, ed. W. W. Skeat. Part III. (*See* E.S. 21.)	,,
O.S. 68.	Cursor Mundi, in 4 Texts, ed. R. Morris. Part V. (*Reprinted* 1966.) £2·00	1878
69.	Adam Davie's 5 Dreams about Edward II, &c., ed. F. J. Furnivall. (*Out of print*.)	,,
70.	Generydes, a Romance, ed. W. Aldis Wright. Part II. (*Out of print*.)	,,
E.S. 30.	Lovelich's Holy Grail, ed. F. J. Furnivall. Part IV. (*Out of print*.)	,,
31.	The Alliterative Romance of Alexander and Dindimus, ed. W. W. Skeat. (*Out of print*.)	,,
32.	Starkey's England in Henry VIII's Time. Part I. Starkey's Life and Letters, ed. S. J. Herrtage. (*Out of print*.)	,,
O.S. 71.	The Lay Folks Mass-Book, four texts, ed. T. F. Simmons. (*Reprinted* 1968.) £4·50	1879
72.	Palladius on Husbondrie, englisht, ed. S. J. Herrtage. Part II. £2·10	,,
E.S. 33.	Gesta Romanorum, ed. S. J. Herrtage. (*Reprinted* 1962.) £5·00	,,
34.	The Charlemagne Romances : 1. Sir Ferumbras, from Ashm. MS. 33, ed. S. J. Herrtage. (*Reprinted* 1966.) £2·70	,,
O.S. 73.	The Blickling Homilies, ed. R. Morris. Part III. (*See* O.S. 58.)	1880
74.	English Works of Wyclif, hitherto unprinted, ed. F. D. Matthew. (*Out of print*.)	,,
E.S. 35.	Charlemagne Romances : 2. The Sege of Melayne, Sir Otuell, &c., ed. S. J. Herrtage. (*Out of print*.)	,,
36, 37.	Charlemagne Romances : 3 and 4. Lyf of Charles the Grete, ed. S. J. Herrtage. Parts I and II (*Reprinted as one volume* 1967.) £2·70	,,
O.S. 75.	Catholicon Anglicum, an English-Latin Wordbook, from Lord Monson's MS., A.D. 1483, ed., with Introduction and Notes, by S. J. Herrtage and Preface by H. B. Wheatley. (*Out of print*.)	1881
76, 82.	Ælfric's Lives of Saints, in MS. Cott. Jul. E vii, ed. W. W. Skeat. Parts I and II. (*Reprinted as Volume I* 1966.) £3·00	,,
E.S. 37.	Charlemagne Romances : 4. Lyf of Charles the Grete. Part II. (*See* E.S. 36.)	,,
38.	Charlemagne Romances :5. The Sowdone of Babylone, ed. E. Hausknecht. (*Reprinted* 1969) £2·50	,,
O.S. 77.	Beowulf, the unique MS. autotyped and transliterated, ed. J. Zupitza. (Re-issued as No. 245. *See under* 1958.)	1882
78.	The Fifty Earliest English Wills, in the Court of Probate, 1387–1439, ed. F. J. Furnivall. (*Reprinted* 1964.) £2·50	,,

E.S. 39.	Charlemagne Romances : 6. Rauf Coilyear, Roland, Otuel, &c., ed. S. J. Herrtage. (*Reprinted* 1969.) £2·10	1882
40.	Charlemagne Romances : 7. Huon of Burdeux, by Lord Berners, ed. S. L. Lee. Part I. (*Out of print*.)	
O.S. 79.	King Alfred's Orosius, from Lord Tollemache's 9th-century MS., ed. H. Sweet. Part I. (*Reprinted* 1959.) £2·75	"
79 b.	*Extra Volume.* Facsimile of the Epinal Glossary, ed. H. Sweet. (*Out of print*.)	1883
E.S. 41.	Charlemagne Romances : 8. Huon of Burdeux, by Lord Berners, ed. S. L. Lee. Part II. (*Out of print*.)	"
42, 49, 59.	Guy of Warwick : 2 texts (Auchinleck MS. and Caius MS.), ed. J. Zupitza. Parts I, II, and III. (*Reprinted as one volume* 1966). £5·50	"
O.S. 80.	The Life of St. Katherine, B.M. Royal MS. 17 A. xxvii, &c., and its Latin Original, ed. E. Einenkel. (*Out of print*.)	"
81.	Piers Plowman : Glossary, &c., ed. W. W. Skeat. Part IV, completing the work. (*Out of print*.)	1884
E.S. 43.	Charlemagne Romances : 9. Huon of Burdeux, by Lord Berners, ed. S. L. Lee. Part III. (*Out of print*.)	"
44.	Charlemagne Romances : 10. The Foure Sonnes of Aymon, ed. Octavia Richardson. Part I. (*Out of print*.)	"
O.S. 82.	Ælfric's Lives of Saints, MS. Cott. Jul. E vii, ed. W. W. Skeat. Part II. (*See* O.S. 76.)	1885
83.	The Oldest English Texts, Charters, &c., ed. H. Sweet. (*Reprinted* 1966.) £5·50	
E.S. 45.	Charlemagne Romances : 11. The Foure Sonnes of Aymon, ed. O. Richardson. Part II. (*Out of print*.)	"
46.	Sir Beves of Hamtoun, ed. E. Kölbing. Part I. (*Out of print*.)	"
O.S. 84.	Additional Analogs to 'The Wright's Chaste Wife', O.S. 12, by W. A. Clouston. (*Out of print*.)	1886
85.	The Three Kings of Cologne, ed. C. Horstmann. (*Out of print*.)	"
86.	Prose Lives of Women Saints, ed. C. Horstmann. (*Out of print*.)	"
E.S. 47.	The Wars of Alexander, ed. W. W. Skeat. (*Out of print*.)	"
48.	Sir Beves of Hamtoun, ed. E. Kölbing. Part II. (*Out of print*.)	"
O.S. 87.	The Early South-English Legendary, Laud MS. 108, ed. C. Horstmann. (*Out of print*.)	1887
88.	Hy. Bradshaw's Life of St. Werburghe (Pynson, 1521), ed. C. Horstmann. (*Out of print*.)	"
E.S. 49.	Guy of Warwick, 2 texts (Auchinleck and Caius MSS.), ed. J. Zupitza. Part II. (*See* E.S. 42.)	"
50.	Charlemagne Romances : 12. Huon of Burdeux, by Lord Berners, ed. S. L. Lee. Part IV. (*Out of print*.)	"
51.	Torrent of Portyngale, ed. E. Adam. (*Out of print*.)	"
O.S. 89.	Vices and Virtues, ed. F. Holthausen. Part I. (*Reprinted* 1967.) £2·00	1888
90.	Anglo-Saxon and Latin Rule of St. Benet, interlinear Glosses, ed. H. Logeman. (*Out of print*.)	"
91.	Two Fifteenth-Century Cookery-Books, ed. T. Austin. (*Reprinted* 1964.) £2·10	"
E.S. 52.	Bullein's Dialogue against the Feuer Pestilence, 1578, ed. M. and A. H. Bullen. (*Out of print*.)	"
53.	Vicary's Anatomie of the Body of Man, 1548, ed. 1577, ed. F. J. and Percy Furnivall. Part I. (*Out of print*.)	"
54.	The Curial made by maystere Alain Charretier, translated by William Caxton, 1484, ed. F. J. Furnivall and P. Meyer. (*Reprinted* 1965.) 65p	"
O.S. 92.	Eadwine's Canterbury Psalter, from the Trin. Cambr. MS., ed. F. Harsley, Part II. (*Out of print*.)	1889
93.	Defensor's Liber Scintillarum, ed. E. Rhodes. (*Out of print*.)	"
E.S. 55.	Barbour's Bruce, ed. W. W. Skeat. Part IV. (*See* E.S. 11.)	"
56.	Early English Pronunciation, by A. J. Ellis. Part V, the present English Dialects. (*Out of print*.)	"
O.S. 94, 114.	Ælfric's Lives of Saints, MS. Cott. Jul. E vii, ed. W. W. Skeat. Parts III and IV. (*Reprinted as Volume II* 1966.) £3·00	1890
95.	The Old-English Version of Bede's Ecclesiastical History, re-ed. T. Miller. Part I, 1. *Reprinted* 1959.) £2·70	"
E.S. 57.	Caxton's Eneydos, ed. W. T. Culley and F. J. Furnivall. (*Reprinted* 1962.) £2·50	"
58.	Caxton's Blanchardyn and Eglantine, c. 1489, ed. L. Kellner. (*Reprinted* 1962.) £3·15	"
O.S. 96.	The Old-English Version of Bede's Ecclesiastical History, re-ed. T. Miller. Part I, 2. (*Reprinted* 1959.) £2·70	1891
97.	The Earliest English Prose Psalter, ed. K. D. Buelbring. Part I. (*Out of print*.)	"
E.S. 59.	Guy of Warwick, 2 texts (Auchinleck and Caius MSS.), ed. J. Zupitza. Part III. (*See* E.S. 42.)	"
60.	Lydgate's Temple of Glas, re-ed. J. Schick. (*Out of print*.)	"
O.S. 98.	Minor Poems of the Vernon MS., ed. C. Horstmann. Part I. (*Out of print*.)	1892
99.	Cursor Mundi. Preface, Notes, and Glossary, Part VI, ed. R. Morris. (*Reprinted* 1962.) £1·75	"
E.S. 61, 73.	Hoccleve's Minor Poems, Part I, ed. F. J. Furnivall and Part II, ed. I. Gollancz. (*Reprinted as one volume* 1970.) £3·15	"
62.	The Chester Plays, re-ed. H. Deimling. Part I. (*Reprinted* 1967.) £1·90	"
O.S. 100.	Capgrave's Life of St. Katharine, ed. C. Horstmann, with Forewords by F. J. Furnivall.	1893
101.	Cursor Mundi. Essay on the MSS., their Dialects, &c., by H. Hupe. Part VII. (*Reprinted* 1962.) 35*s.* £1·75	"
E.S. 63.	Thomas à Kempis's De Imitatione Christi, ed. J. K. Ingram. (*Out of print*.)	"
64.	Caxton's Godefroy of Boloyne, or The Siege and Conqueste of Jerusalem, 1481, ed. Mary N. Colvin. (*Out of print*.)	"
O.S. 102.	Lanfranc's Science of Cirurgie, ed. R. von Fleischhacker. Part I. (*Out of print*.)	1894
103.	The Legend of the Cross, &c., ed. A. S. Napier. (*Out of print*.)	"
E.S. 65.	Sir Beves of Hamtoun, ed. E. Kölbing. Part III. (*Out of print*.)	"
66.	Lydgate's and Burgh's Secrees of Philisoffres ('Governance of Kings and Princes'), ed. R. Steele. (*Out of print*.)	"
O.S. 104.	The Exeter Book (Anglo-Saxon Poems), re-ed. I. Gollancz. Part I. (*Reprinted* 1958.) £2·75	1895
105.	The Prymer or Lay Folks' Prayer Book, Camb. Univ. MS., ed. H. Littlehales. Part I. (*Out of print*.)	"
E.S. 67.	The Three Kings' Sons, a Romance, ed. F. J. Furnivall. Part I, the Text. (*Out of print*.)	"
68.	Melusine, the prose Romance, ed. A. K. Donald. Part I, the Text. (*Out of print*.)	"

O.S. 106.	R. Misyn's Fire of Love and Mending of Life (Hampole), ed. R. Harvey. (*Out of print.*)	1896
107.	The English Conquest of Ireland, A.D. 1166–1185, 2 Texts, ed. F. J. Furnivall. Part I. (*Out of print.*)	,,
E.S. 69.	Lydgate's Assembly of the Gods, ed. O. L. Triggs. (*Reprinted* 1957.) £2·10	,,
70.	The Digby Plays, ed. F. J. Furnivall. (*Reprinted* 1967.) £1·50	,,
O.S. 108.	Child-Marriages and -Divorces, Trothplights, &c. Chester Depositions, 1561–6, ed. F. J. Furnivall. (*Out of print.*)	1897
109.	The Prymer or Lay Folks' Prayer Book, ed. H. Littlehales. Part II. (*Out of print.*)	,,
E.S. 71.	The Towneley Plays, ed. G. England and A. W. Pollard. (*Reprinted* 1966.) £2·25	,,
72.	Hoccleve's Regement of Princes, and 14 Poems, ed. F. J. Furnivall. (*Out of print.*)	,,
73.	Hoccleve's Minor Poems, II, from the Ashburnham MS., ed. I. Gollancz. (*See* E.S. 61)	,,
O.S. 110.	The Old-English Version of Bede's Ecclesiastical History, ed. T. Miller. Part II, 1. (*Reprinted* 1963.) £2·75	1898
111.	The Old-English Version of Bede's Ecclesiastical History, ed. T. Miller. Part II, 2. (*Reprinted* 1963.) £2·75	,,
E.S. 74.	Secreta Secretorum, 3 prose Englishings, one by Jas. Yonge, 1428, ed. R. Steele. Part I. (*Out of print.*)	,,
75.	Speculum Guidonis de Warwyk, ed. G. L. Morrill. (*Out of print.*)	,,
O.S. 112.	Merlin. Part IV. Outlines of the Legend of Merlin, by W. E. Mead. (*Out of print.*)	1899
113.	Queen Elizabeth's Englishings of Boethius, Plutarch, &c., ed. C. Pemberton. (*Out of print.*)	,,
E.S. 76.	George Ashby's Poems, &c., ed. Mary Bateson. (*Reprinted* 1965.) £1·50	,,
77.	Lydgate's DeGuilleville's Pilgrimage of the Life of Man, ed. F. J. Furnivall. Part I. (*Out of print.*)	,,
78.	The Life and Death of Mary Magdalene, by T. Robinson, *c.* 1620, ed. H. O. Sommer. £1·50	,,
O.S. 114.	Ælfric's Lives of Saints, ed. W. W. Skeat. Part IV and last. (*See* O.S. 94.)	1900
115.	Jacob's Well, ed. A. Brandeis. Part I. (*Out of print.*)	,,
116.	An Old-English Martyrology, re-ed. G. Herzfeld. (*Out of print.*)	,,
E.S. 79.	Caxton's Dialogues, English and French, ed. H. Bradley. (*Out of print.*)	,,
80.	Lydgate's Two Nightingale Poems, ed. O. Glauning. (*Out of print.*)	,,
80A.	Selections from Barbour's Bruce (Books I–X), ed. W. W. Skeat. (*Out of print.*)	,,
81.	The English Works of John Gower, ed. G. C. Macaulay. Part I. (*Reprinted* 1957.) £3·00	,,
O.S. 117.	Minor Poems of the Vernon MS., ed. F. J. Furnivall. Part II. (*Out of print.*)	1901
118.	The Lay Folks' Catechism, ed. T. F. Simmons and H. E. Nolloth. (*Out of print.*)	,,
119.	Robert of Brunne's Handlyng Synne, and its French original, re-ed. F. J. Furnivall. Part I. (*Out of print.*)	,,
E.S. 82.	The English Works of John Gower, ed. G. C. Macaulay. Part II. (*Reprinted* 1957.) £3·00	,,
83.	Lydgate's DeGuilleville's Pilgrimage of the Life of Man, ed. F. J. Furnivall. Part II. (*Out of print.*)	,,
84.	Lydgate's Reson and Sensuallyte, ed. E. Sieper. Vol. I. (*Reprinted* 1965.) £2·50	,,
O.S. 120.	The Rule of St. Benet in Northern Prose and Verse, and Caxton's Summary, ed. E. A. Kock. (*Out of print.*)	1902
121.	The Laud MS. Troy-Book, ed. J. E. Wülfing. Part I. (*Out of print.*)	,,
E.S. 85.	Alexander Scott's Poems, 1568, ed. A. K. Donald. (*Out of print.*)	,,
86.	William of Shoreham's Poems, re-ed. M. Konrath. Part I. (*Out of print.*)	,,
87.	Two Coventry Corpus Christi Plays, re-ed. H. Craig. (*See under* 1952.)	,,
O.S. 122.	The Laud MS. Troy-Book, ed. J. E. Wülfing. Part II. (*Out of print.*)	1903
123.	Robert of Brunne's Handlyng Synne, and its French original, re-ed. F. J. Furnivall. Part II. (*Out of print.*)	,,
E.S. 88.	Le Morte Arthur, re-ed. J. D. Bruce. (*Out of print.*)	,,
89.	Lydgate's Reson and Sensuallyte, ed. E. Sieper. Vol. II. (*Reprinted* 1965.) £1·75	,,
90.	English Fragments from Latin Medieval Service-Books, ed. H. Littlehales. (*Out of print.*)	,,
O.S. 124.	Twenty-six Political and other Poems from Digby MS. 102, &c., ed. J. Kail. Part I. (*Out of print.*)	1904
125.	Medieval Records of a London City Church, ed. H. Littlehales. Part I. (*Out of print.*)	,,
126.	An Alphabet of Tales, in Northern English, from the Latin, ed. M. M. Banks. Part I. (*Out of print.*)	,,
E.S. 91.	The Macro Plays, ed. F. J. Furnivall and A. W. Pollard. (*Out of print; see* 262.)	,,
92.	Lydgate's DeGuilleville's Pilgrimage of the Life of Man, ed. Katherine B. Locock. Part III. (*Out of print.*)	,,
93.	Lovelich's Romance of Merlin, from the unique MS., ed. E. A. Kock. Part I. (*Out of print.*)	,,
O.S. 127.	An Alphabet of Tales, in Northern English, from the Latin, ed. M. M. Banks. Part II. (*Out of print.*)	1905
128.	Medieval Records of a London City Church, ed. H. Littlehales. Part II. (*Out of print.*)	,,
129.	The English Register of Godstow Nunnery, ed. A. Clark. Part I. (*Out of print.*)	,,
E.S. 94.	Respublica, a Play on a Social England, ed. L. A. Magnus. (*Out of print. See under* 1946.)	,,
95.	Lovelich's History of the Holy Grail. Part V. The Legend of the Holy Grail, ed. Dorothy Kempe. (*Out of print.*)	,,
96.	Mirk's Festial, ed. T. Erbe. Part I. (*Out of print.*)	,,
O.S. 130.	The English Register of Godstow Nunnery, ed. A. Clark. Part II. (*Out of print.*)	1906
131.	The Brut, or The Chronicle of England, ed. F. Brie. Part I. (*Reprinted* 1960.) £2·75	,,
132.	John Metham's Works, ed. H. Craig. £2·50	,,
E.S. 97.	Lydgate's Troy Book, ed. H. Bergen. Part I, Books I and II. (*Out of print.*)	,,
98.	Skelton's Magnyfycence, ed. R. L. Ramsay. (*Reprinted* 1958.) £2·75	,,
99.	The Romance of Emaré, re-ed. Edith Rickert. (*Reprinted* 1958.) £1·50	,,
O.S. 133.	The English Register of Oseney Abbey, by Oxford, ed. A. Clark. Part I. (*Out of print.*)	1907
134.	The Coventry Leet Book, ed. M. Dormer Harris. Part I. (*Out of print.*)	,,
E.S. 100.	The Harrowing of Hell, and The Gospel of Nicodemus, re-ed. W. H. Hulme. (*Reprinted* 1961.) £2·50	,,
101.	Songs, Carols, &c., from Richard Hill's Balliol MS., ed. R. Dyboski. (*Out of print.*)	,,
O.S. 135.	The Coventry Leet Book, ed. M. Dormer Harris. Part II. (*Out of print.*)	1908
135 b.	*Extra Issue.* Prof. Manly's Piers Plowman and its Sequence, urging the fivefold authorship of the *Vision.* (*Out of print.*)	,,
136.	The Brut, or The Chronicle of England, ed. F. Brie, Part II. (*Out of print.*)	,,

E.S. 102.	Promptorium Parvulorum, the 1st English-Latin Dictionary, ed. A. L. Mayhew. (*Out of print*.)	190
103.	Lydgate's Troy Book, ed. H. Bergen. Part II, Book III. (*Out of print*.)	,,
O.S. 137.	Twelfth-Century Homilies in MS. Bodley 343, ed. A. O. Belfour. Part I, the Text. (*Reprinted* 1962.) £1·40	190!
138.	The Coventry Leet Book, ed. M. Dormer Harris. Part III. (*Out of print*.)	,,
E.S. 104.	The Non-Cycle Mystery Plays, re-ed. O. Waterhouse. (*See Supplementary Series* I. 1970.)	,,
105.	The Tale of Beryn, with the Pardoner and Tapster, ed. F. J. Furnivall and W. G. Stone. (*Out of print*.)	,,
O.S. 139.	John Arderne's Treatises of Fistula in Ano, &c., ed. D'Arcy Power. (*Reprinted* 1969.) £2·25	191C
139 *b, c, d, e, f, Extra Issue*.	The Piers Plowman Controversy : *b*. Dr. Jusserand's 1st Reply to Prof. Manly ; *c*. Prof. Manly's Answer to Dr. Jusserand ; *d*. Dr. Jusserand's 2nd Reply to Prof. Manly ; *e*. Mr. R. W. Chambers's Article ; *f*. Dr. Henry Bradley's Rejoinder to Mr. R. W. Chambers. (*Out of print*.)	,,
140.	Capgrave's Lives of St. Augustine and St. Gilbert of Sempringham, ed. J. Munro. (*Out of print*.)	,,
E.S. 106.	Lydgate's Troy Book, ed. H. Bergen. Part III. (*Out of print*.)	,,
107.	Lydgate's Minor Poems, ed. H. N. MacCracken. Part I. Religious Poems. (*Reprinted* 1961.) £3·50	,,
O.S. 141.	Erthe upon Erthe, all the known texts, ed. Hilda Murray. (*Reprinted* 1964.) £1·50	1911
142.	The English Register of Godstow Nunnery, ed. A. Clark. Part III. (*Out of print*)	,,
143.	The Prose Life of Alexander, Thornton MS., ed. J. S. Westlake. (*Out of print*.)	,,
E.S. 108.	Lydgate's Siege of Thebes, re-ed. A. Erdmann. Part I, the Text. (*Reprinted* 1960.) £2·50	,,
109.	Partonope, re-ed. A. T. Bödtker. The Texts. (*Out of print*.)	,,
O.S. 144.	The English Register of Oseney Abbey, by Oxford, ed. A. Clark. Part II. (*Out of print*.)	1912
145.	The Northern Passion, ed. F. A. Foster. Part I, the four parallel texts. (*Out of print*.)	,,
E.S. 110.	Caxton's Mirrour of the World, with all the woodcuts, ed. O. H. Prior. (*Reprinted* 1966.) £2·50	,,
111.	Caxton's History of Jason, the Text, Part I, ed. J. Munro. (*Out of print*.)	,,
O.S. 146.	The Coventry Leet Book, ed. M. Dormer Harris. Introduction, Indexes, &c. Part IV. (*Out of print*.)	1913
147.	The Northern Passion, ed. F. A. Foster, Introduction, French Text, Variants and Fragments, Glossary. Part II. (*Out of print*.) [An enlarged reprint of O.S. 26, Religious Pieces in Prose and Verse, from the Thornton MS., ed. G. G. Perry. (*Out of print*.)	,,
E.S. 112.	Lovelich's Romance of Merlin, ed. E. A. Kock. Part II. (*Reprinted* 1961.) £2·25	,,
113.	Poems by Sir John Salusbury, Robert Chester, and others, from Christ Church MS. 184, &c., ed. Carleton Brown. (*Out of print*.)	,,
O.S. 148.	A Fifteenth-Century Courtesy Book and Two Franciscan Rules, ed. R. W. Chambers and W. W. Seton. (*Reprinted* 1963.) £1·50	1914
149.	Lincoln Diocese Documents, 1450–1544, ed. Andrew Clark. (*Out of print*.)	,,
150.	The Old-English Rule of Bp. Chrodegang, and the Capitula of Bp. Theodulf, ed. A. S. Napier. (*Out of print*.)	,,
E.S. 114.	The Gild of St. Mary, Lichfield, ed. F. J. Furnivall. £1·35	,,
115.	The Chester Plays, re-ed. J. Matthews. Part II. (*Reprinted* 1967.) £1·90	,,
O.S. 151.	The Lanterne of Light, ed. Lilian M. Swinburn. (*Out of print*.)	1915
152.	Early English Homilies, from Cott. Vesp. D. XIV, ed. Rubie Warner. Part I, Text. (*Out of print*.)	,,
E.S. 116.	The Pauline Epistles, ed. M. J. Powell. (*Out of print*.)	,,
117.	Bp. Fisher's English Works, ed. R. Bayne. Part II. (*Out of print*.)	,,
O.S. 153.	Mandeville's Travels, ed. P. Hamelius. Part I, Text. (*Reprinted* 1960.) £2·00	1916
154.	Mandeville's Travels, ed. P. Hamelius. Part II, Notes and Introduction. (*Reprinted* 1961.) £2·00	,,
E.S. 118.	The Earliest Arithmetics in English, ed. R. Steele. (*Out of print*.)	,,
119.	The Owl and the Nightingale, 2 Texts parallel, ed. G. F. H. Sykes and J. H. G. Grattan. (*Out of print*.)	,,
O.S. 155.	The Wheatley MS., ed. Mabel Day. £2·70	1917
E.S. 120.	Ludus Coventriae, ed. K. S. Block. (*Reprinted* 1961.) £3·00	,,
O.S. 156.	Reginald Pecock's Donet, from Bodl. MS. 916, ed. Elsie V. Hitchcock. (*Out of print*.)	1918
E.S. 121.	Lydgate's Fall of Princes, ed. H. Bergen. Part I. (*Reprinted* 1967). £3·15	,,
122.	Lydgate's Fall of Princes, ed. H. Bergen. Part II. (*Reprinted* 1967.) £3·15	,,
O.S. 157.	Harmony of the Life of Christ, from MS. Pepys 2498, ed. Margery Goates. (*Out of print*.)	1919
158.	Meditations on the Life and Passion of Christ, from MS. Add., 11307, ed. Charlotte D'Evelyn. (*Out of print*.)	,,
E.S. 123.	Lydgate's Fall of Princes, ed. H. Bergen. Part III. (*Reprinted* 1967.) £3·15	,,
124.	Lydgate's Fall of Princes, ed. H. Bergen. Part IV. (*Reprinted* 1967.) £4·50	,,
O.S. 159.	Vices and Virtues, ed. F. Holthausen. Part II. (*Reprinted* 1967.) £1·40 [A re-edition of O.S. 18, Hali Meidenhad, ed. O. Cockayne, with a variant MS., Bodl. 34, hitherto unprinted, ed. F. J. Furnivall. (*Out of print*.)	1920
E.S. 125.	Lydgate's Siege of Thebes, ed. A. Erdmann and E. Ekwall. Part II. (*Out of print*.)	,,
126.	Lydgate's Troy Book, ed. H. Bergen. Part IV. (*Out of print*.)	,,
O.S. 160.	The Old English Heptateuch, MS. Cott. Claud. B. IV, ed. S. J. Crawford. (*Reprinted* 1969.) £3·75	1921
161.	Three O.E. Prose Texts, MS. Cott. Vit. A. XV, ed. S. Rypins. (*Out of print*.)	,,
162.	Facsimile of MS. Cotton Nero A. x (Pearl, Cleanness, Patience and Sir Gawain), Introduction by I. Gollancz. (*Out of print*.)	1922
163.	Book of the Foundation of St. Bartholomew's Church in London, ed. N. Moore. (*Out of print*.)	1923
164.	Pecock's Folewer to the Donet, ed. Elsie V. Hitchcock. (*Out of print*.)	,,
165.	Middleton's Chinon of England, with Leland's Assertio Arturii and Robinson's translation, ed. W. E. Mead. (*Out of print*.)	,,
166.	Stanzaic Life of Christ, ed. Frances A. Foster. (*Out of print*.)	1924
167.	Trevisa's Dialogus inter Militem et Clericum, Sermon by FitzRalph, and Bygynnyng of the World, ed. A. J. Perry. (*Out of print*.)	,,
168.	Caxton's Ordre of Chyualry, ed. A. T. P. Byles. (*Out of print*.)	1925
169.	The Southern Passion, ed. Beatrice Brown. (*Out of print*.)	,,

.S. 170. Walton's Boethius, ed. M. Science. (*Out of print.*) 1925
171. Pecock's Reule of Cristen Religioun, ed. W. C. Greet. (*Out of print.*) 1926
172. The Seege or Batayle of Troye, ed. M. E. Barnicle. (*Out of print.*) ,,
173. Hawes' Pastime of Pleasure, ed. W. E. Mead. (*Out of print.*) 1927
174. The Life of St. Anne, ed. R. E. Parker. (*Out of print.*) ,,
175. Barclay's Eclogues, ed. Beatrice White. (*Reprinted* 1961.) £2·75 ,,
176. Caxton's Prologues and Epilogues, ed. W. J. B. Crotch. (*Reprinted* 1956.) £2·70 ,,
177. Byrhtferth's Manual, ed. S. J. Crawford. (*Reprinted* 1966.) £3·15 1928
178. The Revelations of St. Birgitta, ed. W. P. Cumming. (*Out of print.*) ,,
179. The Castell of Pleasure, ed. B. Cornelius. (*Out of print.*) ,,
180. The Apologye of Syr Thomas More, ed. A. I. Taft. (*Out of print.*) 1929
181. The Dance of Death, ed. F. Warren. (*Out of print.*) ,,
182. Speculum Christiani, ed. G. Holmstedt. (*Out of print.*) ,,
183. The Northern Passion (Supplement), ed. W. Heuser and Frances Foster. (*Out of print.*) 1930
184. The Poems of John Audelay, ed. Ella K. Whiting. (*Out of print.*) ,,
185. Lovelich's Merlin, ed. E. A. Kock. Part III. (*Out of print.*) ,,
186. Harpsfield's Life of More, ed. Elsie V. Hitchcock and R. W. Chambers. (*Reprinted* 1963.) £5·25 1931
187. Whittinton and Stanbridge's Vulgaria, ed. B. White. (*Out of print.*) ,,
188. The Siege of Jerusalem, ed. E. Kölbing and Mabel Day. (*Out of print.*) ,,
189. Caxton's Fayttes of Armes and of Chyualrye, ed. A. T. Byles. (*Out of print.*) 1932
190. English Mediæval Lapidaries, ed. Joan Evans and Mary Serjeantson. (*Reprinted* 1960.) £2·50 ,,
191. The Seven Sages, ed. K. Brunner. (*Out of print.*) ,,
191A.On the Continuity of English Prose, by R. W. Chambers. (*Reprinted* 1966.) £1·25 ,,
192. Lydgate's Minor Poems, ed. H. N. MacCracken. Part II, Secular Poems. (*Reprinted* 1961.) £3·75 1933
193. Seinte Marherete, re-ed. Frances Mack. (*Reprinted* 1958.) £2·50 ,,
194. The Exeter Book, Part II, ed. W. S. Mackie. (*Reprinted* 1938.) £2·10 ,,
195. The Quatrefoil of Love, ed. I. Gollancz and M. Weale. (*Out of print.*) 1934
196. A Short English Metrical Chronicle, ed. E. Zettl. (*Out of print.*) ,,
197. Roper's Life of More, ed. Elsie V. Hitchcock. (*Reprinted* 1958.) £1·75 ,,
198. Firumbras and Otuel and Roland, ed. Mary O'Sullivan. (*Out of print.*) ,,
199. Mum and the Sothsegger, ed. Mabel Day and R. Steele. (*Out of print.*) ,,
200. Speculum Sacerdotale, ed. E. H. Weatherly. (*Out of print.*) 1935
201. Knyghthode and Bataile, ed. R. Dyboski and Z. M. Arend. (*Out of print.*) ,,
202. Palsgrave's Acolastus, ed. P. L. Carver. (*Out of print.*) ,,
203. Amis and Amiloun, ed. McEdward Leach. (*Reprinted* 1960.) £2·50 ,,
204. Valentine and Orson, ed. Arthur Dickson. (*Out of print.*) 1936
205. Tales from the Decameron, ed. H. G. Wright. (*Out of print.*) ,,
206. Bokenham's Lives of Holy Women (Lives of the Saints), ed. Mary S. Serjeantson. (*Out of print.*) ,,
207. Liber de Diversis Medicinis, ed. Margaret S. Ogden. (*Reprinted* 1970.) £2·10 ,,
208. The Parker Chronicle and Laws (facsimile), ed. R. Flower and A. H. Smith. (*Out of print.*) 1937
209. Middle English Sermons from MS. Roy. 18 B. xxiii, ed. W.O. Ross. (*Reprinted* 1960.) £3·75 1938
210. Sir Gawain and the Green Knight, ed. I. Gollancz. With Introductory essays by Mabel Day and M. S. Serjeantson. (*Reprinted* 1966.) £1·25 ,,
211. Dictes and Sayings of the Philosophers, ed. C. F. Bühler. (*Reprinted* 1961.) £3·75 1939
212. The Book of Margery Kempe, Part I, ed. S. B. Meech and Hope Emily Allen. (*Reprinted* 1961.) £3·50 ,,
213. Ælfric's De Temporibus Anni, ed. H. Henel. (*Reprinted* 1970.) £2·10 1940
214. Morley's Translation of Boccaccio's De Claris Mulieribus, ed. H. G. Wright. (*Reprinted* 1970.) £2·75. ,,
215, 220. English Poems of Charles of Orleans, Part I, ed. R. Steele and Part II, ed. R. Steele and Mabel Day. (*Reprinted as one volume* 1970.) £3·75
216. The Latin Text of the Ancrene Riwle, ed. Charlotte D'Evelyn. (*Reprinted* 1957.) £2·25 ,,
217. The Book of Vices and Virtues, ed. W. Nelson Francis. (*Reprinted* 1968.) £3·75 1942
218. The Cloud of Unknowing and the Book of Privy Counselling, ed. Phyllis Hodgson. (*Reprinted* 1958.) £2·00 1943
219. The French Text of the Ancrene Riwle, B.M. Cotton MS. Vitellius. F. vii, ed. J. A. Herbert. (*Reprinted* 1967.) £2·75 ,,
220. English Poems of Charles of Orleans, Part II, ed. R. Steele and Mabel Day. (*See* 215.) 1944
221. Sir Degrevant, ed. L. F. Casson. (*Reprinted* 1970.) £2·50 ,,
222. Ro. Ba.'s Life of Syr Thomas More, ed. Elsie V. Hitchcock and Mgr. P. E. Hallett. (*Reprinted* 1957.) £3·15 1945
223. Tretyse of Loue, ed. J. H. Fisher. (*Reprinted* 1970.) £2·10 ,,
224. Athelston, ed. A. McI. Trounce. (*Reprinted* 1957.) £2·10 1946
225. The English Text of the Ancrene Riwle, B.M. Cotton MS. Nero A. xiv, ed. Mabel Day. (*Reprinted* 1957.) £2·50 ,,
226. Respublica, re-ed. W. W. Greg. (*Reprinted* 1969.) £1·50 ,,
227. Kyng Alisaunder, ed. G. V. Smithers. Vol. I, Text. (*Reprinted* 1961.) £3·75 1947
228. The Metrical Life of St. Robert of Knaresborough, ed. J. Bazire. (*Reprinted* 1968.) £2·10 ,,
229. The English Text of the Ancrene Riwle, Gonville and Caius College MS. 234/120, ed. R. M. Wilson. With Introduction by N. R. Ker. (*Reprinted* 1957.) £1·75 1948
230. The Life of St. George by Alexander Barclay, ed. W. Nelson. (*Reprinted* 1960.) £2·00 ,,
231. Deonise Hid Diuinite, and other treatises related to *The Cloud of Unknowing*, ed. Phyllis Hodgson. (*Reprinted* 1958.) £2·50 1949
232. The English Text of the Ancrene Riwle, B.M. Royal MS. 8 C. 1, ed. A. C. Baugh. (*Reprinted* 1958.) £1·50 ,,
233. The Bibliotheca Historica of Diodorus Siculus translated by John Skelton, ed. F. M. Salter and H. L. R. Edwards. Vol. I, Text. (*Reprinted* 1968.) £4·00 1950
234. Caxton: Paris and Vienne, ed. MacEdward Leach. (*Reprinted* 1970.) £2·10 1951

O.S. 235. The South English Legendary, Corpus Christi College Cambridge MS. 145 and B.M. M.S. Harley 2277, &c., ed. Charlotte D'Evelyn and Anna J. Mill. Vol. I. Text, (Reprinted 1967.) £3·15   1951
236. The South English Legendary. Vol. II. Text, (Reprinted 1967.) £3·15   1952
[E.S. 87. Two Coventry Corpus Christi Plays, re-ed. H. Craig. Second Edition. (Reprinted 1967.) £1·50]
237. Kyng Alisaunder, ed. G. V. Smithers. Vol. II, Introduction, Commentary and Glossary. (Reprinted 1970.) £2·50   1953
238. The Phonetic Writings of Robert Robinson, ed. E. J. Dobson. (Reprinted 1968.) £1·50   "
239. The Bibliotheca Historica of Diodorus Siculus translated by John Skelton, ed. F. M. Salter and H. L. R. Edwards. Vol. II. Introduction, Notes, and Glossary. £1·50   1954
240. The French Text of the Ancrene Riwle, Trinity College, Cambridge, MS. R. 14, 7, ed. W. H. Trethewey. £2·75   "
241. Þe Wohunge of ure Lauerd, and other pieces, ed. W. Meredith Thompson. (Reprinted 1970.) £2·25   1955
242. The Salisbury Psalter, ed. Celia Sisam and Kenneth Sisam. (Reprinted 1969.) £4·50   1955–56
243. George Cavendish: The Life and Death of Cardinal Wolsey, ed. Richard S. Sylvester. (Reprinted 1961.) £2·25   1957
244. The South English Legendary. Vol. III, Introduction and Glossary, ed. C. D'Evelyn. (Reprinted 1969.) £1·50   "
245. Beowulf (facsimile). With Transliteration by J. Zupitza, new collotype plates, and Introduction by N. Davis. (Reprinted 1967.) £5·00   1958
246. The Parlement of the Thre Ages, ed. M. Y. Offord. (Reprinted 1967.) £2·00   1959
247. Facsimile of MS. Bodley 34 (Katherine Group). With Introduction by N. R. Ker. £3·15   "
248. Þe Liflade ant te Passiun of Seinte Iuliene, ed. S. R. T. O. d'Ardenne. £2·00   1960
249. Ancrene Wisse, Corpus Christi College, Cambridge, MS. 402, ed. J. R. R. Tolkien. With an Introduction by N. R. Ker. £2·50   "
250. Laȝamon's Brut, ed. G. L. Brook and R. F. Leslie. Vol. I, Text (first part). £5·00   1961
251. Facsimile of the Cotton and Jesus Manuscripts of the Owl and the Nightingale. With Introduction by N. R. Ker. £2·50   1962
252. The English Text of the Ancrene Riwle, B.M. Cotton MS. Titus D. xviii, ed. Frances M. Mack, and Lanhydrock Fragment, ed. A. Zettersten. £2·50   "
253. The Bodley Version of Mandeville's Travels, ed. M. C. Seymour. £2·50   1963
254. Ywain and Gawain, ed. Albert B. Friedman and Norman T. Harrington. £2·50   "
255. Facsimile of B.M. MS. Harley 2253 (The Harley Lyrics). With Introduction by N. R. Ker. £5·00   1964
256. Sir Eglamour of Artois, ed. Frances E. Richardson. £2·50   1965
257. Sir Thomas Chaloner: The Praise of Folie, ed. Clarence H. Miller. £2·50   "
258. The Orchard of Syon, ed. Phyllis Hodgson and Gabriel M. Liegey. Vol. I, Text. £5·00   1966
259. Homilies of Ælfric: A Supplementary Collection, ed. J. C. Pope. Vol. I. £5·00   1967
260. Homilies of Ælfric: A Supplementary Collection, ed. J. C. Pope. Vol. II. £5·00   1968
261. Lybeaus Desconus, ed. M. Mills. £2·50   1969
262. The Macro Plays, ed. Mark Eccles. £2·50   "
263. Caxton's History of Reynard the Fox, ed. N. F. Blake. £2·50   1970
264. Scrope's Epistle of Othea, ed. C. F. Bühler. £2·50   "
265. The Cyrurgie of Guy de Chauliac, ed. Margaret S. Ogden. Vol. I, Text. £5·00   1971

Forthcoming volumes

266. Wulfstan's Canons of Edgar, ed. R. G. Fowler. (At press.) £1·50   1972
267. The English Text of the Ancrene Riwle, B.M. Cotton MS. Cleopatra C. vi, ed. E. J. Dobson. (At press.) £3·50   "
268. Of Arthour and of Merlin, ed. O. D. Macrae-Gibson.(At press.) £2·50.   1973
269. The Metrical Version of Mandeville's Travels, ed. M. C. Seymour. (At press.) £2·50.   "
270. Fifteenth Century Translations of Chartier's Le Traite de l'Esperance and Le Quadrilogue Invectif, ed. Margaret S. Blayney. Vol. 1. Text, (At press.) £2·50   1974
271. The Minor Poems of Stephen Hawes, ed. Florence Gluck and Alice B. Morgan. (At press.) £2·50   "

Other texts are in preparation.

Supplementary Series

S.S. 1. Non-Cycle Plays and Fragments, ed. Norman Davis. £3·00.   1970
2. Caxton's Book of the Knight of the Tower, ed. M.Y. Offord. £2·75.   1971

The Society will issue books in the Supplementary Series from time to time as funds allow. These will not be issued on subscription but members will be able to order copies before publication at a reduced rate; details will be circulated on each occasion. The books will be available to non-members at listed prices.

May 1971.